Praise for *Conscious, Capable, and Ready to Contribute: A Fable*

Catherine Allen and Ed Offterdinger outline perfectly how a focus on people development and employee engagement results in superior performance. Their compelling advice is practical, accessible, and a must-follow for any leader who is looking to develop a conscious and capable organization.

MIKE CORKERY
CEO and President, Deltek

If you want to build a "people-first" culture in your organization, where, as Ed and Catherine say, you "build it so they will want to come, flourish, and stay, knowing that someday they may leave," then this is the book for you! Immerse yourself in this story that shows you how investment in your people will make your organization and your community a better place—every day.

MONICA MODI DALWADI
Managing Partner—D.C. Metro Region, Baker Tilly US

This book's big idea—that developing your people is the best way for organizations to contribute to society—is not only true, but it's inspiring and perfectly timed. The practical advice on how to build a conscious culture that Ed and Catherine offer is both enjoyable and actionable.

MIKE ROBBINS
Author of *We're All in This Together*

I started reading Conscious, Capable, and Ready to Contribute at 2:30 in the morning after waking abruptly. Two hours later my wife asked me why I was still up! This tale about how Andrew Hyde and his colleagues built a conscious development culture is a fun and thought provoking read. Ed Offterdinger and Catherine Allen have given me new perspective and practical ideas about how to be a conscious leader.

GARY KRAUTHAMER
Founding Partner, Krauthamer & Associates
Former Chairman and Board Member, the Omega Institute

D0649275

A perfectly crafted fable, expertly wrapped around real life and woven into a narrative packed with lessons learned and tangible how-tos and whys. The newest addition to the required reading . . . for my team.

DAN SIMONS
Cofounder, Founding Farmers Restaurants

The story of an organization verging on either collapse or transformation draws you in and takes you deep into a world of inspiring and practical ideas. Kudos to Ed and Catherine for showing us how to move beyond implementing learning programs to building a true culture of development.

TODD STOKES
Managing Partner, People Solutions, Baker Tilly US

Conscious leadership with a mission to develop people for the benefit of themselves, their organizations, and society—it seems almost too good to be true! In this immensely readable book, Ed and Catherine bring to life a story that illustrates why development is vital and how leaders can embed such learning into the fabric of their organizations for the good of all. The authors seamlessly tie together the individual development journey and the systemic forces that accelerate development. As a leader of a coaching company helping organizations scale their learning culture, I consider this is a must-read for organizational leaders, HR professionals, and coaches alike.

PAM KRULITZ
Founder and CEO, Optify

Catherine and Ed are true practice leaders, driven by their vision, passion, and experience unlocking the power of people development. Their book illustrates the compelling case for a conscious, strategic, integrated approach, and then lays out tangible, practical considerations for how to implement it in your organization. This is a valuable resource for leaders who want to make a bigger contribution to society.

DAVID SPACH
President—North America, The Leadership Circle and Full Circle Group

Now more than ever, our country and communities are looking to businesses to be forces for good, and to do more than simply deliver value by providing goods and services. *Conscious, Capable, and Ready to Contribute: A Fable* not only makes the case for *why* successful business leaders must focus on the professional and human potential of their employees, but it is chock-full of thought-provoking anecdotes and ideas on *how* to do so. Focusing on the "employee life cycle"—from recruiting and onboarding to skills development and performance management [to] retention and ultimately offboarding—Offterdinger and Allen's clear, authentic storytelling and insights make this book not only an enjoyable read, but an essential read for every business owner and leader.

BRIAN L. SCHWALB, ESQ.
Partner-in-charge—Washington, DC, Office, Venable LLP

Aligning individual vocation, work, and company purpose is a key objective of the Economics of Mutuality approach championed by my organization. Allen and Offterdinger move companies in a similar direction with their very readable take on how companies that consciously help enable their employees to fulfill their purpose will keep them and find their businesses are more resilient, and even more profitable. It's all about the people, and without conscious development and nurturing, today's employees will wither rather than flourish; they will simply move on if their purpose is not met through their work.

DR. JAY JAKUB
Author of *Completing Capitalism: Heal Business to Heal the World*
Chief Advocacy Officer, Economics of Mutuality Foundation

World-class education is the cornerstone of the Chief Executives Organization, and my team supports a membership with an insatiable curiosity and thirst for knowledge and experience. *Conscious, Capable, and Ready to Contribute: A Fable* has inspired me to reaffirm my commitment to ensuring my team also has opportunities for heightened individual achievement.

JENNIFER LEHMANN WENG
President and CEO, Chief Executives Organization

As someone who has spent almost thirty years in the human capital space, I was excited to read *Conscious, Capable, and Ready to Contribute: A Fable*. Being very fond of the authors and the subject, I was prepared to learn. What I was not prepared for was to learn and at the same time be absorbed by an amazing fable that made the learning enjoyable and relatable. I recommend this book to anyone focused on taking their organization and people to the next level!

TODD DORFMAN
K&A

After twenty-five-plus years as a newscaster, I grew tired of telling viewers every day about the worst of the worst happening in our world. I founded my own company because I wanted to work with change-makers showcasing good news and driving solution-based stories and projects.

Reading Ed and Catherine's book has helped me appreciate that conscious leadership is another way of defining my purpose, mission, and work—and that of my clients. There's nobody better than Ed and Catherine at showing how and why using your business for good is good business.

LAURA EVANS
CEO and President, Laura Evans Media

If you want to grow as a leader, develop better relationships with your colleagues, and mature your business, *Conscious, Capable, and Ready to Contribute: A Fable* is a must-read. Ed Offterdinger and AO People Partners have helped me personally and professionally over the last four years. Catherine and Ed practice the Conscious Capitalism principles in their business and set a great example for all of us to follow. I am recommending this book because I know they will help you and your business grow as much as they've helped me and IronArch.

JOE PUNARO
CEO, IronArch Technology

Our global community finds itself at a moment in time when we need people operating at their highest levels of consciousness. In *Conscious, Capable, and Ready to Contribute: A Fable: How Employee Development Can Become the Highest Form of Social Contribution*, Ed and Catherine share a powerful vision of the role organizations can play and practical guidance on how to build an organizational culture that helps employees grow in order to meet the rapidly changing needs of our complex world.

BILL PULLEN
Academic Director, Institute for Transformational Leadership
Georgetown University/President
BPA Coaching and Consulting

The workforce is evolving. Those that create a culture of consciousness and cohesion will thrive, and those that don't will fall behind the eight ball. This book takes you on a journey to discover what sparks world-class contribution to thrive. It's a must-read for those interested in developing teams and people in the workforce.

BRIAN LEVENSON
Executive Coach, author of *Shift Your Mind*

A compelling vision that employee development is the highest form of social contribution. The authors provide us with a solid framework for embedding conscious people development right into your organization's culture. They invite us to consider that developing your people might just be a core part of why your organization exists, and that growing employees who achieve not just success but also significance might be a key part of your company's purpose.

GINA HAYDEN
Executive Coach
Author of *Becoming a Conscious Leader: How to Lead Successfully in a World That's Waking Up*

As a TV reporter for fifteen years and now the president of a corporate coaching and content business, I believe strongly in the power of stories to define leaders and organizations. So I love the innovative storytelling Ed and Catherine use in the first half of this book to allow readers to see themselves and their own challenges and envision a path to success.

The second part of this book is incredibly valuable, too, because it offers a detailed road map on how to weave humanity, compassion, connection, and learning into the workplace, rebrand so-called soft skills to stress their critical importance, and foster and prioritize critical communication skills for individual and organizational success.

JENNIFER DAVIS
Founder and President, Jennifer Davis Media Group

What if your workplace culture reinforced learning and development in ways that grew capabilities for communicating, and strengthened emotional and social intelligence while contributing solid value to your key stakeholders and bottom line? And what if you discovered those same skills nourished a sense of meaning and purpose to the lives of your employees? What might your organization gain? *Conscious, Capable, and Ready to Contribute: A Fable* tells the story and shows the way to unify our human needs for meaning and value with a company's need to survive and thrive—while making a positive contribution to the world.

LLOYD RAINES
Executive Coach and Principal, Integral Focus

Conscious, Capable, and Ready to Contribute: A Fable is not an ordinary business book. Instead, Offterdinger and Allen use a fictional story to demonstrate the practical need, yet profound impact, of developing people in the workplace. A must-read that follows a CEO's journey to passionately invest in his employees—it will make you think differently about how we're all responsible for contributions for the greater good.

ANNELI WERNER
President and Creative Director, The Jake Group

Conscious
Capable
and Ready to
Contribute

A FABLE

CONSCIOUS
CAPITALISM
PRESS™

Ed Offterdinger
Catherine Allen

Conscious
Capable
and
Ready to
Contribute

• A FABLE •

How Employee Development Can Become
the Highest Form of Social Contribution

Conscious Capitalism Press
www.consciouscapitalism.org/press

Round Table Companies
Packaging, production, and distribution services
www.roundtablecompanies.com

Executive Editing	**Agata Antonow**
Cover Design	**Christy Bui**
Interior Design	**Christy Bui, Sunny DiMartino**
Proofreading	**Adam Lawrence, Carly Cohen**

Printed in the United States of America

First Edition: September 2021
10 9 8 7 6 5 4 3 2

Library of Congress Cataloging-in-Publication Data
Conscious, capable, and ready to contribute: a fable: how employee
development can become the highest form of social contribution
/ Ed Offterdinger, Catherine Allen.—1st ed. p. cm.
ISBN Hardcover: 978-1-950466-25-2
ISBN Paperback: 978-1-950466-26-9
ISBN Digital: 978-1-950466-27-6
Library of Congress Control Number: 2021907091

Conscious Capitalism Press is an imprint of Conscious Capitalism, Inc.
The Conscious Capitalism Press logo is a trademark of Conscious Capitalism, Inc.

Round Table Companies and the RTC logo are trademarks of
Writers of the Round Table, Inc.

We dedicate this book to Spencer, Sydney, Olivia, Danny, and Charlie, and the generations of young people who will create workplaces committed to conscious people development.

Contents

The Fable

1

How to Shift

173

Understand the Role of Leadership 176
Align Business and People Strategies 181
Define Conscious Development Culture Principles 185
Identify Core People Capabilities 189
Embed Conscious Development throughout the Employee Life Cycle 196
Conscious Development Employee Life Cycle Model 197
Managing the Shift 212

Behind the Fable

215

About AO People Partners 221
Acknowledgments 223

The Fable

One

Andrew sat in his office for three hours, poring over materials for the upcoming executive committee meeting. He studied the monthly financial statements and analysis, disappointed to note eroding margins and flattening revenue. He reached into the tipping-over stack of documents in front of him to pull out the latest HR report; it highlighted rising turnover and lower-than-expected employee engagement scores.

Andrew started sorting all the reports featuring bad news to the right of his desk, his "to take action" file. Turning to the marketing report, he saw that client satisfaction scores had dropped for the third month in a row in all sectors of Shift's business. The declines were slight, but the trend was troubling. The marketing report also highlighted a new player on the scene known as Axxcel. Led by Pamela Turner, a former partner from one of the major global advisory firms, this two-year-old consultancy was winning large contracts in Shift's core markets. Andrew was embarrassed that he had never heard of them. *Have I not been paying attention? How did I miss this?*

Taken separately, none of the reports were especially worrisome. But piled on the right side of his desk, they towered over the tiny pile of papers on the left-hand side. They made Andrew's stomach lurch. He picked up the phone to call Pat Carter, his partner and the cofounder of Shift Advisors. Then he put the phone down.

Instead of calling Pat, he stood and stared out the window, looking out at the Washington, DC, skyline and adjusting his silver cuff links. *Three years ago, I would have known about all of this. Now that we've grown*

Conscious, Capable, and Ready to Contribute

1

and keeping up on day-to-day operations is someone else's responsibility, am I letting important things drop? Has Pat even seen these numbers? What now?

His internal conversation was ended abruptly by a knock behind him. He turned to find Leslie Weaver, one of the specialists on the Change Management team, standing in his doorway. Leslie had joined Shift seven years earlier. Andrew smiled at Leslie as he recalled Pat's interview assessment. "We MUST hire Leslie. Notre Dame grad. Big Irish Catholic family has prepared her well for tough conversations with change-averse clients. Excellent blend of brains, people skills, and poise."

"Bad time to talk to you? Your assistant, Meg, said you had a minute . . ." Leslie tucked a strand of her red hair behind her ear and looked around.

Andrew smiled, chasing away his worries. He gestured to one of the chairs in front of his desk. "Not at all. I keep this hour open every day. What's on your mind?"

Leslie lowered herself into the chair, and Andrew did his best to clear his mind of his worries. He realized he hadn't done a very good job when he heard just the tail end of Leslie's words. ". . . I know this is an important client, but I feel uneasy with the way the client's point person talks to our team members. I don't feel like him yelling at us, saying the latest report was 'something a five-year-old could have written' is acceptable. It's not in alignment with what we stand for. That's just one of my concerns, but if the team and I could step back and just get reassigned to a project where we feel valued and can do our best work . . ."

Andrew focused on the words, realizing he wasn't even sure which client Leslie was referring to. *I used to know which team was working on each project. Is this what growth feels like? When did I start getting out of the loop? Don't we teach our team members how to handle difficult clients— wouldn't that have helped here?*

"I hear you, Leslie," he began, grasping for the right words, trying to remember if he had heard what led to the client's comments. "Right now, though, Shift is at an important juncture, and one of the things we really admire about you and the Change Management team is your resilience. You can do this."

Leslie looked like she was about to say something, but her mouth closed with a click.

Andrew took that as a sign he was on the right trajectory. "Personality differences are difficult. I completely understand. But it's important not to get reactive. Try to focus on providing the best care and value for our clients. You know that our number one core value is to provide exceptional service and care for our clients." Andrew pointed to the values framed behind his desk. "Cared for and seen" stood out in elegant script. "Our job is not just to support clients as their companies make U-turns but to make each client feel like part of the Shift family."

Leslie nodded and smiled a little crookedly. "That's exactly what our team is trying to do, but . . ."

Just then, Andrew's phone beeped, and he cursed himself for not putting it on mute as he typically did for this "open door" hour of his day. He glanced at the screen and saw Pat's name.

"Sorry, Leslie. It's Pat." He scanned the words on the text: **Big problem with the Jackson contract. Come to my office the second you get this!**

He glanced up, apologetic, feeling a genuine pang at not being able to guide Leslie through her problem and learning more about the challenge at work. "Sorry, Leslie, but could you wait here just five minutes? Pat has an urgent situation we need to take care of with a client we're bringing on tomorrow, but your issue is important to me, too. I'd love to discuss your team's challenges more. Just five minutes."

Leslie had started to say something, but Andrew didn't quite hear her as he dashed down the hall to Pat's office.

The crisis with Pat turned out to be that the new client had added in an unexpected clause to Shift's standard contract; it took twenty minutes to resolve. By the time Andrew got back to his office, Leslie was gone. Instead, Leo Vincent was standing at the office door.

Leo Vincent had led the Change Management service line for the past seven years. When Leo and his team swept into a company, creating plans for how to turn around leadership or fix a flawed business plan, Andrew marveled at Leo's ability to gain the team's trust and create excitement for change. Just last week, one of their clients had called to sing Leo's praises. "Working with Leo has meant we're all rolling out of bed thrilled to come to work to tackle changes to our company culture. We're happy to sign on for six more months if you can promise us we can keep working with him."

Conscious, Capable, and Ready to Contribute

"Andrew, I need to tell you something," Leo's mouth was pursed, as though he had just swallowed the last cold sip of hours-old coffee. "Well, actually, a few things."

"Sounds serious. Come on in."

Leo closed the door and took a seat at Andrew's mahogany conference table. Andrew walked over and joined him.

It took a few seconds for Leo to look up and start talking. "Don't believe your press clippings. Remember when you told me that?"

"I also told you clients may be thrilled with your work, but you still need to keep pushing." Andrew recalled coaching Leo to avoid excessive self-promotion of his own accomplishments. "Clients expect and deserve excellence on every project, every day."

Andrew rested his elbows on the shiny table, folded his hands in front of his face, and said, "Leo, what's going on?"

"You need to stop kidding yourself." Leo's voice cracked. His chest and hands were shaking. "Shift Advisors is not what it used to be, and it sure isn't worthy of the company of the year awards being handed out at that breakfast tomorrow."

The words pushed the air from the room. Leo had never spoken to Andrew like that before, and hearing them from the kind, affable man made Andrew feel he'd just stepped into the twilight zone. "Leo. Wow. Used to be—?" Andrew began, but Leo kept talking, his voice rising with each statement.

"When you and Pat recruited me seven years ago, your vision was crystal clear. You two left BCC because you were going to build a consulting firm that cared more about its people and clients than partner profits. But you've changed. You've lost sight of Shift's core purpose and your vaunted core values—"

"Whoa, slow down. I—Where are you going with all this?" Andrew said, squinting his eyes like he was trying to bring the conversation into focus. His mind was trying to piece together the words Leo was saying, but it felt like they were having two different conversations. Worse, the conversation Leo was having was effectively flinging mud at Shift. Andrew felt the pain of each hurtful word about Shift, as though Leo were landing physical blows.

Leo's face looked drawn, and he leaned forward so much he was practically coming out of his seat. "I'll tell you where I'm going. Where *we're* going. But first, let me ask you a question . . ."

"Answer my question, first! What is this all about?"

Leo waved him off. "Did you even read the feedback provided in the latest employee engagement surveys?"

Andrew was on his feet. "Tell me what you mean, 'where we're going.'" Glancing at the door, he wondered if others could hear the ruckus.

Leo stared at Andrew. "Have you noticed turnover rising? We've lost several senior managers and directors. And it's happening right in your backyard, too. Your head of communications quit. She told HR, 'Andrew either blows off meeting requests or rewrites everything. He's impossible.' And Pat's last two assistants left with no notice. Reason given? 'Severe exhaustion.' Look, Pat's nice, but who could possibly keep up with the hours she works? Have you read what's being posted on Glassdoor?"

Andrew glanced to his left toward his MacBook Pro.

Leo laughed. It was not a warm sound. "I didn't think so, but I was hoping I was wrong. Take a look; I'll wait."

Andrew opened the laptop and found the Glassdoor website, aware of Leo's eyes on him. His heart sank. "'We used to be visionary, now we're mercenary'?"

"I wouldn't make too big a deal about your nomination tomorrow. You can be sure it was given primarily because of Shift's financial performance."

"Leo, I had no idea. I've spent the last few hours immersed in the reports for the EC meeting. I can see we have challenges. Let's work on figuring out solutions together . . ."

In a quiet voice, devoid of any emotion, Leo said, "Andrew, I won't be here. That's what I'm here to tell you. To be honest, I've been playing the field for about six months. I'm leaving today, and my team will be giving notice as well. We've engaged counsel, and we don't believe your noncompete and nonsolicitation agreements are valid."

Andrew could feel his heartbeat in the veins on his neck. He stared at Leo and said nothing for a few seconds. "Over those six months playing the field, what prevented you from walking in here, confronting me, and giving us all a chance to change our direction together? No courage? Or do you respect me so little?"

Conscious, Capable, and Ready to Contribute

Leo looked at the door but said nothing.

"Damn it, Leo! Say something. You're going to crater the whole Change Management practice we handed you? And what—steal all our clients? We do the work of bringing them on—and you're going to poach them and just waltz off?"

"Yelling at me won't help. My decision has been made. Oh, and by the way, if you want people coming to you with problems, maybe you need to create a place where your team feels comfortable doing that. You're so proud of your open-door hours, but what have you done to make team members come to you? I've probably heard more about our company from our people than you have in the past month."

Leo took a deep breath, visibly reining himself in. "Anyway. We are leaving and going to join Axxcel. We start Monday. And we're not 'stealing all your clients.' Who do you think attracted them and made them want to work with us in the first place? And who covered for you while you were apparently not paying attention to the people you claim to care so much about?"

Andrew slammed his laptop shut with enough force that he felt a sharp twinge in his wrist. It matched the pain in his head. He turned away from Leo, unable to look at him. He took a few deep breaths, his pulse like a drum at his temples. *Axxcel! First clients, now our people?*

As his pounding heart calmed, he turned around. "Leo, we've been together a long time. Will you do me one favor?"

Leo's eyes narrowed. "I will try."

"I appreciate that. Please wait until the day after tomorrow to officially quit—until after the awards breakfast and the tenth anniversary party. You know I need to sleep on things. Maybe you could, too. Meet me at the house for coffee the day after tomorrow? Julia's away. So it will be just us. If you still feel like leaving after we chat, I'll support your transition. Will you do that for me?"

Leo looked down, closed his eyes, and took a deep breath. "I will. But don't be too optimistic, Andrew. It may be too late for me. Maybe it's not too late for you and Shift."

Leo stood to leave. "I'm going to skip the tenth anniversary party. I'm not that good an actor. I'll email Pat that I feel the flu coming on."

"I'll see you at seven thirty the day after tomorrow. Can you close the door on the way out?"

Andrew looked at his phone to see if he had any texts from Julia. There were none. He missed hearing from his wife, and he badly needed her to tell him it would all be okay, but he also didn't want to text and bother her. Julia was with her mother, and Andrew didn't want to text Julia when she was by what could turn out to be her mother's deathbed. Andrew's phone flashed the time at him like an accusation. "Whoa. Five forty-five." He stood up slowly, feeling more seventy than fifty. *Is there any chance of tomorrow not being a total disaster?*

Two

The next day, Andrew felt as if he were dressing for a funeral.

As the CEO of a fast-growing, successful management consulting firm, Andrew knew how to act the part. After all, when clients turned to Shift to help them transform their business or pivot in their industry, they needed to see a leader who was in charge. Andrew channeled that leader now—the one who could take a company with flagging products and turn it around. He put on his favorite gray Canali suit. He looked in the mirror as he slipped on his cuff links. With his crisp blue patterned shirt, blue-and-black-striped tie, and his favorite shiny black Allen Edmonds Oxford dress shoes, he looked every inch the successful fifty-year-old executive. He wanted to look his best for the Company of the Year awards breakfast, even if their recent performance disqualified Shift from winning. The team had been looking forward to the anniversary party and awards breakfast for so long. Both taking place on the same day had required intense planning, but the party had been on the books a year in advance, and he hadn't been willing to say "no" to the awards breakfast when the invitation arrived over the summer.

"Just think of what it will mean to everyone on our team if we win," he had told Pat months ago, when they had been planning both events.

Pat had smiled at that. "You're getting soft. You must mean *when* we win, right?"

How things had changed.

Walking into the massive Marriott Marquis ballroom, Andrew felt a deep ache in his solar plexus from Julia's absence. He took three deep breaths and put on his game face—the one he usually only needed for important sales pitches—then started chatting with a few clients.

"Hello, hello, good to see you."

"Good luck. Hope we are both big winners!"

He found the Shift table, said a round of hellos to everyone, and plopped down next to Pat. She leaned over and whispered, "Nice look. And without Julia's help! I'm proud of you."

Before diving into his breakfast, Andrew texted Julia. **At breakfast. Wish you were here. Madly!** He watched his phone, hoping for a quick reply. He hadn't told her about Leo. She had enough on her plate. As the award ceremony started and winners were announced one after the other, he continually checked, but his phone remained stubbornly silent.

Andrew looked around at the tables filled with laughing, smiling business leaders. *Do any of these CEOs, company owners, and founders ever feel like frauds? Do they keep an eye on everything at their company?* Andrew couldn't quite keep yesterday out of mind. He still had that sinking feeling, as though he had been doing his best to be a caring leader and live up to the values he still felt at his very core, but at some point he had gotten busy landing more clients, growing the company, and had stopped paying attention. He was slowly allowing his company to get worse for it. *How could I have let that happen? I work my butt off every day for Shift. I care about my people and my values. I thought I was doing the right thing by helping the company grow for all of us. What did I miss?*

The meal was surprisingly good, even if most of the speeches were not. *Is it hard to serve quality scrambled eggs for four hundred people?* he wondered, entertaining himself during a particularly standard acceptance speech thanking all the usuals. Taking a sip of orange juice, he scanned the audience. He noticed his friend Gary Norris, a well-respected investment banker, sitting across the room. Andrew also recognized most of Gary's tablemates, including several partners and clients. The one new face at the table was an attractive blond who looked to be in her mid-forties.

Pat noticed her, too, and whispered, "Who's the woman with Gary?"

"No idea," Andrew whispered back. "I was thinking the same thing."

"I wonder how she got that dress," replied Pat with the raising of one eyebrow. "I saw it on Saks's website. Preorder only. She has good taste—it's stunning."

Andrew's attention moved from the mystery woman to the front of the room, where the emcee was taking control of the microphone again. "Now, for our final award—Professional Services Company of the Year! Among the more than one hundred nominations received, our judges looked for performance in four overall categories: revenue growth, quality of services, financial performance, and corporate social responsibility."

"Good luck, partner," Pat whispered. "Remember: you do the talking!"

Andrew responded to Pat with a casual thumbs-up. Time seemed to slow down as he looked around the table at his team and landed on the one empty seat where Leo would have been. Their conversation repeated in his mind. *Playing the field for six months?* How could Andrew not feel betrayed? And Leo threatened to take his entire team. *That was not okay.* So much heat was now rising in Andrew's face that he didn't notice when the spotlight hit their table.

He looked to his left as Pat leapt up in slow motion. Her smile was huge, and for a moment he could see how she must have looked as a seven-year-old child—exuberant, as she raised her face to the sky and stretched her arms wide. The heat in his face dissipated quickly when he saw the explosion of joy in Pat and the other members of the Shift team, all of whom were now on their feet clapping furiously.

Why are they so happy? he found himself wondering. He thought of the times he'd seen laughter spread across a room even when not everyone had heard the joke.

Pat was yelling at him now, her smile morphing into concern as she leaned down toward him. But her words were muddied in Andrew's ears like the teacher from Charlie Brown: "Wah wah wah."

And just like that, the world snapped back into real time as he made out her words.

"We won! We won!"

Andrew moved into gear. Pat held up her hand, and he looked her in the eye as he met her high five, making sure to keep smiling to chase the worried look from her face. Then together, they made their way to the stage, his adrenaline kicking in. Andrew stood tall as he shook hands with the publisher of the *DC Business Weekly*. Together, they posed for a picture, his extensive experience at the front of the room propelling him forward as though on autopilot. As the crowd settled back into their seats, Andrew stepped forward to the podium, unprepared to speak.

He looked out at the crowd and smiled at a few friends. The glare of the bright lights made him squint as he cleared his throat. He was thirsty, so thirsty, as he felt a bead of sweat crawling down his temple.

"As some of you know, Pat and I started Shift Advisors ten years ago today. We had big dreams. We—"

Andrew looked back to his team's table just as Leo slid into his empty seat. Another team member leaned over, and the two exchanged a few words. Andrew's pulse was rising, and he took a step back from the microphone, out of concern it would pick up the thumping in his chest.

"We—"

"We—" He stood a little straighter, tore his eyes from Leo and caught Pat's concerned gaze. He continued. ". . . wanted to create a strategy and change management consultancy to help businesses shift into high gear. We intended to do right by our clients, our people, and our community. We expected to grow—but to have three hundred and fifty consultants delivering over one hundred million dollars in services in our tenth year? No way. And of course, we couldn't have imagined winning an award like this—there are so many incredible professional services firms in DC." Andrew paused, eyeing the water glass on his table, twenty steps away.

"Congratulations to everyone in this room."

With an awkward smile, Andrew raised the award in the air and then stepped away from the podium. He didn't meet Pat's eyes as he walked past her and headed back to their table. By the time he returned to his seat, Leo was gone from the table. Quickly scanning the room, Andrew noticed Leo standing to the side, watching the attendees. Andrew felt relief, but he could still feel himself sweat in his suit. Had Leo said anything to the rest of the team? Did everyone else know that a third of the company had left?

His team members rose to meet him, cheering him and Pat on. Andrew wouldn't remember later what was said—only that he had picked up his water glass and downed it in one go, focusing on keeping his hands from visibly shaking.

Conscious, Capable, and Ready to Contribute

After the breakfast ended, as he and Pat walked to the door, Andrew kept an eye out for Leo, who was speaking with some people Andrew had never met. Several colleagues slapped Andrew on the back and congratulated the pair. Reaching the lobby, Andrew heard a familiar voice yell, "Hold up, big winners!"

Andrew and Pat turned to see Gary Norris and his mystery guest walking briskly toward them. "Congrats, you two. I'm thrilled for you."

Andrew grinned. "Thanks, Gary!" He reached out his right hand toward the blond woman standing beside Gary. "Hi, I'm Andrew Hyde, and this is my cofounder and partner, Pat Carter."

"Yes. I know," the woman laughed. "I think everyone in the room knows who you two are. Congratulations. My name is Pamela Turner, CEO of Axxcel."

Andrew's near-incapacitating thirst returned with a vengeance. His mouth dropped open for a moment as he heard Pat say, "Hello Pamela. It is so nice to meet you. I have to confess that Andrew and I both noticed you sitting with Gary. Your dress is gorgeous. So happy that Gary grabbed us before we left."

"Well, thanks. I have a friend at Saks who owed me a favor. You and Andrew looked great up there. I can only hope that my firm can win that award someday. We're pretty new to town, but who knows? Maybe we can catch up to Shift."

"I would love to learn more about Axxcel. It's always good to know the competition. Lunch, sometime? I know Andrew would love to join us."

Andrew felt faint, desperate to end the exchange with Pamela. *Would she mention Leo? "I'm so thrilled to have Leo on my team. He speaks so well of you."* Andrew wished he could turn back the clock one hour so he could pull Pat aside and tell her about Leo. *How could I have kept this from her?*

Pamela flashed a smile at Andrew. "That would be lovely. I've been learning a lot about Shift recently. It will be fun to hear from the two visionaries. In fact . . ."

Andrew managed to croak, "Sure. Sounds great."

"Well, I need to get going," Pamela said as she handed her business card to Pat and Andrew. "Nice to finally meet you two. I know we will be talking."

The Fable

12

As Gary and Pamela walked away, Pat turned to Andrew. "She was awesome. You okay?"

Do I tell her now? No. I can convince Leo to stay.

"I'm good. A bit dehydrated from my morning run. Voice is shot from all the chatting and the speech. Ready to get back to the office?"

"Sure. See you there. Way to go, partner. Told you we'd win!"

Andrew flashed her a thumbs-up and headed to his car.

Driving, he no longer felt thirsty. He told himself that the run was the cause of his symptoms at breakfast. But underneath everything, he felt a nagging fear. There was something under the surface, scratching to get out. His mind kept reviewing the numbers from HR, marketing, and finance, looking for solutions. *The team at Shift always looks happy. Everyone at the breakfast was smiling and laughing. What am I missing?*

His thoughts turned to the tense exchange with Pamela Turner and the moment he had wondered whether she would mention Leo. Suddenly, he felt himself sitting up taller than he had in a long time, endorphins making the ends of his fingers tingle and his chest expand the way it did when he ran. He had to do this—had to turn it all around.

First, he needed to rally the team. Walking into the celebration dinner at Pat's house, he felt confident and committed to what was possible. With the winds of the award at their backs, everyone in the room teemed with optimism. "Where's Julia?" was the hardest question of the evening.

"She's in Sarasota," Andrew offered. "Her mom may be nearing the end. Alzheimer's. She couldn't take the chance."

He was immediately met with nods from some and hugs from others, along with comforting words like "I'm so sorry, Andrew," and "Please give her our love."

Pat's husband, Tim, owned several successful restaurants, and his catering division had transformed his and Pat's home into an intimate version of his famous Chesapeake Bay–themed restaurant, Easton on Penn. As usual, Tim's food was sublime. As coffee and after-dinner drinks were being served, Pat stood up and tapped a wine glass with her dessert spoon. As her guests put their conversations on hold, she looked around the room, making eye contact with each of them. Later, some would say it felt like she was chatting with them one-on-one in a small booth at the back of Easton's.

Conscious, Capable, and Ready to Contribute

13

"I know Andrew has a few things to say, but tonight, I'm going first! He's become more patient over the last decade, but I don't want to take a chance that he steals all my good lines."

"First, thank you, Tim. I'm lucky to be married to you. It's a bonus that you're the best chef in DC!" There were whistles, and several partners stomped their feet. One or two seemed to be catapulted from their chairs. The rest of the room followed suit.

Tim blushed, pressed his hands together and bowed as if to say *namaste*. He mouthed "Thank you."

After a minute or two, the Shift partners and their guests returned to their seats. Turning to her left, Pat's eyes locked on Andrew. Those seated at his table would have described the look on her face as a mixture of admiration, gratitude, and joy. Others saw the love of a sister. Pat held up a standard business envelope high in the air and asked a question: "Anyone know what's inside?"

"Bonus checks for all the partners?" shouted Will Parsons, the co-leader of Shift's Strategy practice. The crowd roared its approval.

"Not all the partners, Will." She winked and continued. "Just the high performers." Again, the partners laughed; a few slapped Will on the back. "Maybe next year, Will," deadpanned his wife.

"Inside this envelope is pure gold." Pat paused, letting her words quiet them down. "Truthfully, it's fifty-four written words."

Will tried again. "The recipe for Julia Hyde's famous chocolate chip cookies?"

From day one at Shift, Andrew's wife, Julia, appeared at the office periodically with freshly baked cookies, still warm from the oven. She delivered them personally to each team member and partner; it was a tradition everyone loved, and one that had continued year after year.

"Will, you can stop sucking up. But let's raise a glass to Julia, Shift's secret weapon. We wish you were with us tonight, and we send our love to you and your mother."

Turning toward Andrew, the crowd cried out "Julia!"

Andrew nodded his head, overwhelmed at the gesture. He noticed his long-time executive assistant, Meg, was recording Pat's comments on her iPhone. He looked forward to sending the video to Julia, to share this crazy day with her.

"My friends, inside this envelope is a memo—but not just any memo. No, ladies and gentlemen, it's a memorandum we received ten years ago from the BCC managing partner—our boss at the time. But what's important is what Andrew and I wrote on the other side. Yes, my friends, this is the original Shift Advisors business plan penned by Andrew and me on one cold night in Wisconsin. By the way, every night is cold in Wisconsin."

"You kept it for ten years?" Andrew shouted. He was standing now.

"Yes, partner. These fifty-four words changed my life. They changed our lives. This simple business plan—vision, values, and dreams—has worked for a decade. I treasure it. When I feel a bit lost, I pull out our big plan and read it slowly, reflecting on each word."

Every set of eyes was on the two founders. Andrew looked up, closed his eyes, and opened his mouth to speak. Everyone could see his tears. Still blinking, he stepped to Pat and hugged her the way childhood friends do when they meet unexpectedly on the street.

When the embrace finally ended, Andrew spoke. "Thank you, Pat. You're a phenomenal partner—brilliant, genuine, and kind. And you have a great eye for talent," he said, gesturing to the group. "I look forward to another decade of shifting with you. Let's raise a glass. To Pat."

"To Pat!" the crowd roared.

Andrew fought off the urge to just sit down and enjoy the party. "When I think back to that night at the Pfister hotel in Milwaukee, I remember we were exhausted. Pat and I had worked for BCC since business school. The hours were always long, but those last few months had been more grueling than usual. Neither of us had been home in two months. As one colleague said, we were 'sick and tired of being sick and tired.' And the client? Let's just say the client's team was a lovely combination of overconfident and underqualified.

"One night I was talking to Julia on my phone when housekeeping came in for turn-down service. It was about eight thirty. The maid said, 'I'm sorry Mr. Hyde. You're not usually home at this time.' That felt like the last straw. I had to ask myself, when had this hotel become 'home'? Had I been there so long housekeeping knew my schedule?

"When Pat and I met for drinks that night, we were both feeling discouraged. But more than that, we were at our lowest. We'd worked eighty-hour weeks for two months straight. We felt unseen and unheard. Truthfully, we were feeling mean. A few cocktails fueled that indignation. Earlier that day, we had received a memorandum from our fearless leader. *Do this. Don't do that. Get more billable hours. Let's specialize while being a one-stop shop. There's no 'I' in team. Blah. Blah. Blah.* For a while we just vented to each other, as we penned brilliant responses to his edicts in the margins. 'No shit, Sherlock' seemed to be as creative as we could get."

Pat pointed to a corner of the memo paper she was still holding. "You'll notice my handiwork with the caricature of the BCC managing partner in the corner!"

"After laughing like teenagers at our pithy responses, we realized that we were just in a really bad, dark place. Pat had the good sense to order coffee, and then she flipped the memo over and started scribbling. For the next two hours, our vision for a firm of our own took shape. We saw a future with happy, fulfilled partners and employees. With better clients and challenging assignments. With talented employees. We were ready to make a difference in the community. And while it was never about the money, we knew we could create a very profitable enterprise."

Andrew paused, looking down at the floor to his left, letting his eyes close. He pushed the mental image of Leo away. After about ten seconds, he opened his eyes and smiled. "Tonight is about celebrating all we have accomplished together so far. It's been a good run. Let's keep it going for another decade!"

Will jumped to his feet and, in a voice fueled by an abundance of red wine, shouted, "To the company of the year!"

The room exploded with "Shift! Shift! Shift!"

Andrew pumped his arm like a big rig trucker pulling his air horn, feeling like a kid. For the moment, his earlier worries were gone. Pat grabbed him, and the two danced to the rhythm of The Beatles' "Birthday," which was blaring from the ceiling speakers. The crowd clapped as Andrew dipped Pat perilously close to the shiny hardwood floor.

Twenty minutes later, he snuck out of the party. It was only ten o'clock. Ten years ago, he would have been forced into a taxi by the host. His overwhelming need to be one of the boys would have meant a sheepish next-morning call to mumble an apology and ask about the whereabouts of his keys.

Not tonight. As he walked down Tim and Pat's crumbling driveway, buttoning his suit jacket and ducking around a slightly overgrown rhododendron, he couldn't remember the last time he had stayed to the last minutes of a party.

Driving home, he thought about Pat's speech and their journey together. She was always a brilliant thinker and worked harder than everyone around her. Before the pivotal night in Milwaukee, that's about all he knew about her—and that she had been high school valedictorian and earned a merit scholarship to UVA, where she had a perfect grade point average. As they brainstormed their future, Pat opened up about growing up as the middle child and only daughter in the Wilson household. "Dad was a bigwig at GE. Mom played the doting wife and hostess role as if Dad had chosen her from central casting. My older brother, Chip—yes, as in 'chip off the old block'— was good looking, good at sports, and lazy as hell. And could do no wrong. I covered for him all the time—alibis, proofreading, sometimes writing entire papers. The main thing I did to help him was *not* talk about my successes."

Turning into his neighborhood, Andrew remembered thinking, *Sounds lonely*. Out loud he had said, "Well, you seem to have turned out okay!"

"Thanks. Therapy, coaching, a strong female mentor—a client, actually—turned me around. But I'm a work-in-progress. So just know as we start this venture that I've got some hardwiring to keep in mind. I will need your trust and support. And I need us to be equal partners."

"I haven't held up my end of the bargain lately, have I Pat?" Andrew muttered to himself now, as he approached his home.

Pulling into his driveway, he sighed, turned off the car, and trudged into the house, suddenly exhausted. He dropped his keys, wallet, and phone onto the black granite kitchen island and walked to the front door. He knelt to pick up a small Amazon box when something shiny in the garden caught his eye. He laughed when he saw the crystals. Julia always 'recharged' her crystals when the full moon came around. Andrew had no idea what that meant, but he believed in her magic.

Looking up at the clear September sky, he recalled Julia's reference to the harvest moon on their call earlier that day. "And babe, it's a blue moon. Crazy energy today," she had exclaimed. "Be prepared for anything. And try and remember your dreams."

Conscious, Capable, and Ready to Contribute

Heck of a day, Julia, he offered to the glorious sky. He carried the small box into the house, shut the door firmly, and set the security alarm. Andrew walked into the kitchen where he picked up a notebook sitting next to some of Julia's stones. Julia had written a message.

"Look at the configuration of these stones as you read the explanations. You'll know what they're telling you to remember."

Julia's note continued in her flowing cursive handwriting. "The four crystals are:

Clear quartz—amplifies energy and intention, protects against negativity.

Datolite—the green color signifies true potential for learning and seeking knowledge.

Carnelian—stimulates creativity and gives courage.

Citrine—a stone of abundance and manifestation. It attracts wealth, prosperity, and all things good. It also encourages generosity and the sharing of good fortune."

In that moment, Andrew would have given half his annual salary just to have Julia by his side. Even one thousand miles away, she was looking out for him, sending him encouragement. He felt he needed all the knowledge, creativity, energy, and courage he could get.

As he walked up the stairs to the bedroom, he remembered that Leo was coming for coffee at seven thirty the next morning. Just like that, the heaviness set back in. Shift Advisors was about to become a company without a team to help clients shift. As he got into bed that night and pulled up the covers, he felt like he was slowly inching toward the top of a rollercoaster. He closed his eyes. It was a long way down.

Three

Andrew rarely dreamed, but when he did, the pattern was almost always the same. He was shown framed images in rapid succession, like he was scanning an old reel of film, one scene at a time. This night's cinematic voyage started with black-and-white newspaper headlines, like the spinning news flashes he recalled from the campy *Batman* TV show of the 1960s. But in this dream, there was no caped crusader.

Shift: Mercenary not Visionary!

All Hyde cares about is bottom line: "profits before people" claims key employee

Company of the Year award rescinded!

Shift employees and clients bail on struggling consulting firm

Glassdoor reports: Shift ranked Worst Place to Work

The rotating headlines stopped with an abrupt ding as an elevator door opened. Andrew saw himself step out gingerly, glancing around as if expecting a mugger to leap from the shadows.

Andrew felt his body slip into the film just as he turned from the lobby toward his office. The dim lights flickered on and off. A constant annoying hum like an electrical transformer filled the air. As Andrew experienced the dream, he thought of Julia, who refused to watch horror movies. *This is so creepy*, he could picture her saying.

It looks like Shift, he thought. *But why is it so hot in here? Is the A/C out? "Hello?"*

At the end of the hall, Andrew turned right and gasped. A vast floor opened up before him. Andrew was sweating profusely, and his heart began to pound. Body odor, human waste, rotting food—the smells rose up like living things and almost made him gag. Everywhere he looked, Andrew saw people bent over work stations, their hands in frantic motion. Some stitched clothing; others welded parts together, sparks shooting out from their machinery. Hot on the heels of the stench, the deep boom and whine of the industrial machines reached him. Andrew covered his ears in an attempt to muffle the din.

Most of the male workers wore dirty overalls and raggedy shirts. Their leather boots were scuffed. As one worker moved around his worktable, Andrew noticed how the tongue on his left boot flopped, causing him to shuffle. Despite the oppressive heat, nearly all the boys wore the types of hats Andrew had seen in documentaries about nineteenth-century British factory workers.

"My God. At least half of these workers aren't over the age of thirteen."

Suddenly, a loud whistle pierced the air. The workers came to an abrupt stop. An older man on a platform in the corner yelled, "Next shift!" The boys and men staggered to a door that had opened at the far end of the hall. Just then, Andrew was nearly trampled as the next group of workers pushed their way down the hall. The new batch entered the plant and found their way to their stations. Another whistle blew and furious activity resumed. The noise and smell swelled like a wave around Andrew.

Without any warning, Andrew was whisked to a different location in the building. Standing behind a pillar in the Shift Advisors lunchroom, he eavesdropped as two of Shift's best-performing Change Management specialists huddled at the end of the room waiting for coffee. Andrew recognized Leslie Weaver at once by her bright red hair. She was doing most of the talking while her colleague, Elena Núñez, was still. He could also see that Leslie was sobbing. Elena's lips were taut, and her face was red.

"Elena, I don't know what to do. They've got me working on the 3745 account. I knew it was going to be rough when Andrew assigned me. It's worse than I could have imagined."

Elena asked, "Did something specific happen?"

Leslie blushed a bit and stared at the floor.

"You can tell me."

Leslie looked straight into Elena's eyes. She took a deep breath. "The CEO hit on me. He was subtle. But . . . it was easy to see what he had on his mind."

"What'd you do?"

"Getting him to back off was fairly easy. Not my first rodeo."

"Go on, Leslie."

"I still can't believe they are a client. I can remember Andrew and Pat always saying how they will only choose clients whose values match ours. In my second year at the company, they turned down a four-hundred-thousand-dollar contract because the client set unrealistic deadlines. We could have met the milestones, but it would have meant working twelve-hour days for over a month. Any other hungry start-up would have enthusiastically said yes. But not Pat and Andrew. They cared about our well-being. We were all amazed and proud. What has happened to that Shift?"

Elena was looking at Leslie, who had turned away to stare at the ceiling. "There's more, isn't there?" After a few moments, her shoulders sagged as she turned back to face Elena.

"Tom's—we were almost at five years of remission. We were planning to go away for a weekend to celebrate that milestone." Leslie paused and let out a deep sigh. "His doctors want to start chemo next week."

"Oh, Leslie. I'm so sorry. Can I help you with the kids, or jump in on some of your projects while you're off taking care of Tom?"

Leslie burst into tears again. "That's just it. When I told Andrew that I was going to need some time off, or at least a little flexibility in my schedule, all he could say was, 'I don't know, Leslie. We're at a pretty critical juncture on the 3745 project.'"

"You're kidding me. What did you say?"

"I was stunned. Before I could respond, he got a text and said, 'Listen, I've got to go see Pat. I'll think about what you've said but—' Then he blew out of his office, leaving me to just show myself out."

Elena slammed her coffee cup on the counter, hard enough to cause the ceramic to shatter. Shards flew about. Thankfully, none hit Leslie or Elena. "We've got to do something. Let's go see Pat today—" She stopped mid-sentence and looked at the crestfallen Leslie. "That won't help, will it?"

"Pat was just as excited when Andrew accepted 3745 Real Estate as a client. Even with all the indictments and their reputation for suing everyone who works for them. And she just promoted Will to senior partner. Will used to be a phenomenal mentor. Now, all he cares about are the bonuses and having the newest BMW. I don't think there is anything I can do, and I need this job. Tom's going to be out of work for a while. Our insurance is through Shift."

Andrew was just getting ready to reveal himself when Leslie and Elena vanished. He ran to the door and looked up and down the corridor. They were nowhere to be seen.

Just then, Andrew heard loud voices and the steady, repetitive buzz of machines in constant use. He walked toward the source of the clamor. After a few turns, he found himself in a large conference room full of shredders. The noise was nearly deafening. Scanning the room, Andrew saw approximately twenty Shift employees manning the machines. Boxes of records were piled high. These were clearly marked "Woodson Pharma." Some employees were hauling bright green bags of shredded confetti out to a loading dock, which was somehow built into the far end of the conference room.

Andrew saw Will Parsons, colead of Strategy, in the midst of the organized chaos. "Will, what's going on?" Andrew screamed over the cacophony.

"What do you mean, Andrew? We're taking care of the lawsuit problem, just like you wanted us to," Will responded.

"That's crazy. What do you think I 'wanted' you to do?"

Will gave Andrew a baffled look. "I seem to recall someone saying, 'They can't prove any billing inconsistencies if we happened to lose the accounting support.'"

"What are you talking about? Who said that?"

"Right. Maintain 'plausible deniability.' Smart move, boss."

Before Andrew could respond, he realized he was back asleep in his bed. He watched Leo walk into his office and tell him about Axxcel. Each word was exactly as had been spoken the day before. However, as Andrew observed his emotional exchange with Leo, different thoughts began to bubble up. It was as if two separate movies were being screened and he could participate fully in both at the same time. Andrew's left brain talked to Leo, while his right hemisphere started imagining a whole new Shift.[1]

We've lost sight of what's important. How did this happen? There's a lot of work to do!

1   For more on this subject, we recommend Daniel H. Pink's *A Whole New Mind: Why Right-Brainers Will Rule the Future* (New York: Riverhead Books, 2006).

Conscious, Capable, and Ready to Contribute

Four

Andrew's eyes popped open, and he sat up so fast he knocked the bedside clock to the floor. Then it came again: a loud noise below his and Julia's bedroom window. The blue light of the clock blinked 5:03 at him from the floor.

He heard a rustling and another crash. *Raccoons in the trash again*, he thought.

The dream!

Andrew jumped out of bed, scrambling to find a pen and something to write on. No luck. He sprinted down the stairs, pausing to push the start button on the coffee machine before opening and closing drawers and peeking into shelves in his frenzied search for paper.

He noticed Julia's crystal grid displayed on the kitchen table next to the notepad where she set intentions and explained the stones she'd chosen.

Flipping to an open page of the notepad, he scrawled fast, his writing getting blocky as he tried to make sense of the images he had seen.

Is Shift a sweatshop?

Are we taking on bad clients?

Is everything about the bottom line?

Andrew tapped his chin with the pen as he reflected on his dream. It would have been so easy to dismiss the dream as just the product of overindulging in Tim's peach cobbler, but Andrew felt like an invisible force was tugging at his heart. It was if he had nudged his own mind—as though a solution was stirring just below the surface. He had had enough brainstorms in the shower, while running, or while sleeping to know he shouldn't discount anything his mind could come up with when he wasn't paying attention to it.

Continuing his furious scribbling, Andrew wrote a few more lines:

People first. Then clients.

Glassdoor: Need to understand what employees are saying.

Who is approving clients?

What do our people need?

Development?

People. <u>It's all about people.</u> People as *people*. Care for them! We can't be too busy to help our people and then claim we care for them. When we turn our backs on who they are as people, we're acting like they are factory machinery, where they're all cogs.

Higher purpose. (What is Shift's? What do we stand for right now? We had values—those don't feel like enough right now.)

Andrew tapped the page and looked at the last few lines. He closed his eyes, and his mind took him back to the day he and Pat held their first staff meeting. The two partners and their five junior colleagues had gathered in the small conference room of their shiny, but tiny, new office. Working from the outline they'd written in the Milwaukee bar, the seven had created the vision and core value statements that could be found in Shift's offices and in virtually all recruiting and promotional materials. It was a day filled with laughter and good-natured banter about word selection. He especially remembered the young intern, Elena Núñez, challenging the group to commit fully to its employees and their development. "It's why I am here. You sold me on the idea that I would really grow as a person and a professional."

Suddenly, his mind replayed the queasy feeling in the dream, of being invisible and hearing the people at Shift hurting. If Leo wanted to leave, how many others wanted to leave? And if they left, would there even be a Shift? How could he better care for everyone on the team?

This felt big. Andrew circled the words "people" and "development" twice. He drew a circle of stars around them, leaned back, and scanned the paper. *How do I create the sort of place where no one feels the way that dream felt?*

Conscious, Capable, and Ready to Contribute

Andrew's internal conversation was interrupted by a buzz from his iPhone.

Be there in 10. Leo.

"Damn." Andrew smoothed down his hair and reluctantly put down the pen. Was it enough? More importantly, did it make sense? *If Leo and his team leave, we are in serious financial trouble.* Andrew's first inclination was to cut costs and do everything he could to keep the clients happy. But just thinking about that felt wrong. That sort of thinking had made Leo want to leave. Had hurt the company.

Andrew pushed back his chair and headed for a refill. He took a few steps then stopped dead in his tracks. *The shredder!* What could he do as a leader to ensure people were making ethical, conscious choices? Where was he not living up to being the leader he needed to be? The doorbell intruded on any further thoughts.

"Come in. It's unlocked."

Andrew had his head in the refrigerator when he heard footsteps in the kitchen. "I assume that's you, Leo. Bagel? I'm looking for cream cheese. I know we have some." Andrew found what he was looking for and closed the door to find Leo standing by the kitchen island, holding a manila envelope and a notepad.

"Hey, Andrew. No bagel, I'm good. Just water."

"No coffee?"

"I've been up a while. No more caffeine needed."

"Not a great night for sleeping, I guess," Andrew replied. "Lemon? Julia says it's good for overall health."

"Sure. Thanks."

Andrew handed Leo a full glass of water from the filtered tap next to the sink in Julia's gourmet kitchen, making sure to squeeze in a generous amount of lemon. He poured himself the same thing and spread cream cheese on the bagel, which had popped up in the toaster. "Let's sit over here," he said, gesturing to the kitchen table.

"So, Leo, it's been a couple days since our talk. First, I want to apologize for raising my voice with you. No excuse. I just don't want you to leave Shift. You've been such a great leader and—"

The Fable

Leo cut him off. "Apology accepted. I know this is a tough situation for all of us. And I'm sorry it has come to this. I'm sorry if I came across a little strong—I was nervous. But look, nothing's really changed. I've got the formal resignation letter here." He started to open the folder.

"Hold on." Andrew put his hand out the way he had stiff-armed corner-backs in his high school football days. "Talk me through this. Before you hand that to me, please give me a little more information. What happened?"

Leo paused, glancing at the crystal grid. He closed the folder and his chest expanded in a deep breath.

"Okay, I do owe you an explanation. First, I'm grateful to you and Pat for giving me a chance. Until the last nine months, I truly enjoyed being at Shift. Remember how we'd all meet up on Fridays for cocktails at the Ebbitt to compare notes on what we'd learned that week? Or the group tubing adventure down Antietam Creek? Or the year we won the softball championship?"

Andrew laughed. "Despite my two-run error in the eighth inning!"

"Well, I was going to skip that detail. But, seriously, it wasn't just the social stuff," Leo continued. "I will never forget when you assigned me to our first hotel client. We were hired to help them move their five traditional hotels to an extended stay concept. I walked into the kick-off meeting with nothing but question marks for notes. I hadn't slept all night because I was so nervous . . ."

"And we got through it together, didn't we Leo?"

"Yes. And your patience and willingness to teach me started that day. I could always count on you to give me guidance yet hold me accountable. Working at Shift was everything you said it would be, but then . . ."

Leo stopped talking for a moment. He looked at Andrew. "It wasn't just one thing. It was more like death by a thousand cuts. For me, I think it really started when we took on O'Maley Industries as a client. And then 3745 Real Estate Group. I was shocked. Everyone knew about them both—there were scathing write-ups in the *Wall Street Journal*, *Forbes*, and the *Financial Times*. O'Maley routinely looked the other way on safety matters and fired employees who complained. And 3745—the *Journal* described them as "predators"—they routinely evict lower-income tenants at their properties, leaving hundreds of people homeless." Leo paused, as though expecting Andrew to pounce.

Conscious, Capable, and Ready to Contribute

Andrew just nodded his head. "Honestly, I was sleeping at the switch. That's no excuse, of course, but I did learn that O'Maley Industries was active in promoting college education and offering millions in scholarships, and they built that park for downtown and created a camp for lower-income kids. And 3745 was creating tons of jobs and donating to good causes. I saw them doing some good, and I ignored the bad. But I admit it—these are lucrative contracts. And their seemingly charitable activities are just so they can check the corporate social responsibility box. I should have known better and investigated more. But why didn't you come to me before?"

Leo raised his left eyebrow slightly. "Yes, you should have known better! And do you think it would have made any difference if I had spoken up?"

"Look, I . . ."

This time, Leo thrust his palm at Andrew, whose mouth snapped shut. "And there's more, Andrew. I'm still reeling from the decision to cancel the leadership development program and cut the overall training budget by fifteen percent. From day one, training has been part of the Shift special sauce. On my first day, I recall the slide that showed Shift was investing fifty percent more per person in learning and development when compared to the global consulting firms. Not anymore. Now, after a quick tutorial on how the accounting and CRM systems work, we just throw the new staff into the pool and see if they can swim."

Leo took a quick sip of his water. "And about the new leadership program: Shift needs people growing their skills, not staying stagnant. My team wanted and needed that training. I was working with Janine and the HR team to develop it, you know. I had seen gaps in how our team was handling clients. I was noticing problems with unclear proposals and poor writing skills, as well as difficulty coping with challenging clients. Having that program in place would have made our team better. We all knew the training would also give them more opportunities for advancement. Without development of their skills, how are people supposed to go further in their careers? Why should they stay when there's no chance to advance?

"And another thing . . . so many talented staff are leaving because you and Pat are tolerating bad behavior from the partners as long as they sell new work and get high marks from the client." Leo's voice was getting louder with each word. "It's not what I signed up for. It's not the Shift I loved for so many years."

Andrew's feet were tapping the floor, and he was starting to squirm as he listened to Leo's indictment. Leo was right, but he was reacting to who Andrew was before he saw the reality of what was happening at Shift. Andrew couldn't hold back any longer. "Leo, I'm not sure what you mean about bad behavior from partners. I know a few of them, like Will Parsons, have a temper, and a few others push the staff a bit too hard but . . ." Andrew paused. Leo's dead eyes stared back at him. "But you're right—we've lost our way a bit. I've been doing a lot of thinking since we talked. It's time for a new Shift, and you can help me make it happen!"

Andrew paused. *Should I tell him about the dream? He'll think I'm nuts. But what the hell.*

For the next ten minutes, Andrew outlined the slowly evolving vision he had for Shift: a "people-first" Shift based on values—not just values written on a wall but ones that would show up every day. Leo listened quietly, his face once or twice showing keen interest and cautious hope; but mostly Andrew saw the dispassionate eyes of an experienced professional poker player.

"Well, I know it needs a lot of work. But hey, this is just the start of my idea. Pretty good, right? It will be like the early days of Shift, only better. Want in?"

Leo's face was stony. "Andrew, it sounds good. In fact, it sounds great, but . . ." Andrew knew right then that he had lost Leo.

"Go ahead, Leo, it's okay."

"It's too late. Pamela and Axxcel already *have* a 'people-first' culture. She says she left the big company to build a friendlier consulting firm. She had a vision to create a firm where people could thrive and get to work on projects that matter. You may get Shift to be all you have described. Axxcel is already there. I want to be a part of that."

Andrew noticed that his body was oddly calm, the way it had been in the dream. No pounding heart; no dry mouth. He figured he had one last card to play. "Leo, you know me. I'm serious about getting Shift back on track. Do you really know Pamela Turner?"

Leo responded like a baseball batter who had stolen the signs. He

Conscious, Capable, and Ready to Contribute

pounced on Andrew's pitch. "Look, here's what I do know. She's brilliant. I've talked to several of Axxcel's clients. Talk about raving fans! And she's generous. Since coming to DC, she's gotten involved in a bunch of social causes, made sizable contributions and . . ." Leo paused to catch his breath. "All while raising her half sister. *And* while growing Axxcel at a twenty-five-plus percent annual clip."

Andrew sat back in his chair, laced his fingers behind his head, and looked up at the ceiling. After a moment, he leaned back toward Leo and said, "Sounds like you really believe in her."

"Andrew, listening to you today, I actually do believe in you too. One problem is that much of Shift is going to fight you on this. And you still need to come up with a solid plan you can implement."

Andrew grinned and said, "Well, then I'm going to need the best change management consultant on the face of the planet! We still have good people—many of them will back this new wave. We built Shift from scratch, so I know we'll be able to change course. After all, it's what we help clients do."

At this, Leo laughed for the first time. "Thanks for the compliment, but the answer is still no. Pamela is making me chief operating officer and head of the Change Management practice. She says she's grooming me to be CEO. You already have Pat, Andrew. I hope you'll see what a great opportunity this is for me."

Two thoughts crossed Andrew's mind: *I'm not going to win this one.* And *I want to be the kind of leader that Leo will look back on and think well of. I do want former employees to look back fondly on their days at Shift.* "All right then," he said as he stood up with his right hand outstretched. Shaking Leo's hand, he said, "I truly wish you the best. I'll take the letter now."

Leo let out a breath in a whoosh. "Thanks, Andrew. I do appreciate all you've done. I hope this dream of yours comes to pass." They walked to the door. Leo started to extend his hand again but instead leaned in for a hug. "Good luck."

Andrew pushed the door closed and then leaned back against it, his shoulders slumping. *I need to get to the office to tell Pat about my ideas. But first: how in the world am I going to tell her we've lost Leo and his entire team?*

The Fable

Five

Andrew was out the door in a matter of minutes, eager for a run to clear his head. He stretched briefly on the front steps, adjusted his New Balance 990s, and headed down the driveway toward the Potomac River. It was later than his preferred running time, which meant he had to navigate some commuters on MacArthur Boulevard before arriving at his favorite running path. He smiled as he realized that the path was less crowded. Looking over at the busy road to his right, he thought, *They're all in their cars!*

As he headed north toward Bethesda, Andrew's mind began to replay the dream and the conversation with Leo. He envisioned the conversation yet to come with Pat and the others. Andrew was surprised at how calm he felt about the financial impact.

And now that he was thinking about what Leo said, he felt guilty about cancelling the leadership development program and his decision to arbitrarily slash Janine's training budget. He winced as he recalled his dismissive reaction to Shift's long-time chief human resources officer's concerns. "We don't need a fancy program. Just have them spend more time working for clients, and they'll get hands-on know-how. That's how I learned. They'll learn what's important if they crank up the billable hours."

Janine had made an impassioned pitch, pointing out that "we need more leaders at every level of Shift. To become a great leader requires more than just experiences in the field; we can teach many of the required skills." She said that Shift might get left behind if it wasn't growing. Andrew seemed to recall her exact words were "if our people and culture aren't

Conscious, Capable, and Ready to Contribute

31

growing, they're dying." Now he was thinking he needed something bigger and grander than training alone. *But what?*

Andrew grabbed his phone and started his recording app, as he frequently did when he wanted to dictate ideas that came to him on his longer runs. Depending on the topic, he would have Meg type up his musings. She'd often provide additional commentary about wildlife heard in the background. They laughed about how freely she offered opinions about Andrew's fitness level based on his breathing. She had once written, "You need to ease up on Italian food with Julia. You wheezed for ten minutes here." Another time, she had written, "You've still got that cough you've had for two weeks. I found one empty spot in your schedule and booked you for a physical with your usual doc."

Andrew pushed the record button and continued his run. "Do we have a 'mercenary' culture? What culture do I want us to have? What do our people need to succeed at Shift? What capabilities need to be developed? It feels like we're missing something, and I wonder if training programs alone would turn that around—what if we as a company learned together what we needed to know to make us and the company better? If it's about learning together, what do we need to learn, and how do we teach it? It won't just happen by itself."

Andrew felt tightness in his hamstrings as he tried to settle into the run. "Meg, when you transcribe this, remind me to stretch more. Okay, continue transcribing. Is this a pie-in-the-sky idea? Leo didn't seem fully convinced, and I know we need to make up the revenues from Leo leaving. Pat would tell me to hunker down and focus, and she'd be right. We need to do that. But isn't that what got us into this mess?"

As he rounded the bend at mile marker 8, Andrew could see two other runners approaching side by side. Knowing that the unwritten rules of the road called for one runner to fall back behind the other when encountering other runners, Andrew was surprised when the men kept running directly at him. He stopped his dictation and was preparing to call them out when he noticed the red strap that connected the two young men.

"Hey, man. Nice day, eh?" called out one of the runners. Andrew recognized the red beard and the bald head of the man speaking.

"Bob?" Andrew was sure it was his friend from DC Runners Club, a group he hadn't been able to contribute much time to since work got busy at Shift.

The man turned to his running companion and said, "We're stopping here for a minute. We'll take a few steps to your right. This is an old friend."

His companion replied, "Got it," and reached into his backpack for a silver water bottle.

"Andrew, wow. It's been what, five years?"

"At least. I've gotten so busy at work that all my runs are solo. Who's your friend?"

"Oh, pardon me. Richard, say hello to Andrew Hyde." As Richard reached out his untethered left hand, Andrew noticed that both men wore royal blue running shirts emblazoned with the words "Eye Run for DC" and a logo depicting two runners crossing a finish line arm in arm.

"Hi, Andrew. Nice to meet you."

"Pleasure. Beautiful day for a run," Andrew replied and then winced as he realized that Richard was visually impaired.

"Yes, thanks to your pal, Bob, I can enjoy this glorious trail again."

Bob took a sip from his own water bottle. "The club connected us up. We're a perfect match. Six forty-five pace. I never liked running alone. And we live in the same neighborhood."

"Bob's being modest. Having someone I can trust out here is crucial. We run four days a week. It's a true collaboration, a partnership. Honestly, I didn't think I'd run again until I met Bob."

"Well, that's really cool. Under seven-minute miles. Wow, that's not easy."

"Resilience. This dude never gives up, Andrew." Bob leaned over, panting as if he were winded from the run.

Richard laughed and said, "My first boss always used to say, 'misery is optional.' Little did I know how much I'd need that mindset as I reached my forties."

Bob glanced at his Coros runner's watch. "We need to get moving. Shoot me a text sometime, Andrew. The club misses you."

"Will do. Nice to meet you, Richard. Good luck."

"Be well, Andrew," Richard said as he and Bob started down the path toward DC.

As he headed in the opposite direction up the tow path, Andrew's brain crackled with activity. His happiness at seeing an old friend was paired with guilt and a little sadness at how he'd allowed work to replace the joy the club's camaraderie had provided. He also felt hard-to-explain envy of Bob and Richard's friendship. It was clearly a relationship that had started with Bob's willingness to help another human being but that evolved into something that looked like friendship. *When was the last time I spent some time with a friend where work wasn't involved? What was the point of leaving BCC and starting Shift if I'm working the same hours? Shouldn't this feel better?*

Andrew thought about Richard's resilience and his refusal to allow his disability to keep him from something he loved.

"Misery is optional." That really grabbed Andrew in the gut since it was a favorite phrase of his coach, Dave.

As he settled back into the run, Andrew recalled Pat and him closing their first big deal. For thirty minutes, the two had pitched an automotive megadealer group on a change management project. Pat covered the projected high six-figure savings while Andrew explained how Shift would do it. Back and forth they went, often pausing at just the right moment for the other to offer a compelling anecdote or hard fact. Andrew grinned as he remembered how the CEO had told them they had won the assignment.

"You two are like yin and yang. It's so obvious that you are true collaborators. Everyone else has brought lots of experts to meet with us, but it felt like we were interviewing a rock and roll supergroup. All solos and no harmony."

What happened to us? Victims of our success? Divide and conquer seemed like the only way to continue our growth. It wasn't conscious; it just happened. Can we recapture that mojo?

As he continued his run along the river and neared Lock 11, Andrew spotted a young boy and a man about his own age.

The man was crouching in front of the boy, watching him thread a wiggling worm onto the hook.

"Go ahead," the father said, indicating how to push the hook through. Andrew could almost see the man's chest expand with pride.

"Now watch me cast." The boy pulled the rod over his shoulder and sent the worm, weight, and bobber flying into the nearest tree.

The father went up to the tree to start untangling the line. "It's okay. Just try again. Remember how I taught you."

"Mom says I need to listen better."

"Well, buddy, you're doing a great job today."

Andrew gave the dad a thumbs-up as he looked back over his shoulder to see if the boy got a second chance to cast. Suddenly, he had another flashback to growing up with his father, Ted.

Although Ted wasn't much of a fisherman, one of his favorite sayings was "Give a man a fish, and you feed him for a day. Teach him how to fish, and you feed him for a lifetime." Andrew's mind wandered the streets of his memory, recalling the many ways in which Ted's teachings had influenced the choices he'd made, the roads he'd taken. Andrew's entrepreneurial itch was in his DNA. Ted had run his own insurance business and was an inventor on the side. The table alongside Ted's favorite reading chair was piled high with books about the development of Velcro, Post-it Notes, and the Hula-Hoop.

Andrew wished his dad were alive so he could talk about all that Andrew was going through. But Ted had been gone for more than thirty years. One night he had walked in the house for dinner, did his usual Ricky Ricardo imitation, "Lucy, I'm home," and dropped dead of a heart attack.

Andrew could still recall hearing his mom's panicked sobs as she called 911. He also remembered the way his legs had gone rubbery and his stomach had ached as the grief overtook him. He had stood still, so shocked by the still form in the hallway, that he hadn't even been able to cry. Ted had been just fifty-one.

Realizing he had run several more miles out than planned, Andrew shook off the sadness and a bit of worry about his own heart's health and turned to head back home.

He was surprised to see the young boy he had seen earlier now reeling in a fat catfish as his father grabbed the net. Both of them let out whoops of joy. The little guy yelled, "It's a keeper, right, Dad?"

Andrew yelled, "Congrats! Great job," as he passed. The two were so focused on making sure not to let their prize flop out of the net that they didn't hear him.

The run back always felt different. It reminded him of the way it took forever to get to a vacation, but the trip back was always too fast. Today's return was especially quick because Andrew's mind and mouth had been activated by all he'd seen that day. And his memories of Ted.

"Okay, Meg. Let's see what you have to say about my recording today:

What do we need to teach our people? What do we want them to get better at? It has to be bigger than training.

What capabilities do they need to develop?

Do they . . . we . . . I know how to listen like that little boy?

Are we being intentional?

Are we making conscious decisions like the little boy, casting exactly where the fish like to eat?

Purpose. My friend Bob and the boy's dad were happy. Why were they so happy? They had purpose. They were sharing with another human.

They were contributing.

And their contribution was by helping.

Contribution. Is that what it's all about? I'm sure it can't be about money and just the bottom line. We've been so focused on profits and growth that we've missed the real point somehow. We can't stay on that trajectory. We're Richard—and we need Bob in order to move forward.

"Okay Meg. I'm starting to run out of gas. Enjoy listening."

Andrew stopped the recording, slowed his pace, and eased through the last miles of the run through his neighborhood.

As he stretched a bit on the front porch, he sent the audio file to Meg. That ought to keep her chuckling, he thought. And it will be good to dig into those thoughts after I tell Pat about Leo. *Hope she doesn't kill me!*

Six

Andrew pulled into the parking garage beneath the Washington, DC, office building where Shift occupied the top four floors and started to head to the office before he backtracked to grab a sandwich.

Andrew had picked up his usual turkey and swiss on rye when he heard his name being called. Andrew turned to see a former Shift consulting manager marching up the sidewalk.

"Hey, Mitch. How's it going?"

"Really good. I'm thoroughly enjoying working at Benson."

Thankful that Mitch had reminded him which client had hired him, Andrew said, "What's it been? Nine months? I'm glad you're with a client, but sure wish you hadn't left."

"Really?"

"What do you mean 'really?'" Andrew replied.

"Well, I sent you two requests for a 'one-on-one' to talk the offer through. All I heard was crickets chirping."

Andrew's internal search function scanned his memory bank. Nothing.

"Did you get my email the day I left? I laid out all my concerns about Shift and how much it was changing. By now I guess you've figured all that out, what with Leo leaving and all."

"Leo! How do you know about that?"

"Come on, Andrew. DC's the smallest big city in the world. Everyone knows everything."

Andrew stared at Mitch. His first instinct was to lash out. *Don't you have anything better to do than gossip?* But as he looked into Mitch's concerned face, all he saw was kindness, and that made him feel awful about his internal thoughts. *When did I become so harsh to people?*

"Uh, thanks, Mitch. I'm sorry we didn't talk when you reached out. Maybe I could've convinced you to stay." Andrew put on his best sales call smile and added, "It's not too late to come back."

Mitch laughed. "The funny thing is, Andrew, I was bitter and hurt. But Benson is exactly where I need to be."

"Oh?"

"Well, first, the work is plenty challenging, but check this out. I'm on a two-month secondment to a charity that provides financial and job coaching to men and women in DC's Ward 8."

"Wow. That's a place where unemployment always runs really high."

"Over a third of the residents live below the poverty line. Median household income is about thirty-five thousand dollars."

Despite the warm September sun, Andrew felt a sudden chill like a door had opened on a windy, cold January day. His eyes were drawn to his shiny Mercedes. He felt like the car's $90,000 price tag was emblazoned on the side of the hood.

Shaking off his guilt, he said, "So, Benson has a contract with the agency?"

"No contract. They are contributing my time."

"Why you?" He laughed nervously. "Not that you aren't ideal for it."

"Not just me, Andrew. Over a two-year period, every employee does pro bono work for at least two months. I chose this charity because it's the one I supported in the evenings and on the weekends when I worked at Shift."

Not wanting Mitch to see all the thoughts and emotions ricocheting around his body like supercharged electrons, he blurted out, "I had no idea you did that on your own time."

"Yes. And I wasn't the only one. And I have to admit it's better when your company supports it, like Benson does."

"Not to be argumentative, just curious: why do they do it? It sounds really expensive."

"I think they know that allowing employees to feed their passions increases morale, which means lower turnover, higher productivity, and better client service. All of which enhances ROI."

The Fable

Andrew was staring into the distance past Mitch's shoulder, toward the Potomac River. "Contribution. That's it," he mumbled.

"Huh?"

"Mitch, I've got to run. You've helped me more than you'll ever know. I'm happy for your success. Sorry about blowing you off. Please stay in touch. I promise to respond to your emails."

During the elevator ride to the eighth floor and his walk through the lobby, Andrew tried to shake off the feeling from the night before, and the lingering sour taste he had from his meeting with Leo. Pat jumped up when Andrew poked his head into her office. "What's so important? Your text sounded urgent."

"Grab a pad. Let's go to my office. Lots to cover."

Ten minutes later, Pat's face was red, and she was pacing back and forth in front of Andrew's desk. "I can't believe you sat on this news for two days. You didn't think the fact that Leo resigned—and is taking his entire team—was something you should share with your partner, the cofounder of this company?"

Andrew looked up at Pat, who just kept shaking her head. She'd close her eyes and rub her forehead from time to time as Andrew tried to offer a response. "Look, Pat—"

"Don't 'Look, Pat' me. What were you *thinking*?" she gasped and put her hand over her mouth as if in horror. "And I can't believe you just let me prattle on with Pamela Turner, knowing what she had done!"

Andrew was flustered. He had expected pushback, but not DEFCON 2. "I'm sorry. I clearly made a mistake. First, I truly didn't want to distract you from enjoying last night's celebration or the award ceremony yesterday morning."

Pat crossed her arms and kept staring down at him. "And?"

"I just knew I'd be able to talk him out of it."

"How'd that work out for you, Andrew? Your self-confidence did you in again. I will try to get over you not telling me, but your judgment—"

"Wait a sec—"

"We could have had a full, multiscenario plan in place by now. But more than that . . . we could have tackled this together—why didn't we?"

Andrew rubbed the back of his neck as he drew in a deep breath. He grimaced. More than her anger, it was the hurt he saw on her face that made his solar plexus cramp up. "Okay, You're so right. Lesson number two."

"What?"

"Bill George. *Seven Lessons for Leading in Crisis.* Number two is 'Don't be Atlas.' Don't try to hold the world on your shoulders. I know better. I should've asked for help."

Pat's eyes narrowed. She seemed to be assessing his sincerity: the way parents zero in on a teenager's profession of innocence after missing curfew. After a long silence, she stood up and said, "Okay. What's done is done. Let's figure out what to do next."

"Thank you, Pat," he said quietly. "We'll figure out the Leo thing."

"Sure," Pat replied in a wary tone, as if sensing there was a second wave of news coming. "Something else you need to tell me?"

"Yes," Andrew exclaimed, sitting up and leaning toward her. "I know you want to rush off and deal with Leo, but first, hear me out. I think the solution to most of Shift's problems came to me last night. After I left your house, I had the most amazing dream."

Pat looked at her watch and then checked her phone. She dropped back into the chair across from Andrew. "Okay," she said with a sigh. "Tell me about this dream."

For the next ten minutes or so, the words gushed from Andrew's mouth like water from an unsealed fire hydrant. He paced around the office, occasionally rushing to his whiteboard to write down a major point. Initially, Pat was just listening, checking her watch from time to time. After a few moments, she began taking notes and interjecting questions. Her face showed interest, but Andrew could see she wasn't hooked yet.

"Even before the Leo situation, I began to realize we've got big problems. I'm sure you've reviewed the various HR, growth, and financial reports." Andrew paused, noting Pat's head nod.

"And the client acceptance decisions? Geez, what were we thinking? And then, cutting vital HR programs?"

"I agree, Andrew, but we do need to be profitable. We're still a business. And speaking of that—don't you think right now we need to focus on the loss of a third of our business?"

"Of course, I do. But that's a short-term problem. Hey, Meg," Andrew yelled.

The door opened. "Yes, Andrew?"

"Please contact the leadership team and ask them to meet in the large conference room at two." He looked at Pat for approval. The meaning behind her glare was unmistakable.

"Make that noon, please. And have lunch brought in," Andrew amended. Pat nodded, her expression thawing.

"You're scheduled to discuss the change management contract over lunch with Mr. Baxter."

"Damn, I forgot. See if we can slide it to five thirty. We can have drinks at Clyde's. Thanks, Meg!"

"Will do," Meg replied. "Anything else?"

"And please ping Janine and ask her to come join us. We need our chief HR officer to help figure all this out," Pat added.

As soon as his assistant was gone, Andrew ran over to the board and wrote in thick black letters:

Higher purpose: Consciously Develop our People's Capabilities so they can Contribute.

Pat read what Andrew had written. "*The* higher purpose for Shift? We already have a mission—to serve our clients. To help them *shift* into high gear! Isn't that our 'higher' purpose? And to be profitable?"

"On one level, sure. But what is the real reason we're here? Our mission is a great business purpose, but I'm talking about a purpose larger than that—our higher purpose to society, not just to our clients or ourselves. What if we made people development our higher purpose? Imagine if we really developed our people—really poured everything into this. Just think about the client service—the client relationships—we'd get."

Just then, Janine Bell knocked on the door frame as she walked in. "I'm not sure what's going on, but Meg made it sound pretty important," she offered as she scanned the whiteboard and looked at Andrew and then Pat.

As their HR leader, Janine had been their first important nonclient-facing hire in the early days of Shift. It was an expensive investment that few companies their size would have made. Andrew recalled Pat saying, "Let's do it. Let's hire her so we start this company the right way. We know that companies who don't take care of their best people end up having those best people drinking in Midwest bars drawing caricatures of the CEO."

Conscious, Capable, and Ready to Contribute

Since that day some ten years earlier, the three had experienced a lot together. Andrew always felt comfortable telling Janine everything on his mind. This time was no different. He took her through the dream, his run, and the resulting higher purpose.

To his surprise, Janine's lips thinned and turned downward. Her brows furrowed. By the time Andrew fell silent, Janine was visibly fuming.

"Just to be clear: you want to make people development the most important thing we do around here? Even though you guys approved the cancelling of the centerpiece of our L&D program *and* slashed our training budget by fifteen percent. And somehow now you're in charge of people? And what do you mean we weren't people-first? My department's entire goal is our people!"

Janine's face was thunder. "I had a good job when you two lured me away to Shift. Sure, it was safe and uninspiring, but it was comfortable. I only left because you made it clear we were going to build a great people culture. I loved the early retreats where we learned the Myers-Briggs personality types and started to train our people on soft skills. We built a fun culture—with retreats and parties—and balanced that with equipping our team with skills they needed to provide exceptional service."

Janine's eyes were flashing as she continued. "What has happened around here? I told you how important it was to develop capabilities in people. I raised my concerns about the rising turnover and repeatedly told you we needed more training to help people succeed in their jobs and feel like they had the opportunity to grow at Shift. Weren't you listening?"

"Wow. I am sorry. But I thought you'd be excited that we've seen the light."

"Andrew, we've been together for ten years. How could you not see that this would be insulting?" Janine looked at Pat as if to say, "Can you believe this guy?"

"She's right, Andrew. Janine has always been pushing us to do more employee training and development. You've . . . no . . . we've been so focused on getting more clients."

"Okay. I get it. Janine, I apologize. It's because of you that Shift has such a strong employee culture. Sorry for being so tone-deaf. I'm just really excited to do more! And I guess what I'm thinking now is more than the training." As he said "more," he watched Janine's eyes narrow.

"More?"

"It needs to be more than a training program—it needs to be about employee *development*. We need to make sure development impacts everything we do at Shift. Will you help? We can't do it without you." Andrew stood still, his head cocked slightly to his left. He smiled as his eyes locked on Janine's.

Janine took a deep breath, smoothing her skirt as she stood. "Well, one thing I hadn't thought of that is pretty amazing is the idea of developing people for the greater good of society. I had mostly been thinking that development would be good for our people and our company, but you're right: developing people is big. Much bigger than I thought in the way it impacts communities and the world. And I've got plenty of thoughts about this subject, but just to be clear: it's going to be expensive and take time. And if you want to do this, HR needs to be driving this."

Pat cleared her throat and started to speak. "Well, I am more than a little concerned about the cost, and we've got the L—"

Andrew spoke just loud enough to drown out the rest of her sentence. "We're happy to have you be the boss on this! Just know this. From now on, Shift plays the long game. We'll figure out the money."

Pat's mouth slammed shut as Janine headed to the whiteboard. Pausing to collect her thoughts, she said, "When I tried to convince you to not cut training, I recommended Robert Kegan and Lisa Laskow Lahey's book called *An Everyone Culture: Becoming a Deliberately Developmental Organization*. Your thoughts are different since you are talking about specific capabilities plus the notion of contribution, but I want to double back to their book for guidance. Please go read that book since we're all on the same page now. For now, let's try this on for size." She neatly printed: **Conscious Development Culture.**

"Yes," Andrew shouted. "That's it. How do we do that?"

Janine stared out the window and twirled the marker like a small baton. "One thing we need to figure out is how to structure it. Actually, I have been thinking about that, even after the budget was cut. Both Leo and I noticed that our team members don't stop needing training and development after onboarding. In fact, their needs for development change, depending on how long they've been with the company and how their work duties change. It made me consider: what if we look at all the steps in an employee's life cycle and see if we could embed development in each one? The employee life cycle is a structure we already have, so we don't have to reinvent the wheel."

Pat cocked her head slightly. "I'm not exactly sure what you mean."

"Okay. I'm thinking we want to make sure development starts the moment an employee is hired—that it becomes part of everything everybody here does, right? So we need something we all share—a common framework. It occurs to me that the employee life cycle provides an existing structure we can use to embed development, so it becomes part of every step for every person here." Janine sketched a large blue circle on the whiteboard. At the top she wrote, "Attraction." She put a small green circle around it. She continued drawing for a few moments until she had completed a circle with words at various points like numerals on a clock:

Attraction
Recruiting
Onboarding
Capability Development
Performance Management
Retention
Offboarding

Andrew spoke first. "I guess the next step is to discuss how development fits into each step. Before we do that, what's the arrow sticking off the left side of the big circle?"

"Honestly, my hand kind of slipped as I reached 'Offboarding.' Then I remembered that your higher purpose statement had the word 'Contribution,' so I left it there. Seems like it could signify our employees giving back to their communities, the world outside of Shift."

Andrew looked at the squiggly arrow. "That's a great way to show it. The circle—the employee life cycle—is not closed. Shift's people grow and develop and contribute to others. Let's call it Social Contribution."

Andrew looked over to his cofounder, "How's this tracking for you, Pat?"

"It's a great idea so far, especially that last point." She paused and cocked her head to the left. Andrew knew to stay silent; he had seen this look so many times before. Something important was about to bubble forth.

"Got it! Strategy. This has to start with the clarity that people development is core to the business strategy. Put that at the top of the circle."

Janine added "Strategy" to the chart. "Anything else, Pat?"

"I am still concerned—this is a larger investment than I even thought when you started speaking. And, Janine, how do we embed development into, say, attraction or hiring?"

Before Janine could respond, Pat jumped up, grabbed a marker, and wrote, "**Follow-Up List**." She then wrote, "Measurement." She placed the red marker back on the tray and said, "Let's face it. We're going to need ways to see what difference all this could make."

"I agree, partner. We'll add ideas to the follow-up list as we flesh this out. Go ahead, Janine."

Janine looked at the diagram and added clockwise facing arrows to the circle. She grabbed her iPhone and snapped a picture.

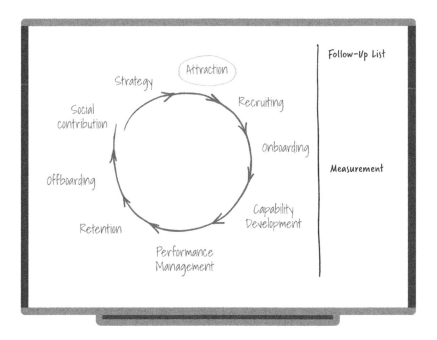

Conscious, Capable, and Ready to Contribute

"Let's start with Attraction. If we really turn Shift into a Development Culture—a place where employees learn and grow—employees will knock down our door to work here."

Pat was up on her feet. "And our hiring decisions would improve, too, if we chose employees who embrace learning and development. They'd want to contribute. They'd want to stay."

"Absolutely," Andrew added, thinking back to the early "problem" hires that still left a sour taste in his mouth. "And I can think of several people I hired who think they know it all. It didn't show up in the interviews, so we'll have to train our interviewers to look for the mindset of continuous learning and development."

Pat glanced again at her watch. "This is a great start. It is exciting, but we have to keep our eye on the prize here, you know. The potential cost is huge, and we need to conserve cash or there won't be a company where you can try these ideas out."

Andrew nodded, saying, "Okay, let's add 'Return on Investment' to the follow-up list."

Pat shook her head. "You're not hearing me. I mean we can't have you just focus on this project. Not while we're in survival mode. If you want to pursue this as a passion side project, I'm all for it. But you need to focus on Shift's finances right now." With a wave of her hand at the board, she said, "And I get veto power over this."

Andrew opened his mouth to protest, feeling a familiar itch of annoyance under his skin, but paused. He needed to choose his battles. *Once I create this program, Pat will say yes. I know it. And Julia green-lighted me to invest more in Shift. I think. Anyway, she always says she believes in me.*

He nodded. "Fair enough. Though I'll add into my plan how companies like Benson are actually improving their bottom lines through contribution. And Janine, please add Contribution—we still need to define that—and Capabilities—Mind Skills, People Skills, Technical Skills to the follow-up list. We can come back to those."

Janine snapped one more photo and said, "'Survival mode'? What's going on?"

Pat was quick to respond. "Yes, this long-term stuff is nice, but we've got a major problem on our hands. Leo has resigned and says he's taking the entire Change Management team to Axxcel. He told Andrew two days ago that they've already retained counsel to fight our noncompetition agreements."

Janine stood up straight and started speaking briskly, instantly in full HR officer battle mode. "We need an aggressive communication plan. And we've got to call Knight Burns to get their legal advice ASAP."

Pat nodded. "My thought exactly. Maybe an injunction against Leo and the others. We have worked too hard to let them just take our clients. And we should go after that Pamela Turner. I knew she was bad news when I saw her sitting there yesterday schmoozing Gary in her expensive dress."

Andrew was unable to stifle his laugh. Pat gave him a death stare.

"Sorry; it was funny. Go channel that energy. I'll see you at noon."

Janine and Pat marched out the door as Andrew called out, "It's going to be all right. In fact, Shift is going to be even better."

Pat was suddenly back in the doorway. "I hope it will, Andrew. But right now, you need to toughen up. Our entire company is at risk." With that, she turned on her heels and was gone.

Andrew grabbed his phone. He hadn't heard from Julia yet today. He was just starting to type a text when he heard three soft taps on his door. Elena Núñez was standing in his doorway holding a few papers and a blue Moleskine notebook.

He got up and gestured toward the table. Andrew sat down while Elena took the seat next to Andrew's usual spot. Andrew noticed that her papers were turned over and her notebook was open. "What's up, Elena?"

As Elena cleared her throat to speak, Andrew recalled interviewing her to become their first intern during her junior year at George Mason University. Her grades and recommendations were exceptional. She had been active on campus while also working thirty hours per week managing the business office of her father's remodeling company. She had been remarkably poised at twenty-one. She had worn a conservative black suit and white blouse buttoned up to the collar. Andrew especially recalled how she had frequently stroked a small cross she wore around her neck as she considered Andrew's questions. "A *quinceañera* gift from my extremely Catholic mother," she laughed as she saw his eyes raise. "Fifteenth birthday. No fancy dresses for the Núñez girls."

Now, some ten years later, Elena Núñez exuded a confidence and depth of character most senior executives never attain. She had worked well on Leo's Change Management team, and electing her to the partnership late last year was an easy decision.

"I guess you know why I'm here. Like Leo and the rest of our team, I've got an offer to join Axxcel. It's a great offer. In fact, take a look." She turned over the papers and slid them to Andrew.

Andrew took less than a minute to read through the details. "Hmm. Twenty percent raise plus four percent equity. Your equity's two percent here, right?"

"Yes, but the financial package is not why I'm thinking about leaving."

Thinking about? So she's not sure!

"I joined in year one of Shift. None of the big consulting firms would hire a Latina whose father was in the trades. They didn't say that, of course, but it was implied at every interview. I hadn't gone to an elite college, and I didn't have family in traditional white-collar 'Corporate America.' Did you know one recruiter asked me how I got into college? As though it wasn't on merit. You and Pat actually embraced who I was and had faith in me." Elena paused, looking like she was planning her next words very carefully. "And until recently, I never thought once about leaving. But lately . . ."

"Elena, I know we've lost some of our mojo. Pat and I were just talking about how to get back on track. We have a plan I really believe in. It's not quite worked out step-by-step, but . . ."

"Well, that's good. The first step is to admit you have a problem."

"Spoken like the wise change management pro you are."

"And the Núñez family knows all about plans and steps—we have experience with the twelve steps, thanks to my father. So we know recovery takes hard work and time. I can hit the ground running at Axxcel. Here? Not so sure anymore."

"Fair enough. The Hyde family knows about plans and steps, too. Alcoholism has scorched the Hyde family for generations. Thankfully, my brother has been sober for ten years. Can I give you a few reasons not to leave?"

"Of course, that's why I'm sitting here. I know you're biased, but I do trust you."

The Fable

Andrew spoke for the next ten minutes about the offer, the little he knew about Axxcel, and the opportunity that Elena had to impact Shift in a big way. He threw in a $20,000 stay bonus, matched the raise, and offered a chance for Elena to buy more equity. As he said the words, he sent up a little prayer that Pat would be okay with the offer.

Elena looked at her notebook and read back to Andrew. "You're right: I've built up political capital here. I'm known and respected. Even with Leo there, I'd be at the starting line once again. I appreciate the financial moves, too, and the bonus. And I like the idea of being part of Shift's new direction. Can you tell me more about that?"

He briefly recounted the issues the company faced, his ideas, and the whiteboarding exercise.

Looking at the "follow-up list," she said, "Looks like you got interrupted before you finished."

"Yes, we did. There's this small crisis going on. You may have heard that about a third of our people are thinking about leaving."

Elena laughed. "Yes, so I heard. And despite that, you're really doing this? Investing all this money and energy on people during a crisis?"

Andrew looked Elena straight in the eye. "Yes. Without great people, we don't have a company, and we need to get serious about developing them and investing in them. Starting now."

Elena looked at Andrew as if she was trying to gauge the strength of his spine. She glanced at the whiteboard again before leaning toward Andrew ever so slightly. In a soft but firm voice she said, "Okay. Here's the deal. I am willing to stay. *If* you let me work directly on this with you, Janine, and Pat—if I get to be a part of turning this around. I know how to do change management, and I love this new higher purpose. Finally, I want you to give a twenty-thousand-dollar stay bonus to every member of my team I keep from going to Axxcel." With that, she stuck out her right hand.

The room was suddenly silent. Andrew hesitated for a few moments before grabbing her hand. "Sounds good to me. I will run it by Pat and confirm within the hour. I know she will be thrilled. Now, go get that team of yours to stay."

Elena stood up and let go of Andrew's hand. "I'm on it."

Conscious, Capable, and Ready to Contribute

Seven

After the lunch session with the executive committee, Andrew walked slowly back to his office, the words of people he had worked with for the past ten years ringing in his ears. He had gone in there so excited about investing in people, developing them, and getting them to stay and make big contributions. Other than Janine and to a lesser extent, Pat, the executive committee had not seen it that way at all. *A dream, really? Can't you see it's the Leo situation that's really important? Well, at least your ideas are creative.* He felt like he had just fought his way to the ten-yard line with Lawrence Taylor draped around his neck.

"Hey, Meg. I'm going to hunker down for an hour or so with my notes from the meeting. Grab the phone, please, so I can focus."

"You got it."

Andrew dropped into his Aeron desk chair, a chair he'd had and loved for the entire history of Shift. Closing his eyes, he pictured the various members of the committee and the range of reactions to the Leo news and Andrew's development ideas. The light from the sunny September afternoon hit him directly in his suddenly watering eyes. Squinting, he stood up and lowered the blinds so he could review the whiteboard covered with ideas from the earlier brainstorming session. *I'm not going to let the unenthusiastic response from the executive committee stop me. I understand their fears, but this is bigger than them. Or me.*

Andrew's heart fluttered and his solar plexus tightened as he thought about the outside investors and how they would react to the loss of the

Change Management practice. "I'm going to need to cut more *and* come up with the money to up the development budget at the same time. How am I going to do that?"

Drawing heavily on his Wharton MBA skills, Andrew dug into Shift's financial statements. In the early days of Shift, he knew those numbers as well as he knew his friends and family. After an hour or so, Andrew put down his pencil and leaned back from his desk. "Well, no wonder the CFO rolled her eyes. We currently spend about 1.5 million dollars on training and development. That includes all payroll, online learning platform subscriptions, outside trainers, and costs like travel and facility rentals. Janine will have to help me, but I think we're looking at doubling that, at least. We've got four hundred and twenty-five employees; no, make that three hundred and twenty-five employees, if all of Leo's team leaves. Doubling the budget would be three million dollars annually. Wow. Can Shift afford that?"

Janine had also told him the money would be only part of the investment: "The costs will not be so much in dollars but in the time and team focus needed to implement this plan."

A calm internal voice that sounded a lot like the former employee, Mitch, spoke to him. "Don't forget that this should lower turnover, raise productivity, help your people be better consultants, sell more. And your brand value will rise. You just need to come up with seed capital."

Andrew looked at the whiteboard and then back at his spreadsheets. He stood up, noticing a shakiness throughout his body. It reminded him of the way adrenaline caused butterflies when he lined up for the start of his favorite Georgetown 10K.

I doubt if any of the other partners will want to put money in right now. I can swing it. But I'll need to get Julia on board.

The loud ding of his phone shook him from his musings.

> **J:** Hey, babe. Looks like Mom is stabilized. Unexpected but happy news. Doctors say I can head home—not much more I can do here. Will be at house by 8:30.
>
> **A:** Awesome. Happy she's stable. Happier that you're coming home. Really miss you. Pick you up?

Conscious, Capable, and Ready to Contribute

J: I'll Uber. Just finish your work
A: Flight number?
J: SW2135, BWI. 7:20 arrival
A: K. I'll keep tabs. Love you madly
J: More

Andrew stood up, feeling buoyed by Julia's text and the usual hearts and unicorns emojis that followed her loving sign-off. *I'm just not the same when she's away. She'll help me figure all this out.*

Andrew was still smiling, settling down at his desk, when his door flew open, slamming against the door jamb so hard that part of it snapped off and landed by Andrew's desk with a small thud. Andrew jumped and looked up.

"You'll bankrupt us all with your crazy dreams," shouted Will Parsons, barrelling into the office, heedless of the door shrapnel on the floor.

Andrew took a deep breath, instinctually drawing on prior experiences with Will and other overly passionate—even angry—Alpha males. He pitched his voice low and slower than usual, hoping to soothe Will. "You need to calm down. Let's talk it out."

He glanced at the phone, keeping it in view in case the situation devolved. As Will paced, gesturing and yelling, Andrew walked up to the door to shut it, brushing a few pieces of splintered wood and plastic out of the way. In the hallway, he saw Meg mouthing, "Sorry. I tried to stop him." Behind her, another assistant was paused in midstep, mouth open and eyes wide.

Andrew closed the door and refocused on Will, who was sweating profusely and gesturing wildly.

"We lose one-third of our business because you're sleeping at the switch, and all you want to talk about is your Ebenezer Scrooge dream! 'Conscious development,' really? You weren't conscious enough to prevent Leo leaving. Maybe I should call Pamela Turner, too!"

Andrew grabbed his phone, pretended to scroll a bit, and said, "Okay, Will. I've got her number right here. Want me to write it down for you? I hear she's hiring."

With that, Will stopped pacing and said, "Damn it, Andrew. It's not funny! How are we going to pay the bills, much less invest in big programs?"

"Will. Let's sit down and talk it through. I want to know what you think we should do."

Will stood still, his torso tensed like a prize fighter waiting for the bell to ring for the fifteenth round. After a few moments, his shoulders dropped, and he fell into one of Andrew's desk-side chairs. "You really want my opinion?"

"I do. But first, let's be clear about something. We are partners; your behavior just now was unacceptable. I have no problem with healthy disagreements. We need to avoid group think, and I respect your ideas as the colead of Shift's Strategy practice. But barging in here, scaring Meg and the others, and damn near destroying my door . . ."

Will looked like a golden retriever who had been swatted across his snout with the morning paper after eating the family's breakfast off the kitchen table. Andrew kept his face impassive. He knew from previous run-ins that Will's temper flamed hot and then sputtered out almost immediately. Redirection almost always worked. Sure enough, Will sulked for a minute and then said, "I'm sorry. No excuse for my approach. I will take care of the door and apologize to Meg and her neighbors."

"Thank you. Now, I am listening."

Will sagged deeper into his chair. "I will think on some specific ideas. For now, I would just ask you to remember that you have a responsibility to *all* the partners. We have mortgages to pay, college tuitions to plan for, and equity buy-ins to fund. As an EC member . . . and as a partner with debts . . . I feel like your comments today were totally tone-deaf." Will slowly rose to his feet. "I've got a Zoom call in five minutes. But do remember that your decisions affect us all. Sorry again about the door," he said, his blond head shaking as he stepped over a piece of what once was Andrew's door jamb.

Andrew sat motionless, his eyes fixed on the spot where Will had been sitting, as Meg's head peered around the doorway. "You okay?"

"Huh? Oh, I'll be fine. We'll all be fine," he said.

Will we? Andrew tamped down on the spike of guilt Will's words brought up. *He's right. My position—a paid-off house, no debts, a secure job, no kids, and a nest egg—is not everyone's reality. I've been so worried about our people. But Will is our people, too. How do I help everyone?*

"Can you see if Dave can meet me around four o'clock? I'll stop by his home office on the way to Clyde's."

"Will do," she said. She hesitated. "I'm sorry about Leo, Will, and all of this. You're a great boss; you'll figure it out. You always do."

"Thanks for the pep talk. You and I make a good team, eh?"

She winked. Glancing at Will's handiwork on Andrew's carpet, she said, just before she closed the door, "I'll see about fixing this mess after you leave."

Andrew acknowledged Meg's comment with a nod of his head as he once again sat down in his chair with a thud. "Be sure to send the bill to Will." Staring at the board, he thought, *Leo was right. They are fighting me. But now I see why. To achieve this new higher purpose, I need to consider everyone's needs.*

Turning his sights to the DC skyline outside his window, he sighed. "Well, I need to pull this off, but it sure won't be easy. And the alternative is pretty ugly."

• • •

Dave Edwards had been Andrew's executive coach for seven years. They had exchanged business cards during the busy lunch rush at the renowned Palm Restaurant on 19th Street in downtown DC. It was well known for its thick dry-aged steaks and walls adorned with caricatures of famous DC politicians and business leaders. One of Shift's early Strategy clients had made the introduction. Andrew noticed Dave's likeness hanging above a booth as he left the restaurant. He recalled thinking that Dave must be a pretty big deal. However, Andrew knew that he needed an outsider's help, so he called Dave the next day and invited him for coffee near Dave's home office on Capitol Hill. He was happy, and a bit surprised, when Dave agreed.

David Michael Edwards was two decades older than Andrew. His wife Nancy was a successful author in residence at one of the many DC think tanks. Dave had retired early from a large Chicago-based financial institution, where he'd held a wide variety of positions. Dave told Andrew his story at their first meeting.

"I've always been an HR guy at heart," he said, stirring his coffee. "When the CEO had a stroke, even I was surprised when the board tapped me to succeed him."

Andrew had studied up on Dave before their coffee, so he knew what Dave was modestly leaving out: Despite a seeming lack of experience, Dave had led the bank through a tough recession and ultimately to a perch near the top of the list of most admired companies in America.

In retirement, Dave had returned to his first love: helping people. Upon arriving in DC, he hung up a shingle as executive coach and advisor. Andrew's research before their first coffee suggested Dave's counsel was sought by Capitol Hill leaders, cabinet members, and many of the major business leaders in DC. His role at the bank had brought him to DC on a regular basis, and he was a natural-born networker. Once permanently ensconced in the federal city, his practice grew quickly. The specific names on his client list were a matter of much speculation. And while Dave honored each client's privacy, there was no doubt that Dave's clientele was the "who's who" of Washington. This point was made abundantly clear as General Colin Powell stopped by the table to say hello to Dave. Andrew had jumped up to shake the hand of one of America's great generals—a man widely respected on both sides of the political aisle. As he had walked away, Powell called back, "See you at six, Dave!"

Two hours into the coffee, Andrew said, "I know you have a full roster of clients, who have much bigger jobs than mine. So I imagine that the answer is 'no,' but is there any chance you'd be willing to coach me?"

"Andrew, you aren't my typical client, but it would be a privilege to work with you on your journey."

Since then, they'd been through a lot together. As Andrew parked, just down the block from Nancy and Dave's house, he thought today's session was going to be their most important yet. As he walked up the steps, he recalled Dave's favorite line, "Pain is inevitable; misery is optional." He said it during that first coffee meeting, and it was the first hint Andrew would get that Dave came at things in both a practical and spiritual manner.

Sporting his usual blue button-down and navy cardigan, Dave ushered Andrew into his office, located just off the foyer. Dave sat in his well-worn, amply cushioned leather chair. Andrew chose a straight-back across from

Dave. Pouring himself a glass of water from the pitcher on the large round coffee table in front of him, Dave spoke first. "Meg said you need to leave at five sharp. Let's get right to it."

For the next fifteen minutes, Andrew talked Dave through the last few days.

Dave sat back in his chair with his hands together, each finger touching its counterpart on the other hand, flexing his hands every so often. Other than an occasional "hmm" and a loud laugh as Andrew described the little boy's first tree-bound cast, the coach displayed no reactions. As Andrew ended his tale with Will's destruction of his doorjamb, Dave reached to his left, grabbed a pen and pad from a side table, and made a few notes.

"And . . . ?" Andrew knew that Dave was about to ask one of his zingers. Dave's preferred style was 90 percent questions, 10 percent advice. "The best learning is self-learning" was one of the many Dave-isms Andrew had learned.

"It sounds like some of Shift leadership, including Will, are responding with fear. What about you, Andrew? What are you feeling?"

Andrew leaned back so hard in the chair that he yelped in pain as he slammed into the stiff back of the wood chair. "Look. I'm not afraid of Axxcel or Leo or Will!"

Dave just raised an eyebrow. "Well, maybe you should be scared. And, really, you didn't tell Pat and you didn't realize that Janine would be hurt? You better wake up, Andrew."

Andrew stood up and then quickly sat back down. "Okay, I *am* worried. That's why I am here. I need your advice. I need you to help me."

"And I will. But like always, you have to do the work." Dave's craggy face took on a quizzical look.

"Thank you, Dave. Another question?"

"Yes. Fixing Shift will take a lot of resources, so you need to connect with your why. It would be easier, certainly, to do what Will says—just focus on partner profits— and not pursue this plan of development. What would happen if you did that? What would you be giving up if you give up your plan?"

Both men sat silently for a minute.

"I may lose the company," Andrew finally mumbled. Raising his voice a few decibels, he said, "I feel like I'm already losing the company." He paused, turned away from Dave for a moment.

"The Shift I love is already lost." He looked at Dave, feeling his eyes sting. The enormity of Andrew's statement hung in the air.

"How did I let this happen? When was the last time I checked in with Leslie or Will or had a real talk with anyone—even Pat? I've been so focused on revenue growth and short-term profits that . . ." Again, Dave allowed the silence.

"I am Shift. The only thing I love more is Julia. And I have been spending so much time at Shift, I can't remember the last time our date night wasn't cut short. I'm done. Change has to come."

Dave spoke next. "Didn't you say Elena referred to AA's twelve steps?"

"What? Yes, apparently her dad is . . . wait . . . can you just tell me the answer for once!"

Dave grinned like the man in The Band's classic song "The Weight." He quietly said, "No."

Rolling his eyes, Andrew turned to face the wall across from Dave. After a long pause, he very slowly said, "The Shift I know is already gone. I just need to accept that and move on to the hard work of reinventing it."

"That wasn't so hard, was it?"

"Easy for you to say, Dave."

"True. What else?"

Andrew paused and, pacing around again, he spoke. "I'm scared that I don't have the right team. What's going on with Pat? Do I have what it takes to execute Shift's new higher purpose? This is going to be expensive and may need more capital. Where will we get it from? It's great to have a dream and all, but what if that's not enough? What if I'm on the wrong path? What if I let them all down? Let myself down? Let Julia down?"

Dave looked at the vintage watch he always wore. This treasured gift from the CEO of Patek Phillipe was one of Dave's very few vanities. "Andrew, you are on a very tight schedule, so just this once I am going to break the first rule of coaching and give you very direct advice." Andrew laughed as he recalled rule number two: never coach someone without their permission and never ever coach your family, friends, or boss—even with permission.

Conscious, Capable, and Ready to Contribute

"Thank you, Dave."

Dave stepped up to the dry-erase board, which covered most of the south wall of his office.

"One, Pat is your partner. Listen to her and get curious and empathetic so you can cocreate this."

"Okay. Like the old days. Seems simple enough."

Dave drew "2." on the board. "The four tenets of Conscious Capitalism can help guide you. So far, I'd say you are focused on Higher Purpose and Conscious Culture. So you want to build a great culture, and you're thinking about the big "why": why your company exists, beyond money. You're working on being a better leader, so you're working on Conscious Leadership. That's fantastic, but don't forget the fourth tenet: Stakeholder Integration. Some call it Stakeholder Orientation. Employees are vital stakeholders, of course, but there are others. Be sure to build a plan that's also good for clients, investors, partners, the community, and the board."

Andrew nodded his head. "Speaking of—I need to call the board chair tonight! You're right; I am missing some stakeholders."

Dave's eyes danced and he nodded. "One more big one, Andrew, and then you better hustle if you are going to get up Wisconsin Avenue in time to meet Baxter.

"Figure out *your* Higher Purpose, Andrew. Whatever it is, it has to be one hundred percent aligned with Shift's."

Dave walked over to his mentee, wrapped his arms around him like a bear, and whispered, "You can get Shift headed in the right direction, but only after you determine your *why*. Now, go meet your client, call the board chair, and get home to that beautiful, wise wife of yours."

Eight

Like most successful leaders, Andrew had always been able to compart-mentalize his thoughts and feelings. This ability to push problems to a temporary holding pen came in handy on this particular day as he shifted into sales mode for his client meeting at Clyde's. Driving through North-west Washington, Andrew felt his spirits rise. He always enjoyed talking to William, "not Bill," Baxter.

At their first get together, Andrew had learned that Baxter had spent twenty years in the Marines. Now, he was CEO of Logistics International, a global company providing a wide array of services to the Department of Defense.

As he eased the car into the parking space, Andrew sent up a silent "thank-you" that the company's COO had recommended Shift to Baxter. Baxter hadn't had any requests for changes to the contract or proposal and had seemed enthusiastic on the phone about having Shift work with Logistics International during their new product launch.

Baxter was waiting near the hostess station at the Chevy Chase loca-tion of Clyde's, a DC institution with locations across the city. Andrew knew the American saloon-inspired menu well; he had been a waiter at the affiliated Old Ebbitt Grill during summers in college.

"Hello, William. Hope I didn't keep you waiting."

"All good," Baxter replied as the hostess walked them past the upstairs bar to a booth in the back of the transportation-themed restaurant. Look-ing around at the vintage automobile replicas and small planes hanging from the ceiling, Baxter said, "I love Clyde's."

Andrew nodded as the waiter appeared.

"How are you this fine day?" Baxter asked the waiter.

"Same as yesterday, Mr. B. Grateful to be upright," the waiter said. "The usual—Clyde's burger, medium rare, no onions, fries, and a Diet Coke?"

"Okay, if we eat and drink, Andrew? My lunch date canceled," Baxter said with a smirk. "If I didn't know better, I'd say he didn't want to hear all my Marine stories from the Gulf War."

"I'm sure that wasn't the problem," Andrew laughed. "Your stories are too good to pass up. And sorry about lunch."

Baxter grinned as he said, "Swap out the Diet Coke for a very dry vodka martini. Tito's."

"Nice to see you, Mr. Hyde. It's been a while. What can I get you?"

"Cup of your famous chili and a crab cake sandwich. The bartender's recommendation from her beers on tap. And fries. I ran today!"

"You got it." The waiter snapped his order book shut.

Like they usually did, Andrew and Baxter spent the first few minutes chatting about their shared passion for convertibles as well as their mutual dislike of all New York sports teams.

"My wife just bought me a flame red 1957 Thunderbird!" Baxter slid over his phone so Andrew could see the shiny car.

"Wow. My dad had a black '56. Always said he sold it so he could afford me!"

Once the drinks and Andrew's starter had arrived, Baxter sat up so straight that Andrew felt as if he was seated across from the battle-tested lieutenant general rather than the fun-loving executive Andrew knew from earlier meetings. Baxter looked him in the eye. "Andrew, we're going to go in a different direction with the project."

Twelve words, and Andrew felt as if his heart had stopped. The hunk of bread he had just swallowed felt stuck midthroat. Gulps of water and then a mouthful of the amber lager didn't seem to help. *Am I going to need the Heimlich maneuver?*

After a few seconds, the lump of dough moved down his esophagus enough that Andrew could respond. "What do you mean by a 'different direction'?"

Baxter paused and popped a vodka-drenched olive in his mouth. His eyes never wavered from Andrew's face as he chewed the green fruit. Swallowing at last, he continued. "We hired Pamela Turner and Axxcel to be our strategy and change management advisors. They start next week. I wanted to tell you in person."

Andrew needed to say something, but his brain seemed to have locked up like an engine in February drained of antifreeze. The awkward silence was broken by the return of the portly waiter, his tray loaded down with their entrées. His "anything else?" was met with a head shake from Andrew and a pleasant "No thanks. This looks fantastic" from Baxter.

Baxter continued. "Shift has a great reputation, and my team was confident in the decision to retain you—but there was some late competition. Our accountants encouraged us to talk to another firm before we signed up for a 5.2-million-dollar multiyear project."

"That's reasonable advice," Andrew said.

"Yes. My plan was to check with one or two others to confirm that Shift was the right choice. When we met with Axxcel," he paused. "Honestly, they were a lot better than we expected, and their bid was thirty-five percent lower."

That's outrageous. Thirty-five percent! He took a big sip of his beer to buy a few seconds of time and to calm his pounding heart. He wanted his voice to sound steady. "Well, that's quite a discount. I see your dilemma. Did they explain how they could do the work for such a low-ball price?"

"I really have no choice. You guys seemed to be the obvious choice, but the numbers are material. I do have shareholders."

Andrew closed his eyes for a second. *Yeah, so do I.* "You mentioned Pamela Turner. Did you meet her personally?"

Baxter's eyes lit up. "She's amazing. No offense . . . She's super intelligent and charismatic. It's clear to see why clients and people are joining her team in droves. Too bad you didn't hire her." Baxter stopped talking. His wince gave him away.

"You know that Pamela has stolen some of our best people?"

"I know that some of your best change management folks will be working on our account. That Leo Vincent seems to be the real deal."

Andrew could feel his face turning red. "You bet he is. I hired him and trained him. Pamela had no right . . ." Andrew's voice trailed off. He took a deep breath.

Conscious, Capable, and Ready to Contribute

"I get it." Baxter chewed his way through another olive. "If I were you, I'd be pissed as hell. I come from a world where loyalty and trust are vital to survival. But, for me, my loyalty has to be to my company. Axxcel is our choice. I know you won't let this situation get in the way of them doing what we need."

"I appreciate you telling me in person. I don't want to make my problems with Pamela and Leo your problems. I understand your decision and hope that we can work together at some point in the future." He stood up and reached for his wallet. "My wife is returning from a long trip tonight. I better get going."

"Put your wallet away. I've got this. You go ahead. I'm going to have an espresso and return a few emails." He shook Andrew's hand and patted him on the shoulder. "Good luck. I sure hope it all works out for you and Shift."

When Andrew reached his car, he leaned against the door for several minutes as he tried to get his bearings. *How did this happen? I need to call the board chair and tell her about Leo and Baxter. Should I call Pat?*

Andrew's hand was shaking as he pushed the automatic starter button on the Mercedes. At this point, he wouldn't have been surprised if his car had refused to start. It had been that kind of day. He took a deep calming breath and thought of Julia. The thought of going back to the empty house to wait for her was suddenly unthinkable. *Julia!* He made a last-minute lane change to turn right on Wisconsin Avenue, jerking the steering wheel and ignoring the litany of outraged honking behind him. *It's an hour to BWI, and I'll surprise Julia at the airport.* He opened his phone voice app to make calls as he drove.

• • •

Andrew scrolled through his iPhone contacts, found "Wendy S. cell" and hit "call."

Wendy Shapiro was a legend in the DC business community. She was managing partner of Knight Burns, an international law firm. Andrew and Pat had known Wendy for over fifteen years; she had helped get Shift organized at the very start.

Although Shift did not have a formal board until taking on a private equity investor in 2018, Andrew and Pat always relied on Wendy as one of their key advisors. When it was decided to name a nonexecutive chair of the newly formed board, Wendy was the consensus choice of the board members.

After one ring, Wendy answered, "Hey Andrew. To what do I owe this pleasure?"

As Andrew cruised up Interstate 95, he gave Wendy the overview of the Leo situation, including the lost Logistics International contract. Wendy was glad to hear that Janine and Pat had already reached out to her employment law colleagues.

"Okay. Let's have a full board video call at eight a.m. day after tomorrow. I will have my EA organize it. You and Pat better get ready for some tough questions."

"No doubt. We'll be ready. Thanks, Wendy."

"Drive safely. See you soon."

The familiar muffled chirp let Andrew know that the call had ended. Thinking through how the board meeting might go, he thought about Wendy and the other outside board members, especially Victor Jones, the founder of VJ Capital, and Roger Coyle. Roger was a former Deloitte Consulting partner whom Andrew had met in B-School. Victor was the founder and CEO of the PE firm that owned 12 percent of Shift. He envisioned their angry faces and outrage about how Pamela Turner had raided the company.

His mind turning as he sped up the highway, Andrew imagined the tough but supportive questioning from Victor, Roger, and Wendy. Then he remembered the two new outside board members who had been added at the beginning of the fiscal year. One was a retired Marine general, Anthony Pagano. His colorful language had livened up the one meeting he had attended. Also joining that first meeting was another VJ Capital partner, Jesse Martin. After the meeting, Pat had dubbed him "the thinker." No one could recall Jesse uttering a single word. *How would they react?*

Andrew's musings ended as the convertible passed under the brightly lit Baltimore/Washington Thurgood Marshall International Airport sign. He maneuvered up the ramp of the short-term parking garage. He turned off the car and hustled down the long hall leading to Southwest Arrivals.

His phone pinged.

J: Just landed. Early. Should be home by 8:15

A: I'll be waiting! Madly

Conscious, Capable, and Ready to Contribute

Andrew scurried to the base of the escalator that deposited the travelers from the Southwest flights. He shifted from foot to foot, checking the gate number and flight status on his phone. His eyes darted back and forth from his watch to the top of the moving stairs. It reminded him of the way he'd constantly looked up and down Old Georgetown Road as he waited for the morning school bus. He laughed out loud. *This is way different. I'm excited to see Julia.*

And just then, he recognized the color of her favorite green jacket. There she was, gliding down the escalator, chatting with an extremely fit forty-something man in a black blazer and jeans. At the bottom of the stairs, Julia smiled. "So nice to meet you, Jim. Enjoyed our talk on the flight."

She turned in the direction of the luggage claim, taking the first step toward the slowly spinning carousel of oversized suitcases, tagged carry-ons, and baby strollers when her eyes landed on Andrew. In the space of a second, her face flickered from focused to shock. After a split second, she beamed the smile that had melted Andrew back in college. Andrew rushed to her, meeting her as she rushed toward him. They half collided and giggled at the impact. Throwing his arms around her small frame, Andrew felt home. The familiar smell of her honey shampoo and the way she squeezed the backs of his arms as she reached up for a kiss made half the fear and confusion of the past hour thaw. Julia's lips tasted of the lemon water she always drank on planes. They stayed wrapped around each other until Andrew heard a muffled complaint from his left.

"Babe, I think we're in the way." Julia pulled away, her hands falling until their fingers linked. She gave his hand a squeeze.

Andrew pulled back and smoothed down his rumpled shirt. He grabbed the carry-on from Julia's hand and smiled at her slightly smudged lipstick. He put his arm around her. "So glad you're home. I can't wait to tell you about all that's going on at Shift."

"Thank you for picking me up. It's been a long week. I'm looking forward to just sleeping in our bed again."

Julia gently pulled her arm away, leaving Andrew's hand feeling cold without her warmth. She zipped ahead, not looking over her shoulder. "Let's get home."

Nine

Andrew blinked his eyes a few times and looked around his and Julia's bedroom. He rolled over to look at his bedside clock. *6:30. Better than 5:03*, he thought. Just then he heard beans being ground in Julia's prized coffee machine. *Julia!*

In the fuzzy moment between dream-state and daily existence, Andrew remembered picking Julia up at BWI. They were both unusually quiet on the ride home. Andrew recalled asking Julia how she was feeling as he pulled out of the parking garage.

"Exhausted. Not sure I can string two coherent sentences together."

"Well, let's just get you home safe and sound," Andrew recalled saying. "Tell you what—I can head into the office a bit late tomorrow. We can drink our coffee and compare notes."

"My coffee. Oh, that sounds so good. First my bed, especially my pillow."

Andrew patted Julia on the thigh and said, "Close your eyes, babe. We'll be home soon."

"Downstairs!" Julia now called. Andrew sat up, swung his legs to the right, and hit the floor. "Happy to hear the thud of those big feet of yours."

The sound of Julia's voice hit Andrew like the first shot of desperately needed morning caffeine. Within a minute, Andrew bounded down the stairs, where he found Julia sipping coffee in front of the crystal grid she had laid out at the kitchen table. Andrew leaned over, kissed the top of Julia's head, and said, "You won't believe how spot-on these crystals were."

"I bet I will," she replied with a wink. "And I can't wait to tell you about

Mom. She made such a remarkable turnaround, and her nurse said . . ."

"Let me grab coffee and breakfast. Don't move. You've got to hear what you missed."

"I'll be here," she said as she lit her votive candles.

After a few minutes, Andrew returned with a banana and a toasted sesame seed bagel loaded with cream cheese. He carefully balanced his water and steaming mug of black coffee. "Same as everyday, Andrew. Such a creature of habit," Julia laughed.

"Good thing for you, you're one of my habits," he responded with a raised eyebrow and a grin. Julia just shook her head, and Andrew knew she had been expecting the corny line. After nearly thirty years, Julia knew him well.

For the next twenty minutes, Julia sipped her latte, listening to Andrew talk about the last few days and about the big changes he had in mind for Shift. "It's not going to be easy, and it may require you and me to invest more in the company. You okay with that?"

"That excitement in your voice reminds me of the Andrew who returned from Milwaukee one night and told me he was quitting BCC. I haven't seen you this happy in a while. I'll take that Andrew over money any day."

"What if the new Andrew wants a Tesla?"

Julia smiled and shook her head.

"But seriously, what do you think? Am I doing the wrong thing? Where are my blind spots here?"

Julia could always be counted on for seeing nuances that Andrew missed. Andrew knew some people underestimated Julia, seeing only her crystal grids and bake sale charm. They hadn't seen what he had—this woman had doubled the profits of a prominent real estate agency with her pioneering ideas about video tours and virtual walkthroughs. Her business mind coupled with her otherworldly intuitions made her an invaluable asset for Andrew.

Julia closed her eyes, as though in silent meditation. After a minute or two, her hazel eyes opened slowly. "Hmm. To me, Elena sounds like the key. I'd invest in her. She and Janine could power the engine for the change you and Shift need."

Andrew had grabbed a pen and began taking notes.

The Fable

"I agree something's going on with Pat. She hasn't been in touch for months. Maybe she has a personal issue going on? I'm glad you wished Leo well. I like him. And it sounds like he was suffering, too. I'm proud of you for showing him compassion."

"What about Will?"

"Oh, dear Will. All hat, no cattle."

Andrew nearly spit out his coffee at that comment.

"My hunch is that with someone like Will, as you succeed, he'll follow along. Just don't expect him to be a leader. Have you talked to Dave about him? You'll need to invest in the development plan and shoring up your clients, but Andrew, I don't think this is going to be easy; Pamela Turner is a formidable foe."

"You know her?"

"Of her. My friend Janet told me that Pamela had joined the 'Beat MS' charity board. She called her 'charismatic, altruistic, wicked smart, relentless—a force of nature.'"

"Interesting. She's definitely at the tip of the spear of Shift's outside problems."

Julia's phone rang. "It's the nurse. I need to take it. Hello? Yes?"

Watching Julia walk to the living room, adjusting her ear pods, Andrew headed out the front door to get the paper. He embraced technology in his work life but still loved the smell and feel of a real newspaper. At the end of the driveway, he knelt to pick up the *DC Business Weekly* and the *Washington Post*. As if on autopilot, he slowly walked back to the house, scanning the *Weekly*. As he stepped into the front hall, he froze. He threw down the *Post* and the main sections of the *Business Weekly*.

"Are you kidding me?"

He ran to the kitchen table where Julia sat staring at the phone on the table in front of her. He flipped the glossy pages of the quarterly special insert to the featured executive profile and tossed the rest of the *Business Weekly* on the table. "Would you look at this crap?"

The New Queen Bee of Strategy: Pamela Turner
How Axxcel and its founder are becoming every CEO's go-to advisor

BY ROBERT JACOBY

Spend an hour or two with Pamela Turner, and it's not hard to see why captains of industry of all shapes and sizes view her strategy firm, Axxcel, as the company to call if you want to dominate your competition. Ms. Turner has assembled a world-class team of strategists and change management experts comparable—she'd say "superior"—to the likes of global firms like McKinsey, Boston Consulting Group, and Bain. "Best of all," she says with a smile that makes her cover-worthy face all the more memorable, "not only do we provide superior talent and deliver excellence, we are able to solve client problems for about two-thirds of what the big boys charge."

When we met in her elegant, yet compact, office in Northwest Washington, DC, earlier this month, Ms. Turner put the emphasis on the word "boys."

"Look, I like men. Most of our clients are men. But let's face it. Women are better strategists. We see nuances in behavior and patterns in data the typical guy wouldn't notice if they bit him on the ass."

During my two hours with her, the "girls versus boys" theme would dominate our discussion. At one point, she hummed a tune while she got up to fill our water glasses. At the time, I thought, this woman sure is comfortable in her own skin. Only later did I recognize it as "Man Smart, Woman Smarter," famously sung by Harry Belafonte and covered by such diverse acts as the Grateful Dead, Joan Baez, and Robert Palmer.

I had done my homework on Pamela Ellen Turner, the only child born to the stormy marriage between old-money Wall Street scion Richard Turner and his second wife, the former it girl of the early '60s, Margaret Ann "Maggie" Wood. Growing up surrounded by extreme wealth and unimaginable chaos, Pamela was shipped off to expensive boarding schools. Her high school soccer career at the Lawrenceville School is legendary. After scoring twice as many goals as any player in the more than two-hundred-year history of this sprawling high school near Princeton, New Jersey, she was heavily recruited by all the elite soccer universities in America. Ms. Turner chose Duke, where she was a three-time all-American.

After pairing a major in finance with a master's in interdisciplinary data sciences, she took the spot that had always been saved for her at her father's investment bank. Pamela said, "Truthfully, I don't really like banking or bankers. But my father never understood the word no—especially from a woman. The good news turned out to be that I was fascinated by the long-term strategic decisions my clients were making: some wise, others not so much. So I applied to Harvard Business School and got in. I was the youngest in my class."

"After B-School, of course, I went to the number one global consultancy," she said with a tone that reminded me of her fondness of the word "superior." "I learned a lot about strategy. And . . ." She paused for the first time, staring out the window at the setting sun above Rosslyn, a sky that evoked in me the memory of John Hiatt's gorgeous love song "Lipstick Sunset." I watched her carefully, wondering if she might hum again. After a moment or two, she whipped her head around again, her blue eyes flashing. "And I learned how not to treat people."

With that as a launchpad, Ms. Turner spent the next few minutes outlining her vision for Axxcel. "The only consulting firm with female owners. People first. Pay at the top of the market. Work/life balance. Great benefits. Opportunities to serve the communities where we live and work. World-class in all we do, including our CSR programs."

CSR, or corporate social responsibility, fills Pamela's voice with passion. She tells me all about the charities her company is involved in and the "generous" Axxcel scholarships set to launch this year.

"And of course, this all means we outserve the competition."

"How?" I asked.

"We have better people. It's not an accident that I founded Axxcel in DC. We really have no competition, other than the local offices of the expensive, impersonal behemoths. And the few great consultants in town . . . well, we're just hiring them away."

"What can you tell me about your clients?" I asked, fully expecting her to give me guarded responses, if any. To my great surprise, she reached into the center drawer of her leather inlaid antique desk and handed me a list of approximately fifty clients. I mentally compared the list with the DC largest public, private, and middle market lists that my employer proudly publishes each year. "Wow, Pamela. Looks like you represent over half of all the leading companies in DC."

Now, to be fair, Ms. Turner did not disclose any details about these companies, the nature of the projects, or Axxcel's fees. But I did wonder if any of these powerful companies' CEOs would object to being named in the *Business Weekly*. [Editor's note: As of publication date, our staff was unable to obtain comments from officials at any of the companies we contacted. Accordingly, consistent with our policy regarding substantiation, we have elected to not publish any of the names provided by Ms. Turner.]

Rereading the words I have typed so far, I must admit that Pamela Turner's confidence sounds excessive. Some might call her arrogant. However, in her presence, this naturally skeptical reporter found her inspiring and charming. Sitting in her office surrounded by pictures of Pamela shaking hands or attending events with famous folks like Michelle Obama, Elon Musk, Sheryl Sandberg, and Brené Brown, I found myself kind of hoping she'd offer me a job.

Pamela Turner is here, DC. And our city may never be the same.

Andrew looked over at Julia, who had been reading along with him. He said, "I think I'm going to throw up."

"I feel sorry for her."

"What?" Andrew coughed, his face turning beet red. He pushed his chair back so hard it crashed to the floor.

"She's trying so hard to create the perfect image, it makes me wonder what's under the gloss. And being an all-star soccer player in a boarding school far from two parents who maybe were caught up in their own drama . . . it sounds awful lonely to me. And . . ." Julia cocked her head as if listening to a private voice. "It must have been hard to work at her father's bank."

Andrew looked at Julia.

"But your job is not about Pamela. Your job is Shift. You need to focus your energy not on this puff piece but instead on the board and making your 'Conscious Development Culture That Contributes' idea a reality. Share this article all over Shift. Your partners will rally around defeating Pamela Turner. And can you imagine Pat and the other women owners' reactions to this?"

"Brilliant! One good strategy is the 'common enemy' plan. Like when Nike set their mission: 'Crush Adidas!'" Andrew grabbed his keys, kissed Julia on her forehead, and sprinted to the door to the garage. Over his shoulder, he yelled, "I love you, Julia Winslow Hyde!"

As she heard the car's engine roar as Andrew sped down their driveway, Julia breathed out a long, loud sigh. "I love you too, Andrew. Maybe tonight we can talk about me and my mother."

Ten

Andrew raced through the lobby and down the hall to his office, where Meg was standing outside the door. "Pat's on her way. What's so urgent? What's all that?"

Andrew carried a load of *DC Business Weekly*s he had procured at several convenience stores on the way into the office. He dropped them with a loud thud on the ledge in front of Meg's workstation. "Follow me," he said, grabbing three copies of the glossy insert.

As he waved at Meg to sit, Pat walked in. "What's so urgent this time?"

He handed her a copy of the magazine. "Recognize her?"

"Of course. That's Pamela Turner. What's she done now?"

Meg was flipping through the publication and blurted out, "You're going to want to read page ten."

Pat sat down and began reading, her face reddening as she bounced up and down in her chair. "What a piece of work," she snapped. "'Better people'? 'No women owners'?" Pat was sputtering out the words, her voice rising. "And the 'few great consultants in town'?—Why didn't she just say 'Podunk' town?—'Well, we're just hiring them away.'"

Pat jumped to her feet. "I'm a woman. Half our partners are women. Talent? I'll show you talent." Andrew winked at Meg and gestured for her to grab the stack of journals.

Pat continued her tirade. "Perfect. I'll be dropping a copy on the desk of each of our female partners and directors. First Leo, then the Baxter debacle, and now this—this is war."

Andrew's glee at Pat's fury ended at the mention of the contract loss. "Yes, do that, Pat. In fact, Meg, see if you can get a copy for *all* the partners. Ms. Turner," he said, sarcasm oozing from every syllable, "has insulted us all and harmed our business. Rally the troops, Pat. I'm going to work on getting ready for the board."

"Game on. Miss all-American goal scorer better be ready to play a little defense," she said, scooping up the papers as she stormed out.

"Nicely played, Andrew."

"Whatever do you mean?" Andrew widened his eyes in his best innocent look. "Will you see if Elena is in?"

Andrew stared at the colorful circle and notes on the whiteboard across the room. Janine's Conscious Development Culture and employee life cycle as an organizing system continued to make sense to him. He walked to the board, grabbed a green marker, and underlined Capabilities in the new Shift higher purpose statement: "Consciously Develop our People's Capabilities so they can Contribute."

In a large open space on his whiteboard, he drew three columns. At the top of each, he wrote Mind Skills, People Skills, Technical Skills. "What capabilities do our people need in order to thrive at work? At home? As citizens?" he asked out loud.

"Great questions, boss."

Elena walked into his office. Impossibly, her smile seemed larger than her entire face. It reminded him of the look on his two-year-old nephew's face when the little boy cried out, "Unky Andew, I did it all by myself!"

"Well, Elena, you look like you've got some news to share." The words had barely left Andrew's mouth when she exclaimed, "Yes! I saved six of the Change Management team members."

"Way to go!"

"And there are another six on the fence." She waved the *DC Business Weekly* at Andrew. "Once they see this, I think we can get all of them to stay. Maybe you can talk to them about this development plan. I think that will help. And Andrew, I really appreciate the faith you have in me and for allowing me to participate in the creating of the new Shift."

"You earned it, Elena."

"Thanks. Now, I've been thinking about all this and diving into some

Conscious, Capable, and Ready to Contribute

research," she said, gesturing to the whiteboard. Reaching into her leather bag, she pulled out a paper. "I started a list of capabilities."

Elena walked to the board, grabbed a green marker. "I like green, makes me think about growth. Okay if I start filling in these columns?"

"Go for it."

For the next few minutes, Elena neatly printed concepts into each of the three "Skills" columns, at times glancing at her notes. She placed the marker down and turned toward Andrew, who was studying her handiwork.

"After our meeting the other day, I dug out a few books, which seemed likely to help us."

"Like what?"

"Your favorite, Tom Friedman, of course. His book *Thank You for Being Late*, about the '*Age of Accelerations*,' gave me some great ideas. That book Janine mentioned—Kegan and Lahey's *An Everyone Culture*—also offered some guidance. And I scanned a few others, like Carol Dweck's *Mindset* and Dan Pink's *A Whole New Mind*."

"And . . . ?"

"They each support the notion that we—as in all people—need to think differently about continuous learning and development if we are going to succeed in this fast-changing world. They offer their own versions of *why* to change and how others have done it." Elena paused, stared at the whiteboard, and said, "This idea—your idea—companies consciously developing people as a form of social contribution is unique. No one seems to be thinking about it that way."

Elena looked thoughtful. "Clients I have worked with train their employees and want them to grow. Sometimes it's because growth makes for better employees. If you're lucky, it's because leaders genuinely care about doing good for their people. But I don't think I've ever seen a company that asked, 'How can we develop our people so they make a difference in their communities and the world?' That's what we're asking, isn't it?"

Before Andrew could respond, Janine walked in. "Wow. Perfect timing," she said as she took in Elena's lists.

"Really impressive." Janine lifted a blue document. "This aligns with the employee life cycle model I've been drafting. We'll get to my stuff later. First, let's brainstorm Elena's list."

At Janine's suggestion, the team added an overarching Core Capability for both Mind Skills and People Skills, as well as working definitions of those two categories.

The three sat quietly for a few moments, taking in their creation.

MIND SKILLS	PEOPLE SKILLS	TECHNICAL SKILLS
• Executive Function Skills (Focus, organizing, etc.) • Growth Mindset • Critical Thinking • Adaptability • Decision-Making • Curiosity	• Emotional Intelligence (EQ) • Communication • Authenticity • Resolving Conflict • Teamwork • Influencing • Integrity	• Digital Readiness • Job-Related Mastery

"Well, Andrew, what do you think?" Elena asked.

"First, this list is spot-on. I'm sure we'll refine it as we work more on it." Squeezing his chin as if to form a dimple as he often did while thinking, Andrew turned toward the board again. "A few questions are popping up for me. How do we help each other develop these capabilities? Are there companies out there that already are doing some or all of this that we can learn from? And—" He paused to look at Janine. "How do we link—no, embed—these capabilities in our culture and into how we work every day? For this to work, development and growth and a focus on our people has to show up all the time consistently in everything we do."

Janine picked up the paper she had brought with her. "Take a look at the life cycle I drew up, based on our earlier meeting."

As Andrew's and Elena's eyes scanned the blue and green graphic that depicted the circle on Andrew's whiteboard, Janine continued. "I was thinking we build development of these capabilities into every step of the life cycle."

Andrew nodded. "As for finding other model companies, I'm going to talk to Dave about getting us in to see a few of the truly great places to work. He has an old-school Rolodex that would choke a horse."

Andrew looked at his watch. "I need to get ready for the board tomorrow morning. So let's adjourn and pick this up again in the next day or so. Great job! I'm fired up for what's next."

Conscious, Capable, and Ready to Contribute

. . .

Andrew looked at Pat, took a deep breath, and clicked the Join Zoom Meeting button on his MacBook. They both were dressed in conservative boardroom-appropriate attire. Pat's black blazer covered a crisp white blouse buttoned to the neck. A charcoal midlength skirt and midheel black pumps completed her professional consulting partner look.

Andrew's own traditional navy-blue suit, white shirt, and blue Repp tie weren't his favorite, but they were what Julia called his "ask for a loan from a sixty-five-year-old bank president" look.

"Good morning, Pat and Andrew," Wendy said.

"Good morning," they responded in near unison, watching the square videos pop up, indicating that Victor, Jesse, and Roger had joined. Each of the directors looked straight into the camera.

"Of course, General Pagano was already waiting," Wendy said, smiling into her camera.

"Yes, ma'am. Five minutes early is five minutes late," replied Gus Pagano.

Wendy laughed and said, "Gus, I've told you that 'ma'am' makes me feel old."

"Yes, ma'am. Oh shit. Sorry!" Gus's smile and wink made Andrew think this slip-up was a deliberate way of winding up Wendy.

Victor Jones exhaled loudly as he shuffled his papers. "I've got a hard stop at nine o'clock, Wendy. Can we please just get started?"

"Yes, of course, Victor."

Wendy grabbed the agenda from the top of a two-inch-high stack of papers on her desk. "As chair, I call to order this special meeting of the board of directors of Shift Advisors, Inc. Have all members reviewed the agenda and the reports that were circulated yesterday?"

"Yes, Jesse and I have. Of course, we didn't have much time."

"I'll fill in the details for you, Victor," Andrew said.

"Good. These reports raise more questions than they provide answers." Victor looked down, as if at some notes.

"Am I reading this right? Approximately one-third of the business is leaving? The most profitable part of Shift?"

Victor Jones's angry face filled the screen. He leaned so close to the camera that Andrew could see the individual hairs on his head. "We invested ten million dollars in Shift just last year so you could expand. And you've managed to let thirty percent of the value just walk out the door? My investors will not understand!"

"Yes, but there is some good news."

Jones cut him off. "Let's hear all the bad news first, Andrew. Wendy, what did your firm's employment lawyers say? Can we keep this Vincent character from stealing our people and clients? Don't we have noncompetition agreements?"

"Shift does require all partners and employees to sign nonsolicitation agreements. But the courts are increasingly siding with employees on this type of matter. We can proceed against Leo and his team, but it'll take a long time, a lot of money, and a lot of luck. We might eventually keep them away from existing clients, but there's no way to keep them from working as consultants for Axxcel or anybody else, for that matter."

Pagano cleared his throat, which caused the Zoom screen to switch to him. He sat ramrod straight as he said, "Damn it, then. We need to go straight at the real enemy. Axxcel."

Pat jumped in. "Sorry, General. But Wendy's law partners made it clear when we spoke that we've got little to no chance to stop Axxcel from taking the people or clients."

"Then you and Andrew will just have to go beat them head-to-head. Make sure people choose you, even when they have Axxcel as an option. You can do that, right?"

Everyone paused to look at Andrew, who was uncomfortably aware they were looking at his image on the screen with hopeful expressions. Andrew's throat was suddenly very dry. His head knew that the board was on his team, but the rest of his body was screaming *danger!*

He wanted to tell them something that would confirm their faith in Shift and in him. They wanted to hear good news, and Andrew realized he needed to tell them about the Baxter loss instead. Andrew flinched and felt his gut drop like the time he and Julia had taken their nephew, Charlie, on the Tower of Terror at Disney World. *Oh God, I hope I don't throw up like I did that day.*

Conscious, Capable, and Ready to Contribute

Eleven

Andrew and Pat looked at the five faces of the other board members, framed neatly into the windowpanes of the Zoom call. Andrew was sure the computer hadn't frozen, but everyone was still. Hearing Andrew admit he'd lost the $5 million contract had resulted in a range of unspoken reactions: wrinkled foreheads, narrowed eyes, pursed lips.

Roger Coyle spoke first. "I've known you two for a long time. Even back at Wharton, Andrew, you always had a plan B. And usually a C."

"Yes, Roger. We do. Of course, these plans are a lot more difficult to put together than what we did back then, charting the weekend's festivities in Philadelphia."

"You bet your ass they are," Victor shouted. "Get to the point."

To avoid the distraction of Victor's sweaty forehead pressed so close to the camera, Andrew spoke to a spot just above the green light. He sat up straight and slipped into full-on CEO mode.

"First, let me acknowledge that we've got short-term challenges. It's not going to be easy. And as each of you know, we have a really strong internal team at Shift. For the last few days, our finance, growth, and HR teams have been working around the clock. Pat's going to lead this discussion, but first, let's be clear about something. Shift is playing the long game here."

Pat looked at Andrew and then the faces staring back at her on the screen. When no one spoke, she said, "I'm going to share my screen with you, so you can see the actions we're taking." A Shift Advisors logoed presentation appeared, titled, "Change Management Practice Situation: Ten-Point Action Plan."

For the next few minutes, Pat and Andrew explained their plans: a return visit to William Baxter with an offer to match Axxcel's price; calls to all of Shift's largest clients to ensure their relationships were solid; and a few cuts in variable costs like internship parties and field trips.

"And we've managed to retain at least a half dozen of Leo's team and are working on another ten," said Andrew.

"Well, that'll be great—*if* you've got work for them. Otherwise, it's just more wasted money." Victor mopped his forehead.

Wendy spoke up. "Jesse, I see you have the 'hand-up' icon pressed. Go ahead with your question. And no need to be so polite."

"Yes, why be polite, Jesse? It seems only a few of us actually know what that icon actually means." Andrew could imagine General Pagano's tone was the one he had used to snap troops into order.

Andrew's attention quickly shifted to Jesse, eager to hear what he had to say. Jesse Martin had been chief technology officer at Victor's company. In his twenties, he had worked at the Defense Advanced Research Projects Agency. While at DARPA, Jesse won several awards for helping create HALOE, a laser-based radar tool that provided high-resolution 3-D geospatial data to military leaders. Victor had wooed him away to Silicon Valley with the promise of a well-funded innovation lab where he could pursue innovation unfettered by Uncle Sam's constraints. When the facial recognition software he had created turned their enterprise into a "unicorn"—a privately owned start-up valued at over $1 billion—he had helped Victor sell it to a federal contractor serving the more clandestine intelligence agencies. Obscenely wealthy at thirty-eight, with no interest in retirement, Jesse had accepted Victor's offer to join his newly formed private investment firm.

"These plans are mostly focused on revenue generation rather than cost reduction. What's plan B? C?"

Pat leaned forward. "We'll have detailed backup plans shortly."

Andrew nodded. "For now, we're running the play while also working on a new long-term strategy focused on development of our people's mind skills, people skills, and technical skills."

Conscious, Capable, and Ready to Contribute

"What the?" Victor snapped. "There will be no 'long term' if you don't deal with the fire burning around you. I don't even know what you mean by 'people skills' or 'mind skills,' but you need to go back and cut more costs. Don't make me wish that banker Gary Norris and our esteemed chair had never introduced us in the first place."

With that, his screen went dark and Victor's square on the screen disappeared. Jesse chimed in with an almost an imperceptible eyeroll. "I better go too. Look, guys, when I was at DARPA, long before I met Victor, we were always visioning the long term. Our boss allowed us that privilege, provided the short-term plan was tightly engineered. Good luck."

After Jesse was gone, Roger and Wendy said their goodbyes, leaving the two cofounders staring at General Pagano.

"Thank you, General. We'll get the plan back to you and the board soon."

"You do that. But don't forget, I served under General James 'Mad Dog' Mattis. He was all about action, and he had some great sayings. None more apropos than 'PowerPoint makes us stupid.'"

Pagano's grin faded. His steel gray eyes bored into the camera. "Make no mistake. You are under siege. Always watch your rear flank, *especially* with a guy like Victor." With that, Gus Pagano's craggy face disappeared.

Ensuring that he and the others had signed off, Andrew slowly closed the laptop. "Well, that sure went well, don't you think?"

Pat burst out in a nervous laugh. "Thank God Victor only had an hour."

"Amen," he said, bowing his head and folding his hands. "We do need to have a plan B with deeper cuts. Hopefully, we won't need them. Most important, we have to deliver on the ten-point plan."

Pat nodded. "We need to execute the short-term plan so well that Victor will want to claim it as his own while . . ."

Andrew waited for her to continue, but she fell silent.

"Hey, what's up?"

Standing up, Pat walked to the window, as though trying to avoid his eyes. "I'm nervous, Andrew, and before we go on, there's something you should know. Tim's restaurants are not all as successful as Easton on Penn. His accountant says he's in default on some loans. Two kids in private universities, personal mortgages, huge loans on the restaurants—and now these challenges." Pat sighed deeply and placed a hand on the glass pane.

"It's all a bit much. We need to focus on the finances now to make sure we have something in the future."

Andrew got up and stood beside Pat, hoping to catch her eye. "Why didn't you tell me about Tim?"

"First, I'm kind of embarrassed and I didn't want to worry you, to let you down. Plus, Tim's a mess. He would be mortified to know I was talking to you. And, he has no idea that all this is going on here. And there was never any time—"

"Hey, I get it. But I tried to be the superhero with Leo, and look how that turned out. I should have told you sooner, and you should have let me know about this. Right now, I need your head one hundred percent in the game. Together, we can meet any challenge. Right?"

"Yes. We've got this." With a more confident smile, Pat looked up and finally made eye contact. "I keep repeating what David Edwards always says: 'When one door closes, another one opens . . .'"

Andrew interrupted, "But it's hell in the hallway!"

Pat gave Andrew a high five and walked quickly out the door.

When she was gone, Andrew allowed the smile to slip from his face. He slumped forward. *Feels like a long hallway, Dave.*

• • •

After the board call, Andrew hunkered down at his desk. He called a few major clients and felt reassured by their positive comments about Shift's performance. He picked away at the short-term plan and thought about Pat's admission—*how long has she been carrying that around with her?*—but his mind kept wandering to the whiteboard across the office. It was as if the center of the employee development life cycle was the sun, pulling him into her orbit.

Just then his phone chirped.

J: Hope you didn't forget date night . . .
A: Nope. See you soon. 7:30 res at Mika's. Madly

Thank goodness Meg made that reservation, Andrew thought, closing down his laptop. *I really have been distracted.*

Conscious, Capable, and Ready to Contribute

Andrew held hands with Julia for the ten-minute walk to Mika's, enjoying the peace of her presence beside him.

"I heard from my mom's nurse today," Julia told him, briefly mentioning the call she had earlier.

"And here we are." Andrew placed his hand on the small of Julia's back as he held the door open for her. "I'm hungry!"

Mika's was their favorite neighborhood bistro. Tables for two were the norm, although locals frequently pushed them together for larger gatherings. The tiny restaurant felt as if it were quietly tucked away on a leafy street in Paris's 18th Arrondissement.

Mika herself greeted them at the door. "It's been so long! But I have your favorite table by the window." She placed the daily menu in front of them. "Veuve Clicquot for the lady. Heineken for you, Andrew?"

Julia laughed. "We are so predictable."

Andrew smiled at the bistro owner. "Something a bit stronger tonight. Bourbon on the rocks. Twist, please."

When the drinks arrived, Andrew took a big gulp. "Whew, that burned a bit."

Julia took a sip of her own drink and placed her hands on the table in front of her.

"What?" he said, taking a more careful sip of bourbon. "I know that look."

"Andrew, after twenty-five years, I can tell when you're jumpy, distracted, dying to talk. Out with it!"

Except for a brief pause to place their orders, and to pick at his meal, Andrew talked nonstop for the next hour. He recounted the details of the board call, including Victor Jones's bulging neck veins, Jesse's surprising curriculum vitae, and Pagano's colorful language. Julia listened as she savored every bite of her meal.

"Something else you need to share?"

Andrew drained the remains of his second bourbon and hesitated. "Apparently, Tim's restaurant empire has some cracks. Pat's worried about money. I'm more worried about you and me."

"Us?"

Julia was a statue, her eyes starting to mist up. Andrew held both hands up. "Sorry, not us, as in our relationship, but maybe our finances. I mean, on top of all my other worries, I've got to prepare for Tim to come to me asking for a bailout. Will it never end?"

"You know, Andrew, sometimes you are so self-absorbed. You should hear yourself." She slowly placed her dessert fork on the edge of her plate as if it suddenly weighed ten pounds. "Your business partner confides in you, and all you can think about is yourself. Of course, I can sure relate to that."

Andrew didn't hear her. His attention was caught by the couple walking by.

Julia followed his gaze to where Gary Norris and Pamela Turner were walking arm in arm, right up to Mika.

Gary Norris's face froze when he looked over at Julia and Andrew.

"Oh, hello, Andrew. Hi, Julia."

Andrew almost laughed at Gary's discomfort. As if sensing Julia's glare, he stood up. "Hello, Gary. Pamela, I'd like you to meet my wife." Andrew was aware his tone and facial expression suggested that he would prefer to be picking up a Chesapeake Bay blue crab by the claw than meeting Pamela, but somehow he couldn't pull off a more cordial greeting.

Julia stepped around Andrew and hugged Gary. "It has been too long, Gary. You look great." Before Gary could respond, Julia released him and turned toward Pamela. "Hi, I'm Julia. So nice to meet you. It was fun to read your profile in the paper. You're even prettier in person."

"Well, thank you." Pamela grabbed Julia's outstretched hand. "Join us for an after-dinner drink?"

Andrew cut in. "We need to go. I've got an early start tomorrow."

Gary fidgeted. His hands were deep in his pockets, and he was shifting side to side slightly. Andrew noticed he had let go of Pamela's arm and taken a small step back. *Interesting.*

Pamela looked at Julia. "Oh, I wish you could have joined us. Gary talks about you two all the time."

"Maybe another time." Andrew pulled out his wallet, handed the waitress three fifty-dollar bills. "The extra is for you. Merci."

Julia pulled her black cashmere shawl over her shoulders and gave Andrew a nudge. "Nice to meet you, Pamela. Take care, Gary."

Conscious, Capable, and Ready to Contribute

As they headed out the door, Pamela Turner's voice followed them. "Maybe next time, then. I would love to chat business."

Andrew stopped, his face reddening. He could feel his heart rate rising. Before he could turn back, Julia's left hand, obscured by the shawl, shoved him in the kidneys. Hard. His mouth snapped shut. "Keep walking," she hissed.

Andrew knew better than to speak on the walk home. Steam seemed to pour out of Julia's ears, and her heels sounded like rapid gunfire on the sidewalk. She walked just slightly ahead, making it impossible to hold hands. Not that Andrew was trying. He was still fuming, imagining all the witty comebacks he could have made when Pamela mentioned "business."

Reaching the foyer inside their home, he couldn't control himself any longer. "Can you believe that guy? How could he do this to me?"

Julia spun around with a glare that could have stopped a tidal wave. "Really? He's in love. Or 'in infatuation.' Give him a break."

"You're taking his side?"

"How are there sides in this? And why is it all about you? After three hours of our date night, would you like to know how I'm doing? How Mom is? Or is this like Pat—you only care how other people impact you? All this talk about people development and contribution to society. That's rich, given how very little you seem to care about people the closest to you."

Andrew didn't say a word, and Julia's frown deepened. She wrapped her shawl closer around herself and grabbed the car keys. "Well, give that some thought. I'm going to the grocery store. *Somebody* finished off all the milk this morning."

Andrew stood motionless as Julia slammed the door behind her. Once he heard the garage door close, he made his way slowly to the kitchen. He sat down hard and let his head drop into his hands, his elbows propped up by his thighs.

I screwed up again. What is wrong with me? If I can't please the people I love most in my life, how on earth can I hope to help others?

Dave's voice resonated in his mind. "Mood follows action, Andrew. You can't think your way to feeling better."

Andrew straightened up in a move that would have made General Pagano proud. *First order of business is the love of my life. I'm not moving until she walks through that door.*

Twelve

The next morning, Andrew headed along the GW Parkway in his convertible. Andrew loved convertibles. He had purchased his first when he was just twenty-three. The beat-up '68 royal blue Corvette was fun for a summer. Within three months, he had to admit that he simply couldn't afford it. This Mercedes was pure luxury, but Andrew never got whistles, waves, and "woohoos!" like he did seemingly every day that summer. One thing was the same: he felt so alive with the wind whipping through the open car, classic rock blaring. And many of his best ideas came to him as he cruised down Canal Road to his office. Today, however, he added a few miles to the trip by heading across the river to the GW Parkway. After yesterday, he needed the extra thinking time.

Julia had returned thirty minutes after slamming the door, with a few groceries. As she started putting the milk and bread away, Andrew launched into apologies.

Julia initially rebuffed his mea culpa. "What are you sorry for? That you acted like an ass? That I'm pissed?"

"No. Well, yes. Those things for sure. But the heart of the issue is that I haven't been supporting you the way you always support me."

Julia kissed Andrew. "Let's get some sleep. I accept your apology. Just keep in mind that how you act going forward is what matters."

"How you act going forward" were words that nagged at Andrew as he sped toward the office.

Andrew was still thinking about Julia as he walked into his office. He was startled to find Pat sitting at his conference table, papers scattered about, reading glasses perched at the end of her nose. She looked up and said, "Yes. I'm aware I look like crap. Didn't get much sleep. Finally gave up at three and came in. The initial revenue and profit forecasts for the rest of the year are pretty grim."

Before Andrew could respond, Meg appeared in the doorway. "Hey. I've reserved the Jefferson conference room for your meeting with Leo's team. It starts in five." She handed him a blue folder. "Here's a list of attendees, their tenure with Shift, clients they've supported, and everything else I think you might need to convince them to stay with Shift. Elena reviewed this info too. She thought it best if she is not with you—might make her peers a bit uncomfortable—but Janine will be waiting for you."

"That's perfect. And thank you as always for making me look great. Sorry, Pat; got to run."

Pat's eyes were still glued to the spreadsheets, as her hand flailed in the air with a dismissive wave. "Sure. What? Oh yeah, good luck."

Walking down the hall, Andrew scanned the information packet that Meg had prepared. *What? Jenny Robinson isn't in the group? Damn, she was my star hire from UVA in 2013. Clients love her. How could Pamela Turner get to her? Leslie Weaver's in the group? Hopefully, I can make amends for blowing her off the other day.* Andrew focused on smiling, hoping he looked more confident than he felt.

The six consultants who had agreed to hear him out turned to greet Andrew as he and Janine entered the room. He scanned their faces, hoping for clues as to their relative openness to what he might have to say. He and Janine slowly worked their way around the table, shaking hands and greeting each by name. Their faces stayed impassive. *Good poker players*, he thought.

"Congratulations," Andrew said as he sat down in the open chair in the middle of the table. "You have been paid a real compliment. Of course, I'm not surprised that someone wants to steal you away from Shift. Each of you are stars."

Andrew paused as he watched some shoulders relax. Some of the fidgeting stopped. A few of the consultants uncrossed their arms. Shelly Madsen, a twenty-nine-year-old graduate of William and Mary, exhaled so loudly that everyone laughed nervously. Her face suddenly looked like she should have slathered on the SPF 50.

"Hey, I get it. You're nervous. You're facing a big decision. Probably the biggest decision of your business lives."

Andrew drank some water and then walked over to the dry-erase board and grabbed a marker. "You're super smart, and I know you're wondering if it's time—whether it's time to stay or go. I trust you'll make the decision that's best for you. My advice is that you ignore the short-term stuff. Sure, our stay bonus of twenty thousand dollars is nice. I am sure Axxcel is paying you well, as are we. But I want you to look a bit further out on the horizon. Let me show you where Shift is headed."

As Andrew started to draw, the consultant sitting next to Janine said, "Andrew, wait a sec."

Andrew turned as Gregory Grantland, a thirty-year-old director, continued. "Andrew, I am definitely leaving. I shouldn't have come to this meeting. So, before you share any trade secrets, I better go." He pushed his chair back, collected his papers, and started toward the door.

"Gregory, please stay. I appreciate your ethical approach to this. But what you will hear is going to be on our website and in recruiting materials for years to come. So no worries about hearing it. And who knows, I might just change your mind."

"Okay. But I'm definitely going to Axxcel."

Andrew smiled at Gregory. "That's totally up to you."

Andrew drew the life cycle prototype on the board. "Janine, would you please come over and help me with the list of capabilities that Elena, you, and I came up with?"

"With pleasure."

As Janine neatly printed the list of Mind Skills, People Skills, and Technical Skills on the board, Andrew used the green marker to write "CONTRIBUTION" in big block letters. She spoke as she wrote. "The research is very clear: to compete in the current world of work, people need to develop their technical skills, people skills, and mind skills. Developing these capabilities at work is also something team members want and something that helps them experience well-being. On top of that, Shift plans to make people development a way to contribute to society."

Turning back to the young consultants, he said, "Imagine that Shift delivered all this development to you and had only one ask in return: that you use these enhanced capabilities—mind skills, people skills, and technical skills—to contribute to society. What would you think and how would you contribute?"

It didn't surprise Andrew that Markiesha Charles, a change management specialist, responded first. She was known as a bit of a visionary and for speaking her mind. Pat had recently described her as one of the best systems thinkers at Shift, a "real dot-connector."

"Andrew, to your first question, any company that invested in me to the extent you just described . . . well, I doubt I'd ever leave. As to contribution, my first thought is, I'd figure out how to teach young people these skills. For example, if I knew how to teach 'critical thinking' and 'growth mindset,' I'd be taking these tools to my community."

Rajesh Patel, one of Andrew's favorite Virginia Tech hires, was vigorously nodding his head. "I need help with 'communication skills' and 'resolving conflict' skills right here at Shift. And I sure could use those at home. Me being a better parent and husband would contribute to society, too, don't you think?"

"You both are on the right track," Andrew replied.

Rajesh paused as if trying to decide whether to say more. After a moment, he looked directly at Andrew and said, "But really, the 'only ask' is that we contribute to society? Really? I don't know . . . You must want us to use these skills at Shift, too."

"Uh. Well, yes, of course. I definitely need to be clearer about that . . ."

Janine spoke up. "Rajesh, to be clear, the way we look at it is if you grow here at Shift, you will provide amazing service to clients, and that itself will be a contribution to society and of course to the company. And if you leave, you'll help your next company. When we help companies grow, they hire more people. And good jobs help people thrive." Janine continued, looking over at Andrew, who was nodding his head in support. "And we feel like these capabilities will help all Shift employees contribute to society during the times they aren't here at work."

"What did the partners say?" asked Vicky Bernstein, one of Pat's favorites. "None of this will work without full buy-in from the senior leaders."

Rajesh rolled his eyes. "And they have to want to develop, too! Not too sure I can see some of your partners changing. Right now, they pay lip service to Janine's training programs. But when it is a question of billable work versus learning . . ."

Vicky continued. "How are you going to embed learning and development goals in the partner's performance management system? How will you incentivize them to support all this? If they don't grow, will they see a hit in their pay?"

"All good questions." Andrew's hands were scribbling fast as he tried to capture the rapid-fire thoughts the group was throwing at him. "We still need to figure these out."

"I feel like Janine has tried lots of this training stuff before. Didn't you just cut her budget? Janine, do you believe Andrew will truly back you on all this?"

Before Janine could respond, Leslie Weaver spoke for the first time. "Andrew, is this something you're seriously considering," her eyes narrowing slightly, "or is this just an academic exercise? You couldn't find time to talk to me about how a client was mistreating me and the staff, but now you are going to make working here all about us? A cynic might say it's just another program from management that gets people excited but then just dies on the vine. Worse, you could just be flashing a shiny object at us to distract us from Pamela Turner."

Rajesh piped up. "And she's a really shiny object." About half the people at the table laughed and the other half looked at Andrew nervously.

Andrew couldn't help himself. After a few moments of laughter, he stood up straight and said, "This is no exercise, Leslie. Janine, Pat, Elena, and I have been working hard on this and making it a practical approach we can implement. And I am sorry that I left you sitting in my office. I was wrong. I will talk to your client."

Andrew looked at his watch and said, "I know today's the day you need to get back to Axxcel." He turned around and pointed to the board and then slowly made eye contact with each of them. "As you each make your decision, I hope you'll take our plans into consideration. I invite you to

Conscious, Capable, and Ready to Contribute

stay and help us create the new Shift, where employee development is the mission and where together we will truly contribute to society. But I respect your decisions, whatever they are, and wish you the best in your futures."

Andrew and Janine collected their materials and notes from the meeting and walked back to Andrew's office. "That's a smart group, Andrew. They made some excellent points."

"No doubt. What's your prediction about who stays?"

"Gregory is obviously gone. Leslie didn't seem to buy your answer. I think you hooked the others. Then again, I was sure I'd see Jenny Robinson there, so take my predictions with a grain of salt."

The two of them stopped outside Janine's office. "Thanks, Janine. Let me know their decisions as soon as you have them."

"Will do."

"Janine. One more thing. I truly am sorry that we cut out your leadership program and made you take deep cuts in your staff. I should have known you were right."

"Thanks. I'm just glad you are starting to see the light."

Andrew flashed her a thumbs-up and headed to his office. Even with the pushback, he was invigorated. The meeting had reminded him of the early days of Shift when every employee had crowded into his office around a small folding table to debate issues and next steps for the fledgling enterprise. These memories carried him as he walked by his fellow Shift team members. He greeted everyone he saw with a smile. He stopped to chat at a few workstations. He felt like he had just achieved a new 10K PR, his body tingling from the endorphins.

As he rounded the corner near his office, Andrew saw Meg waving frantically. She was talking to someone on the phone. "Hurry!" she mouthed, pressing the mute button on her headset. "It's Grayson."

"What did he say?"

"He said he wants to talk about Axxcel."

Thirteen

As soon as Andrew put the phone down, Meg appeared in his office doorway.

"Well?"

"Grayson's a good egg. He just wanted me to know that Pamela Turner tried to get him to move his business to Axxcel."

"And he said no?"

"Thankfully, yes. He wanted to hear directly from me that Shift wasn't 'imploding.'"

"And it's not, right?"

Andrew's head snapped up from the papers he was scanning. "No!" he barked before he noticed Meg's grinning face.

He rolled his eyes, but he couldn't help smiling. "Three things, Meg. Can you get me a kale salad? Yes, a salad. Time for a change in menu to go with all the other changes."

"You got it. What else?" she said as she scribbled in her ever-present pink notebook.

"Let's keep the afternoon clear. I'm going to call a few more clients to see how bad the damage is, send notes to the staff I just saw, and call that jerk client who's been beating up Leslie and her staff." He looked at Meg, who had stopped scribbling and was staring at him. "I'll be calm. I promise."

"Third thing?"

"I committed to Pat I'd only work on the conscious development stuff as a side project. Would you ask Janine and Elena if they can come meet me at six? In fact, see if they can meet every night this week at six. Thanks."

Conscious, Capable, and Ready to Contribute

Meg closed the door on her way out as Andrew began calling Shift's Change Management clients. After what felt like twenty minutes, Andrew looked at his watch and realized he'd been sitting for four hours. He stood up slowly, remembering his oft-committed, rarely kept promise to stretch more. After a few toe touches and quad stretches, he stood at his desk studying the scorecard he had created.

CLIENTS		REVENUE
Contacted		
Staying	12	$10.5 million
Lost	4	$3.75 million.
Unsure	4	$4.55 million
Not Contacted	55	$11.2 million (avg. $204K per)
Total Clients	75	$30 million (avg. $400K per)

Andrew recalled Victor's furious expression on the Zoom call. *He's going to be really angry about the "Lost" clients. He'll go nuts if we don't keep the "Unsure" clients.* The scorecard confirmed that Pat was right when she said "grim." Shift needed to put a full-court press on the four major at-risk clients and the fifty-five smaller Change Management clients.

A wave of fear slammed Andrew, starting with his gut and then heading simultaneously both up and down his spine. "I bet Pamela's calling on the Strategy clients, too, not just the Change Management ones." A cascade of negative thoughts filled his mind. *What kind of leader are you, Andrew? How did you let this happen? Is it too late to stop her?* Andrew's legs felt like they were made from sponges, as though they'd collapse if he stood up. He shook his head and took a deep breath, trying to stop the thoughts.

Suddenly, General Pagano's voice echoed in Andrew's ears. "You will just have to go beat them head-to-head. You can do that, right?" Andrew also heard words that Pagano hadn't actually said but had no doubt been thinking. "Stop feeling sorry for yourself. Or you *will* lose it all."

Andrew pulled up the client list from Shift's CRM system, sorted it by revenue, and began making calls. An hour later, he pushed his chair back and spun it to face the DC skyline.

The Fable

Fifteen Strategy clients called. Every one of them had heard from Pamela Turner. Thanks to loyalty and outstanding service by Pat and her team, Andrew had discovered that only three were thinking about leaving. *Pamela is relentless. I better call Pat to ask her to reach out to the three on the fence.*

Just then, Andrew's Mac pinged, indicating new emails coming in. He had one from Janine, which he opened immediately.

CM Staff Update

Good news. Our pitch worked on four of the six. Of course, Gregory Grantland cleared out his office today, and Leslie Weaver is leaving, too. She sent me the following email:

"Janine, thank you for your time today and all you have done to make this a great place to work. Regrettably, today will be my final day. Please forward this to Andrew.

Andrew, I know you only read short emails, so I'll be brief. Good luck with righting the ship. You once had time for all of us. And you taught us well. Today's meeting reminded me of those early days, but candidly, when you used the word 'conscious,' it made me realize how asleep—unconscious?—you've been. Hope this Axxcel situation is the wake-up call you need. Leslie."

Andrew, I'm sure these comments sting. Let me know if you want to talk. Janine

Andrew crossed his arms on his desk and let his head drop onto his forearms with a thud. He heard Janine and Elena chatting with Meg in the hall and quickly raised his head and smoothed his tie. *No sense in worrying them or making them think I can't handle this.*

"Are you ready for us?" Janine asked. Elena slid to Janine's side and said, "The calvary has arrived!"

"Wow. Six o'clock already? Yes. Come in."

Andrews's phone chirped.

Andrew hesitated a moment, trying to recall if he and Julia had discussed evening plans. *Oh crap. We were going to discuss next steps for her mother.* He winced as he typed his response.

Andrew stared at his phone hoping for a quick response. Nothing. No text came as they settled in for their meeting, and Andrew's phone stayed quiet as Janine passed around updated drafts of the employee life cycle and core people capabilities.

Andrew and Elena scanned the colorful documents. Elena spoke first. "Beautiful design. My research suggests we add 'Creative Thinking' to the Mind Skills list. Many of our teams need to develop that to make sure we're competitive and coming up with solutions other firms aren't."

"Good one—we need to encourage out-of-the-box solutions in life and in work," Janine said, looking at Andrew, who was also nodding his head.

The trio went back and forth discussing and editing the two documents for over an hour before Janine stepped to the almost full whiteboard and started writing. "How to . . ." She paused and took a step back. "'How to' what?" she said to no one in particular.

"'How to *Shift*'?" offered Elena.

"Bingo!" Janine said as she finished her list. "To make this actually show up at Shift, we need to create a conscious development culture. One that makes learning and growing a part of everyday life here. To do that, we need to figure out how to make that culture happen. My research suggests there are five steps we need to follow."

How to Shift

1. Understand the role of leadership.
2. Align business <u>and</u> people strategies.
3. Define Conscious Development Culture Principles.

4. Identify Core People Capabilities.
5. Embed Conscious Development throughout the Employee Life Cycle.

Andrew started to speak just as his phone dinged.

J: Okay. :(Just don't be any later than 8:30.
A: See you soon. Madly.

"I've got about thirty minutes before I need to get home to help Julia figure out next steps for her mother. Let's begin at the top of the list. I guess that starts with me."

"And the other partners," Janine added. "As Vicky pointed out earlier today, we need their full 'buy-in.'"

"We need more than that from them!" Elena said. Andrew and Janine's heads snapped around at the same moment.

Elena blushed. "Oops. That came out a bit louder than I intended. What I mean is I feel like 'buy-in' is too weak. We're talking about leading change. They need to *own* it."

Janine jumped in. "That is much better. And good leaders need to embody the company's values. In this case, we need them to be living examples of conscious development. They need to *model* it."

"And once we put meat on the bones—embed development in all aspects of the life cycle—we need to execute, just like any other strategic initiative. We need to *drive* it." As Andrew completed his sentence, he was on his feet. "*Own, model, and drive.* And it starts with me as CEO."

The three sat in silence as Andrew's words hung in the air. Andrew's mind wandered to Leslie's scathing indictment. Her email hadn't been wrong. He had been sleeping. *What do I need to own about my leadership deficiencies? Where do I need conscious development? What personal changes do I need to model and drive?*

Janine broke the silence. "Looking at the clock, Andrew, I think this is a good place to stop. Tomorrow, let's dive into how to engage the partners. I think it starts with a series of well-thought-out conversations designed to get them to think about how they can own, model, and drive their personal development. But let's sleep on it."

"Sounds like a good plan." Andrew swept up his papers, grabbed his laptop, and threw them into his backpack. "Great meeting. You two have my wheels turning. Own, model, and drive! Speaking of which, I better get in my car now."

Janine laughed. "Go. Even the way you drive, you will need some luck to make it by eight thirty."

Fourteen

Andrew drove home on automatic, his mind spinning through Elena's list of capabilities and taking his own personal inventory, matching the capabilities against his own strengths and weaknesses. As he pulled into the garage, he reached a conclusion: *I've got a lot to work on. To 'own.'*

Andrew burst into the kitchen and found Julia at the table, sipping tea as she perused an inch-high stack of official-looking documents.

Andrew breathed a loud sigh of relief when he saw the microwave clock blink 8:29. "It's two minutes slow, Andrew," she said without looking up.

"What? Really?" Andrew stood frozen in place. "Are you sure?"

"Sit down. I'm kidding. You were right on time." She smiled with arms outstretched for a hug. He leaned over, kissed her, and folded into her embrace. As he pulled away and sat down, his own papers flew out from his backpack, which he had slung onto the table.

Julia ignored the commotion. "Hospice." Her voice cracked on the word. "The doctor says there's nothing else they can do for her. It's a matter of days. Lots of papers to sign. I'm heading out again first thing in the morning."

Andrew immediately pulled the documents Julia had been reading closer to him, quickly scanning each page. He wished he had been home an hour earlier to help her, but he was here now.

"Do we both need to sign? Where is the 'Do Not Resuscitate' medical directive? Do they need the trust documents?"

"Andrew!"

"What? What can I do?"

"You can stop flipping through my papers and actually listen."

Andrew looked up, seeing for the first time the tears on Julia's cheeks and her lips pressed together, as though she could contain all the grief inside herself.

She grabbed and began reading the papers that had spilled out when he had tossed his pack onto the table. "How would you feel if you had something really important to talk about, and I just ignored you?"

Before Andrew could respond, Julia laughed, though her lips were downturned and the laugh had a hard edge to it. "People skills. This is a great list. But it doesn't make me think of you. Ever heard the saying, 'You need to walk the walk before you talk the talk'?"

"Honey, I'm sorry about your mother, and I'm sorry you're upset. You don't sound like yourself and—"

Julia cut him off as she read each capability out loud. After *Listening*, she said, "Andrew Hyde: F! *Balance*: F! *Teamwork*—are you kidding me? F-minus."

Julia's tirade continued. Andrew waited quietly, feeling the grief behind Julia's unkind words. This was not her, not the Julia he knew, but he thought maybe she needed a release from the pain. *And I did screw up. How did I not see she was hurting?*

"And last, but not least, *Empathy*. What's worse than F? Incapable?"

"Can I go back out and come back in? Start this over?"

"No, but you do need to listen."

"Well, I do know how to do that. After all, I'm a consultant."

"No, you don't. You hear words. A good listener focuses completely on what the other person is saying, how they're saying it, what their body is doing, the tone of their voice. In other words, what they're feeling. If you'd truly listened to me, you would know how I'm feeling, and you'd share some or all of those feelings. That's called empathy."

Andrew sat still for a minute or two, allowing what Julia had said to permeate his brain like a puddle of water seeping into the ground after a July cloudburst. Then he slowly reached his arms across the table, palms up, fingers outstretched. "I love you, Julia. Thank you for setting me straight. Can we start at the beginning?"

Julia sat motionless, staring into her teacup. After what to Andrew felt like an interminable length of time, she took his hands and said, "Right around six tonight, Mom's doctor called and recommended we bring in the hospice workers."

Andrew held Julia's hands as they talked for nearly an hour. His eyes were glued to hers. At one point, he burst into tears when he recalled how Julia's mother had called him on every birthday since he and Julia had begun dating. They both laughed at how she was the only person who could get away with calling him "Andy." As Julia described her fear of also suffering from Alzheimer's one day, Andrew gasped. It was as if he was experiencing exactly what she was feeling. And it felt like a thick, hazy cloud covering him.

At around ten o'clock, Julia said, "Let's get a glass of wine and go sit on the back deck. It feels like we haven't done that in years." Andrew poured two glasses of Cakebread Cellars Cabernet Sauvignon and walked with Julia out to their favorite loveseat rocker. As they sipped and gently rocked, Andrew put his arm around Julia's shoulders and said, "I get it now. Thank you for yelling at me and teaching this old dog a few new tricks."

Julia buried her head in his shoulder. "I was awful to you. I'm so sorry. I was frustrated and have been frustrated with everything, but there's no excuse. You don't deserve that."

Andrew leaned over and dropped a kiss on top of Julia's head. "Hey, I'm learning how to listen. As someone very wise once told me, 'A good listener focuses completely on what the other person is saying.' I know you were hurting and just needed to release that. I'm happy we trust each other to be real. And I really did deserve it."

Julia snuggled closer. "Well, I did notice that one of the 'People Skills' on your capabilities list is 'giving feedback.' How did I do?"

"Brilliantly, I'd say. You were direct. You had good intentions and gave me feedback with the 'intent to improve the recipient.'"

Julia laughed. "Indeed I did. My goal was crystal clear: improvement! But I think you're more of a puppy than an old dog."

Before he could respond, Julia patted his leg and said, "Let's go in. My flight to Sarasota is at seven a.m."

• • •

Conscious, Capable, and Ready to Contribute

Andrew was thankful that Julia's flight was out of Reagan National Airport, just across the Potomac from DC. After dropping her off at 5:30, he cranked up the stereo and headed up the GW Parkway and across the Roosevelt Bridge into Northwest Washington.

He reflected on the leadership discussions with Janine and Elena and his conversation with Julia. He was sad about Leslie Weaver's "unconscious" commentary about his recent leadership, but rather than trying to ignore it, he tried to think about it from her perspective. *All the cost-cutting, questionable client decisions, and then I blew her off when she was really hurting.* No empathy, no interest in what Leslie was feeling or curiosity about what had happened with her client.

"I'm awake now," he yelled into the early morning sky. Just then David Bowie's "Modern Love," one of Andrew's all-time favorites, came blaring from the sound system. As he sang along, he thought of Julia and how grateful he was for her.

Andrew pulled into the garage, still humming "Modern Love," and mentally worked to shift himself toward what he needed to do before the next day's board meeting.

As Andrew walked through the dark empty workstations on the way to his office, he noticed that his door was open and the lights were on. *That's odd. It's six in the morning.*

He walked in and saw Pat sitting at his conference table "Again? Are you getting any sleep?" he said as he set his newspaper on his conference table.

"A little. Sleep doesn't feel important right now. Tomorrow's a big day. We have the regularly scheduled board meeting. Being overprepared has always been my modus operandi."

Andrew flashed back to a story Pat had shared years earlier. Starting in sixth grade, her father, the head of government relations for a Fortune 100 diversified manufacturer, required Pat and her three brothers to make a presentation every Sunday evening regarding their upcoming week at school. Naturally, he would check in on Fridays to be sure everything had been accomplished. Andrew shuddered when he recalled Pat's matter-of-fact recounting of one particular "performance report."

"Dad looked me in the eye and said, 'Pat, your brothers are all naturally gifted and will always be one step ahead of you. You'll do fine in life, but you will always have to work harder than them.'" After a long pause, Pat had said, "He meant well."

His mind snapping back to the present, Andrew grinned and said, "That drive of yours has served you and Shift well. Just try and get some more sleep tonight, so we can kick butt tomorrow. Now let's get coffee and dive into it."

After they filled their mugs at the coffee bar, Pat opened her laptop and walked Andrew through the "Ten-Point Plan" presentation.

"I wish I had better news," she said. "We can make some cuts in staff, of course, but unless we get some new projects, we're going to need more capital."

"I recommend we go all in on trying to save all the clients we can." He gave her the rundown on the prior day's calls. "Pamela Turner is definitely out to get us, but I believe we can keep all the Strategy clients and stop the Change Management bleeding. They trust you, Pat."

"Okay. I'll call the at-risk list today. The other partners are contacting their clients too. We'll have a better picture by tomorrow's meeting."

"Any luck on the legal front?"

"Nothing good," she said. "It's Wendy's firm. She'll give her report to the other board members tomorrow." Pat slammed her palm down. "I can't believe that we can't better protect ourselves."

"Well, let's focus on what we *can* control. What do you think about launching a big direct marketing campaign?"

Pat shook her head. "Who's going to pay for that?" Then she gestured at the whiteboard. "It looks like your conscious development project is getting even more expensive. Got a printing press somewhere?"

"No, we aren't going to go into the counterfeiting business. But I do have a few ideas. First, I recognize that not all of the partners are in a position to temporarily reduce their compensation or invest more capital. That said, some may want to, so I think we should offer the partners the opportunity to invest with the same terms we gave Victor. Totally optional, of course."

Pat sat up a little straighter, her eyes no longer skeptical slits. She nodded and said, "Uh-huh. And . . . ?"

"And Julia and I will invest whatever else is needed to stem the tide and get the development program going. Would you be all right with that?"

Pat's lips quivered slightly. "Yes. I just wish Tim and I could do more."

Conscious, Capable, and Ready to Contribute

She wiped the tears from her eyes, dabbing a bit of mascara off her face. "I do love this place—so much. I feel helpless. Worse, I feel cut off from what Shift is. So busy working on the client side and worrying about Tim, I'm not really taking part in what matters."

Andrew let silence be his friend for a moment before he spoke again. "Shift needs your love. There's no Shift without you." He pointed to the whiteboard. "I need your help on this. Frankly, I can't do it without you. Would you be willing to jump in?"

"That would be wonderful. The truth is I do think this is exciting. You know that from day one I have always believed that our people come first. It's just the finances . . ."

Andrew waited to respond, sensing that Pat had more to offer.

"Andrew, I've been spending a lot of time here lately. At odd times, too. It's kind of shocking how many people are seemingly here all the time. Way more than they are at home." Waving at the whiteboard, she continued. "So part of why these capabilities and the life cycle make so much sense to me is the realization that work is where people spend most of their waking hours. So as employers, we have an opportunity and an obligation to help them develop."

His face lit up with a huge grin. He leaned toward Pat. "Yes! That's such a crucial point. See why we need you on this?"

Andrew stood up and walked to Pat's side of the table and wrapped his arms around her. "Thank you, Pat. We can do this."

"Tonight at six, right?" Pat said after the two had finalized the assignments for the board meeting.

"Yep. Let Meg know your dinner order," Andrew called out as Pat left.

He sat down behind his desk and began furiously scribbling his talking points for the board. *We'll be ready for whatever Victor and his crew throw at us.*

• • •

"Good morning everyone. Looks like all members of the board are present." Wendy Shapiro looked like she was headed to court later that day, dressed in an austere blue suit on top of a crisp white blouse. "As chair, I call this meeting to order. Let's start with a review of the minutes from the special board meeting conducted ten days ago. Any questions or corrections?"

None of the other members raised objections, and the minutes were approved. "Andrew and Pat, the floor is yours for a financial and operational update."

Andrew and Pat moved to the end of the table so they could see each of the board members. Andrew spoke first. "Good morning. I will kick off our report with some overall updates. Pat will then run you through progress on the Change Management Practice Situation Ten-Point Plan that was discussed at the last meeting. Then, time permitting, I'd like to give you an update on a longer-term project regarding employee development. Sound good?"

Andrew smiled as he made eye contact with all five of the board members. He noted a few perfunctory head nods and lots of paper shuffling. Most notable was Victor's stonelike face. *Nothing? He's making eye contact and nodding, but those eyes remind me of a hawk fixing on some unsuspecting prey just before plummeting for the feast.*

Andrew had expected Victor to be on attack. This stoic version of Shift's major financial investor caused Andrew to shiver and hesitate for a moment. He pushed the feeling aside and focused on his prepared remarks.

For the next five minutes, Andrew shared the actions he had taken to shore up Shift's business. He reported about the successful meeting with the staff, discussions he'd held with many of the partners, and of course the results of his client outreach calls. Andrew braced for a volley of demanding questions from Victor. However, Victor sat very still, making an occasional note. As Andrew finished speaking, Victor looked up from his notes, smiled, and said, "Thank you, Andrew. Very informative."

Pat took this as a cue to start her presentation. The news was not especially positive, but Pat had prepared well. She spoke with authority. She was candid about Shift's precarious financial position, which "could worsen considerably if these measures aren't fully successful." At that point, Andrew jumped in to say that he, Pat, and the other partners were in discussions about "adding more capital to the business."

As those words left his lips, Andrew recalled something he'd heard from Dave much earlier in his career. "There's a third level of listening, Andrew. If you get good at it, you can literally feel the energy. You'll know what's going on even though there are no spoken words."

Conscious, Capable, and Ready to Contribute

I feel it, Dave. But I don't really know what "it" is yet.

Andrew looked at Pat as she asked the board if they had questions. General Pagano directed a question to Wendy about whether Shift could get damages from Axxcel or Pamela Turner.

"Sorry, General. My team feels like it would be fruitless to even try."

"Ridiculous. Who writes the laws in this damn country anyway?" he grumbled.

Wendy continued. "Pat and Andrew, I don't think there are any other questions. Thank you for this thorough report. I know you mentioned the development plan information you wanted to share, but I'd like to table that for now. Okay?"

She shot Andrew a quick glance but continued speaking. "Let's go into our usual executive session. As you know, Andrew and Pat, that's just for outside board members. I'll text you when we're done so you can return for final comments."

Pat and Andrew stood up slowly. "Thank you. We'll be in my office," Andrew said as he scooped up his papers.

As soon as they had turned the corner and were safely out of earshot, Pat said, "No questions. That's good, right?"

"I think so. You did a really good job, thorough and optimistic without seeming naive."

"Thanks. I'm going to grab a file from my office. I'll be over a in few minutes."

As Andrew walked to his office, he kept thinking about the third level of listening and the lesson in listening he had received from Julia just the night before.

No questions from the board? That silence feels loud for me right now.

Fifteen

Pat and Andrew sat in Andrew's office and made small talk for the first ten minutes. As the executive session stretched on, Andrew updated Pat about the work that Janine, Elena, and he had done defining conscious development, especially the idea of people skills, technical skills, and mind skills. Pat was especially eager to brainstorm the agenda for the planned discussions with the partners.

"Using 'own, model, and drive' as the guiding principle, I suggest we start by honestly sharing where we each are on our personal development journey," she began. "I know I've made a bunch of mistakes recently, and owning up to those seems important to share."

"First, I love the use of the word 'journey.' Change is a process, not an event." Andrew quickly walked to the nearly full whiteboard and squeezed the words **It's a journey** into the upper right corner. "And yes, what you are saying leads to what we called the Core Capability of 'People Skills.' Emotional Intelligence. And major elements of EQ are self-awareness and self-control. I can see how my EQ has been missing in action."

Pat's body shook as she tried unsuccessfully to suppress a chuckle.

"What's so funny?"

"I was just thinking about how I sucked up to Pamela. No self-awareness that I was coming off like she was some kind of Instagram superhot influencer. Ugh. I was so effusive about her damn dress."

Now it was Andrew's turn to laugh. "It's even funnier given what we now know. But hey, you're not alone." His smile turned to a tight-lipped

Conscious, Capable, and Ready to Contribute

grimace. "I let our success get the best of me. Mr. Big Shot. I couldn't see how I was impacting everyone around me. You. Julia. The other partners."

Pat jumped in. "Okay. Enough self-flagellation. We admit all this to the partners and start the conversation of how we are committed to changing."

"Right. Committed to own *our* development. That will be a good way to start the conversation about the Capabilities. Where should we go from there?"

Just then, Andrew's phone chirped.

> **W:** We're ready
> **A:** On our way

"Let's go and find out what they've been talking about for the last hour."

As the two cofounders took their seats, Andrew scanned the faces of the board members. The air felt heavy. Victor wore the same smug smile as earlier. Wendy's blouse's top button had come undone, and her hair was mussed like she'd run her fingers through it over and over. Roger Coyle and Jesse Martin stared straight ahead, as if seated at the World Series of Poker main event. General Pagano, red-faced, was tapping his pen loudly on the table. "Come on, Wendy. Let's get this over with," he snapped.

"Andrew and Pat, after discussion with Victor and the others, I am resigning from the board at the end of this meeting."

"Wendy!" Pat exclaimed. "Why on earth would you do that?"

"I'll tell you why. She's got a conflict of interest," Victor replied before Wendy could open her mouth. "The real issue is that her firm's advice about the employment contracts was faulty. And now a chunk of my investment is just waltzing out the door."

Wendy's face flushed and her eyes flashed. "That's your opinion, Victor. Our employment lawyers are the best in the business. The law is the law."

"So why resign?" Andrew asked. "Pat and I trust you, and we all chose you as chair for a reason."

"I have no choice. Victor announced in executive session that he was considering going after us for malpractice."

"Damn it, Victor. You have no right to . . ." Andrew yelled, his body throbbing with adrenaline. His mind immediately flashed back to his office and the conversation with Pat. *Get it together. Show some self-control.*

"A ten-million-dollar investment gives me lots of rights, Andrew. Don't be so naive. You screwed this up by not paying attention to what your employees and clients needed from you. At the same time, Shift's shoddy legal protections were prepared by the 'best in the business.'"

With that, Victor stood. "Let's go, Jesse. This meeting is adjourned."

As Jesse collected his papers, Victor locked eyes with Andrew. "Sixty days," Victor snarled. "That's how long you have to get this ship back on course."

Andrew resisted the temptation to lash out, as Victor stomped out of the conference room, Jesse on his heels.

The group sat in stunned silence until General Pagano broke the tension. "What a damn jackass. In my world, guys like him die in battle all the time." He paused for a few seconds as the others looked at him—"from gunshots in the back."

Wendy rose while the others laughed at Pagano's perfectly delivered line. "I wish I found it funny. Pat and Andrew, I'll inform my partners today they can no longer support you and Shift on this matter. I'll get you a few other names to consider. But now, I'm late for court." The look on Wendy's face made Andrew's stomach feel hollowed out. She had stood by Shift faithfully for years.

"Wendy, I am so sorry about this. You don't deserve to be treated this way," Andrew said as he wondered how he had ever thought that Victor was the right financial partner.

Wendy walked out silently shaking her head, leaving Pat, Roger, the General, and Andrew staring at the door. Roger was the first to speak. "Don't let all the drama distract you. Let them fight it out. You need to focus on rebuilding the company."

"You're right. And thank you for supporting Pat, me, and Shift."

Pagano turned to face Pat and Andrew. "Wendy showed real integrity as that weasel attacked her. He kept saying that she had to stay and 'fix it.' She kept her cool, and in the end, she stuck to her guns. Integrity and class. That's what I saw."

Roger and General Pagano stood and walked out, talking quietly.

Pat and Andrew sat in the empty conference room. Andrew could feel his heart rate slow as the remnants of the meeting's energy dissipated. He

Conscious, Capable, and Ready to Contribute

felt depleted, like he had been squeezed through an old wooden clothes wringer. Right then, he decided he needed to check in with Dave. *I bet he's seen some version of this movie.*

After a minute or two, Pat broke the silence. "What did Victor mean by sixty days?"

"Next board meeting, I guess. Regardless, we need to get moving. As you said earlier, it's a journey. But right now, it feels more like a trek through the Black Hills."

• • •

"Andrew, I think you are learning a valuable lesson about strategy," Dave said, his weathered face filling the screen of Andrew's laptop.

"Many lessons, Dave. It's like drinking from a firehose."

"And *you* popped the hydrant, Andrew. Think back a year. How did you decide you needed a financial partner?"

Andrew reached into his desk and pulled out the Shift "Plan-on-a-Page." He held it up in front of the camera. "We all decided—the executive committee, with input from the partners—to expand into new markets and service lines," he said. "As a result, one of the plan's overarching strategies was to generate capital for hiring, mergers and acquisitions, and new offices in key cities."

"That all makes sense. So what went wrong?"

Andrew's eyes turned to the plan and then back to Dave a few times before he spoke. "Well, for one thing, I see a beautifully written statement about choosing 'ideal clients and employees who share Shift's core values.' But when it came to finding investors, all I cared about was whether they had the money and whether the terms were acceptable."

Dave was always masterful at posing just the right question. He was also known as the "king of awkward silence." After Andrew had stewed for a few minutes on what he had just figured out, he suddenly leaned closer to the laptop while he grabbed the plan. "Clearly we need to change this. I knew we'd revise the 'Higher Purpose' statement, but now I see we need to rethink this whole thing. We need to have some way of measuring how we take on investors and anyone who touches this company, all the way down to vendors. We also need to create metrics to measure how we're developing people, just like we have key performance indicators for sales and everything else around here."

"Ah, the student is on his game today. What else?"

"I don't have the details yet, but it seems clear we need to create a system where Shift's overall goals are aligned with specific talent development goals. And the rewards need to be crystal clear; development needs to be incentivized top to bottom at Shift."

"Makes sense to me. Know any good strategy consultants that can help you?" Dave said with a wink. He added, "Don't forget the *teamwork* capability. Don't try to go it alone."

"Aye aye, captain," he laughed, just as his phone pinged.

J: Turn for the worse. Call ASAP

"Dave, I have to run. Julia's mom . . . Thanks a million. I'll be in touch."

"Go," Dave said, as he ended the Zoom connection.

Julia answered on the first ring.

"Hi, babe," Julia whispered, "I'm in Mom's room now. The doctor's tending to her. She's barely breathing. Seems like it could be the end."

"What can I do?" Andrew wanted more than anything to be right there beside her. He could picture the way Julia's body would lean into his, the way it did whenever she got really scared or sad.

"Would you contact the family and give them an update? Tell them to expect bad news very soon."

"Sure. Do you want me to come down there?" Andrew was torn. Leaving everything to Pat seemed somehow unfair, but he couldn't picture not being by Julia's side.

"Yes, but no. There's nothing to be done, and we'll bring her right back to DC for services." With that, Julia burst into tears. "I have to go. I'll keep you posted. I love you."

The call ended before Andrew could respond. Andrew held the phone in his hands, picturing Julia on their wedding day, standing beside her mother. He pictured all the family picnics where the tall, elegant woman had brought her famous potato salad and had encouraged him to have that extra oatmeal raisin cookie he'd been eyeing.

Do I go anyway?
Ping.

> **J:** I'm serious. No need for you to come down. Do I know you or what? :)

Andrew smiled, even though his throat felt tight. *I love you, Julia. So much.*

> **A:** Guilty as charged. Let me know if you change your mind. Madly

After Andrew called Julia's two brothers directly, he sent a group email to their extended family, including Julia's mother's few living friends. Except for checking for texts from Julia, which never came, and responding to emails about Julia and her mother, Andrew devoted the remainder of the afternoon to getting ready for the six o'clock meeting. He reviewed each of the Capabilities again, attempting to envision how to teach them.

Some, like *communication*, were fairly simple. But a few of the Mind Skills were actually hard to picture teaching. On the board, he circled a few to discuss with the team:

Growth Mindset
Critical Thinking
Curiosity

How can I teach someone to be curious? Is it even teachable? Are some people just born with a growth mindset? Dave always seems to be learning something new—is that just natural to him?

Andrew looked at his watch. "Five forty-five. Wow."

As he waited for the others, his mind continued grinding. Something was gnawing at him. He knew there was another topic he wanted to explore with Janine, Elena, and Pat, but he couldn't grab it. Suddenly, it hit him.

So Others Might Eat! Julia's mother's favorite charity. The blind runner. Mitch's pro bono work in the poorest section of DC.

Contribution! We need to talk about contribution.

Sixteen

Julia's mother had died during the night. The call he had expected when he put his cell phone on his nightstand jarred him from a surprisingly deep sleep at 3:25 a.m.

The conversation had been brief. "She's really gone, Andrew. I just wanted you to know and to hear your voice. I've got to talk to the doctor. I'll call in the morning. I love you."

"I love you too. Is there anything—?" he began, only to find himself talking to the early morning air. He sat on the edge of the bed for a moment, scenes of good times with his mother-in-law playing in his head. He could picture the Shift launch party ten years earlier, at which his mother-in-law had walked in with a plate of fresh baked chocolate chip cookies. As the scent of gooey chocolate wafted across the room, she had said, "This company will be successful, provided everyone is well fed!" He smiled thinking about how Julia had done her best to follow her mother's admonition.

I guess I will just stay up was his last thought until the familiar ping on his iPhone woke him a few hours later.

Julia's text let him know that she'd be coming home later that afternoon.

> **A:** I'll see you at Reagan. I'm sorry, babe.
> **J:** It was beautiful to be with her, holding her hand as she transitioned. I'm at peace.

Conscious, Capable, and Ready to Contribute

A: So is she.

J: Yes. See you soon. I love you.

Wandering through his and Julia's silent house, Andrew found himself feeling adrift and lost in a sea of dark worry. He moved slowly, as though the resistance of grief were waves tugging at his joints.

The memory of Ted's death grabbed at him, as if pulling him toward the shore of some unnamed fear. He remembered the feeling of numbness as he carried his father's coffin and the nights that followed, when he sat up watching the stars, unable to drift off.

He thought about Julia facing the reality that both her parents were dead. Both had died not really knowing who they were anymore. Julia had shared her own fear of dementia a few times, and it always left Andrew grasping for words and shaky. He knew what she'd gone through with her parents. And because they had never been able to have children, their support system was each other. Would he be able to show up for Julia the way she had for her parents if that became necessary? Always there, never complaining. Spreading kindness to all. *Could I do that?*

For the ten days after that middle-of-the-night phone call, Andrew's schedule was packed with family events. Andrew made the funeral arrangements and helped Julia host her extended family. The house seemed full at all times, so Andrew snuck out one afternoon for a long run to decompress and to collect his thoughts for his eulogy.

The funeral was held on a Saturday in the Basilica of the National Shrine of the Immaculate Conception. When Andrew rose to give his eulogy, the light was streaming in through the stained-glass windows. As he spoke, he watched the congregation's reactions: equal measures of tears and laughter. When he returned to the church pew after his remarks, Julia patted his thigh and squeezed his hand.

A few times, when he couldn't sleep, he saw his insomnia as an excuse to come into the office and work before dawn. His mind quieted when he worked on the details of the people development plan, sent emails to clients, and followed up on current projects. Most days, he'd slip home like a ghost before too many Shift employees started showing up for work. He was surprised how early he needed to leave to avoid anyone.

The Fable

Will Parson's assistant nodded as they passed in the hallway at five, and he became familiar with the cleaning crew he had agreed to hire three years earlier but had never met.

Now, almost two weeks later, Andrew was eager to catch up with Pat to see what progress had been made on stopping the financial bleeding and advancing the conscious development work.

As Andrew pulled into the garage, his left eye began to twitch as it frequently did when he felt anxious. He parked, pushed the automatic off button, and took a deep breath. *Why the twitch?*

Closing his eyes, Andrew attempted to put a name to the feeling that seemed to be lodged in his gut. It took only a second to identify: *Guilt.* "Hardly checked in with Pat last week. And now I'm here when I feel like I should be home with Julia."

A sharp rap on the window, and he snapped forward in the seat. Just to the left of his car, he heard Pat's voice. "You okay, partner? Talking to yourself may scare the employees."

"Yes. Just collecting my thoughts," he said with a big grin. "Miss me?"

"No. Actually, it was quite nice," she said casually.

Before Andrew could sling a retort Pat's way, she continued. "Seriously, I'm glad to see you. We made some good progress but need you to jump back in with both feet."

"I'm ready."

"I'll give you the morning to catch up on your to-do list and to breathe a little. We're headed to visit Warrenton Realty Partners. I called Dave, like you suggested. He says WRP has a culture second to none. They really focus on being deliberately developmental, like the others in the Kegan and Lahey book Janine had us read.[2] If you're feeling up to it, we'd love to have you join us on our field trip."

"Sounds great. And we're meeting at six o'clock with Elena and Janine?"

"Yes. We'll review the agenda for tomorrow's partner meeting." After parting ways with Pat in the lobby, Andrew strolled to his office, where Meg was waiting to review critical emails and other correspondence.

---

2   Robert Kegan and Lisa Laskow Lahey, *An Everyone Culture: Becoming a Deliberately Developmental Organization* (Boston: Harvard Business Review Press, 2016).

After an hour, Andrew pushed back from his conference table. "Well, that wasn't so bad. Thanks for keeping everything moving."

Meg stood up and replied, "That's my job. Keep the trains on the track. Sandwich at your desk before the WRP site visit?"

"I am going to stick with the salad regimen." He patted his belly. "Starting to make a difference!"

Meg gave him a thumbs-up and closed the door behind her.

Andrew spent the next few hours reading through the financial reports for the month. Revenue was down by about a third compared to the prior year—to be expected with Leo and his team's departure. Profits were down even more since Shift's overhead structure was built to support what just a few weeks before was a much larger firm.

Andrew's mood brightened as he discovered that Pat had convinced three of the four of the on-the-fence Change Management clients to ignore Pamela Turner's entreaties. In addition, her staff had contacted all fifty-five of the smaller CM clients. About 15 percent of the clients were leaving for Axxcel. Bad news for sure. But he was buoyed by the fact that while 30 percent of the Change Management people had left, only half that many of the clients planned to defect.

Then Andrew called three other clients, ostensibly to check on the status of Shift's performance. In truth, he wanted to know if Pamela Turner had called any of them; worse yet, would more clients decide to move their business to Axxcel? He was relieved to learn from two clients that their projects were "going well."

Only the last one acknowledged that Pamela had called. "For now, all systems are go, Andrew. But don't let me down." *Not exactly a ringing endorsement, but it beats the alternative!*

Promptly at 12:55, Andrew stood up, straightened his tie, and put on his suit coat. He walked by Meg and waved. "I'll be back no later than five."

"Andrew," Meg called, dashing after him, waving a document. "Take this. It's a briefing on Warrenton Realty Partners and their CEO, Valerie Maguire. Pat said she'd drive so you can get fully prepared."

"Nice. Thanks."

Elena, Janine, and Pat were waiting for Andrew in Pat's eight-year-old dark green Volvo XC60 SUV. Andrew jumped into the front passenger seat, and forty minutes later, Pat eased the SUV into a visitor's parking space in front of a traditional, red-brick four-story office building.

On the ride, Andrew had learned that Warrenton Realty Partners was the largest developer of mixed-use and multifamily real estate on the East Coast, with more than one thousand employees. So he was surprised to look up at a simple red-brick façade with minimal landscaping. Only the roof full of solar panels communicated that WRP might be different than most companies based in the Northern Virginia suburbs.

The four walked into the lobby where a tall casually dressed woman stood next to a young man holding a clipboard. The man's eager smile and slightly wrinkled polo shirt made him look fresh out of college.

"You must be the Shift Advisors team. Hi, I'm Valerie, Warrenton's CEO, and this is my assistant, James. We're happy to see you," the woman said, with one of those smiles that seemed to say *Welcome to our home*.

Valerie led the Shift leaders through the sun-drenched office. Later, the foursome would all agree that it felt alive. Andrew noticed all the individual workspaces housed huge wood table desks, each the same size for partners, managers, staff, and outside contractors, with ample space for everyone to spread out and personalize their surroundings. No exterior offices meant that abundant light poured in through the windows. It was clear that WRP had spared no expense on materials. Andrew noted virtually no plastic and was pretty sure the windows themselves were thermally efficient and met LEED standards. Opposite the windows was a living wall, filled with ferns and a variety of other green and yellow plants. Everywhere they walked, Andrew could tell that Valerie and her company had sustainability in mind.

But it was the color choices that stood out. The walls reminded Andrew of some of his favorite Crayola crayons from growing up. He remembered one Christmas when his grandmother had presented him with a new box. Sixty-four choices! He smiled as he recalled recently looking at his niece's crayons, noting that the deluxe box now had 120 varieties and that a few of his favorites had been replaced with more descriptive versions: hot magenta, pink flamingo, jazz berry jam, granny smith apple. Everywhere he looked at Warrenton, he found bright oranges, greens, and yellows and an occasional pink. *Invigorating*, he thought.

During the course of Andrew's long career as a consultant, he'd walked through many offices with company values and quotes on the walls. With few exceptions, the quotations, whether from famous leaders or that mystery sage "Anonymous," fell flat. Perhaps it was because they were often paired with cheesy stock photos of early morning rowers or bearded mountain climbers. So as Andrew listened to Valerie describe the space, he also paid close attention to what hung on the walls of WRP.

Like the color scheme and design choices, Andrew could imagine that each picture, message, and award had been carefully chosen for maximum impact on the culture.

In Warrenton Realty Partners' reception area, a dozen pictures of company projects hung alongside two placards: WRP's core values and a framed acknowledgment of their status as a founding member of Conscious Capitalism's local chapter. Pat nudged Janine and whispered, "Check out the first two values: 'Development' and 'Kindness.'" As Janine stopped to read, Valerie stopped walking and said, "People often ask us about our values. I think they can't believe a real estate company would embrace a value of 'kindness.'"

"Well, real estate people are known for being pretty ruthless," Elena said. The moment she finished her statement, she slapped her hand over her mouth as if to punish it for speaking without permission. Her cheeks turned pink. "Oh, Valerie, I'm sorry."

Valerie grinned. "Don't apologize. It's true! But not here at WRP." Her face softened. "I always loved the idea of 'practicing random acts of kindness,' but then it occurred to me that I don't want random acts. I want *intentional* acts of kindness. So we preach it, and we teach it."

Janine and Pat exchanged a look.

Valerie laughed. "Yep. We get that, too. People can't believe kindness can be taught. It just happens, right? Well, we've learned, like many things, it's a skill and when we focus on it, we see more of it. And we train people in kindness by seeing kindness as a type of feedback; we train to help us notice interactions between the kindness-giver and recipient. We show everyone how to model the behaviors in our work every day. For example, our leadership development program includes a video session to show how favorably people respond to little things like a thank-you or an offer to get them coffee. Then we role-play scenarios. In fact, we use experiential training exercises a lot around here. In fact . . . I think a workshop is starting in ten minutes. James, will you check, please?"

James stepped to the side and made a call. "Great! Valerie has some guests who want to observe. We'll be up in a few." As he put his phone back in his pocket, he gave Valerie a thumbs-up. "Third-floor training room."

Before exiting the lobby, Andrew pointed to the framed announcement next to the values and said, "So I'm guessing Conscious Capitalism is a big part of the Warrenton Realty Partners playbook?"

"Yes, another thing we have to thank Dave Edwards for."

Moving like a small caravan through the office, Andrew smiled when he noticed none of the usual quotes and stock photos. So of course, when Andrew passed by a conference room of employees celebrating a team member's birthday, the fact that there was one inspirational quote outside the room really caught Andrew's attention.

"See everything and everyone as opportunities to learn.
Everyone and everything are our teachers."
Anonymous

Beneath the quote was a chalkboard with beautifully written notes of gratitude and stories of how a particular WRP person or team had helped another team member to learn. *James, I appreciated the flowers you bought for my client today. She was so moved by your gesture during this tough time for her. Thank you for showing me what empathy and kindness look like.* Andrew recalled seeing an example of such a "wall" created by Round Table Companies for a corporate event. Valerie saw Andrew pause. "Employees are encouraged to send in texts, notes, or emails calling out behavior to be celebrated. A team of artists then updates the wall each day."

What a brilliant way to celebrate learning and development. What would Shift be like in a year if we started doing some of this? Andrew thought, as he snapped a picture of the quote and the wall with his phone. As his thumb hovered over the screen, he noticed the other photo he had taken earlier. "Kindness." *I want to think I'm kind, but am I? How do I talk to Will? How was I speaking to Leslie before she decided to leave?*

Conscious, Capable, and Ready to Contribute

Seventeen

As the Shift team walked into a large open space on the third floor, Valerie gestured to a row of seats in the back. The room was dark except for lights, which flooded a stage some thirty rows in front of them. As the crew settled into their seats, a scraggly-bearded man walked to the middle of the stage. He wore a faded black t-shirt, blue denim jeans, and sandals. His gray hair was pulled back into a ponytail. Eyeglasses perched on the end of his nose completed the look.

"I'm Warren Haley, and yes, I'm from California," he said as his hands outlined his body from head to toe with a dramatic flourish. "The Bay Area, to be precise. I've been doing this improv workshop for fifteen years after a semi-successful career as a TV comedy writer and a completely successful career following Phish."

Laughter erupted from a group of about twenty Warrenton Realty Partners employees seated in the front rows of the darkened hall.

"You're mine for the next four hours. Our goals are pretty simple. Behind me is the single PowerPoint slide you will see today."

Andrew read over three lines that appeared on the screen.

Learn to listen with all your senses.
Learn to speak with all your senses.
Experience discomfort and turn it into something wonderful.

"I call it: feel, adapt, create."

Haley pushed another button on the remote.

Work as a team to achieve a goal as you resolve conflicts, leverage

The Fable

each of your unique qualities, and make decisions as a collective.

"And this last point is the most important," he said with a dramatic wave of the hand-held device toward the screen.

Laugh your ass off!

"You ready?"

Valerie leaned over to Andrew and whispered, "This is the introductory workshop. Everyone starts here. Then we move them through a monthly process to develop a full sketch show in month six. If you like what you see today, please come back for the big show."

Just then Haley yelled, pointing to someone in the audience. "You! Andrew, is it? Give me five sounds you might hear in Central Park."

"Uh," Andrew choked as he shot a look at Valerie, his eyes opened wide like saucers.

Valerie whispered gleefully, "Have fun."

"That's one!" Haley gave the rest of the audience an exaggerated wink.

Andrew's shoulders dropped a bit. He made a mistake of glancing at the audience; several faces looked back at him, faces partially in shadow. His palms started to sweat, and memories of middle school oral reports flooded back. Usually, when he spoke in front of others, he had his notes, Meg's instructions, a presentation. Reaching back, he remembered his media training. He stood up straight, relaxed his posture slightly, took a very deep breath, and then shouted, "Dogs barking. Police horses clopping. Wooden oars slapping the water. Ice skaters . . . falling down. The Foo Fighters playing a free concert."

Warren hopped down to the audience and spoke quietly enough that Andrew couldn't quite hear. A minute later, three audience members returned with Warren to the stage. They stood in a half circle. "Please join us, Andrew."

After Andrew had sauntered to the front of the room, Warren turned to one of the women now on stage and said, "Okay, Sandra, start a story using Andrew's weird sounds."

Sandra dropped her hands to her side and shook her upper body vigorously. Bouncing from one side to the other, she started riffing.

"Dave Grohl's voice pierced the night. Songs of heroes, angels, and devils learning to fly carried Sally to another world, a world of—"

Conscious, Capable, and Ready to Contribute

"Stop. Jill, take it from there."

Jill hesitated for a moment and then launched into a monologue. "A world with no dogs barking, where Sally could sleep all night dreaming of her youth. A time of ice skating with her older brother on the frozen ponds of Northern Minnesota. The clumsy brother who always seemed to fall."

"Cut! Nicely done. Okay, now it gets harder. Samuel, you have to pick up the story, but this time, you have to convey an emotion or feeling that Jill evoked in you. Take a moment."

Samuel stared at Jill and then closed his eyes as if trying to commit to memory all he'd heard and seen. His voice was just a whisper, and yet each sound was clear all the way to the back wall.

"Her brother was always falling. As he hit his teens, his youthful drug experimentation grew to something more insidious. Fun became need, and need became obsession, and obsession became addiction."

Everyone in the auditorium seemed laser-focused on Samuel, as though it were he and not Warren who stood in the spotlight. Samuel didn't seem to notice.

"She awoke from a dream one summer's night, thinking she'd heard police horses clopping up the front steps. She lay still, the ceiling fan whirring overhead, trying to take in every word as her mother answered the front door. 'There must be a mistake, officer. My son knew how to swim. How did he fall?' 'He may have jumped, ma'am. The rowers . . . well . . . they think they heard a splash, but it could've been just the oars slapping the water. We'll keep searching. We're very sorry, ma'am.'"

Samuel stopped, blinked his eyes twice, and looked over at Haley. Andrew felt his own breathing change, become ragged. All he could hear were the sounds of sniffles. He looked up and saw that Valerie, Pat, Elena, and Janine were blinking rapidly and looking everywhere except at each other. Andrew, too, was doing his best to hold it together. Over the past ten days, he had become all too familiar with the tell-tale burning in his eyes.

Warren Haley stood motionless on the stage for a moment and then began to clap. The audience immediately joined in, as if eagerly seeking something to do other than cry. Haley let the noise die down on its own, turned to the audience, and said, "Okay, team, before this group leaves, tell me what you learned. Just shout out ideas."

"Samuel made me feel like I was Sally."

"That's empathy!"

"Jill and Sandra listened to every detail Andrew said. They didn't miss a word."

"Samuel must have listened with his heart because he sure spoke with it."

Haley smiled. "Yes, he sure did. And this first foursome is going to be a tough act to follow."

"Okay, group one. You have your story. Your job is to turn that into a twenty-minute sketch. Your assigned room is 101. I'll check on you from time to time after I get the others started. Of course, we will let Andrew get back to his tour."

As Samuel and the others left the stage, Andrew gave Haley a high five and rejoined his team. Valerie said, "Let's go. There's more I'd like you to see."

Stumbling out into the light of the office, Andrew considered what it felt like to stand there and to share, then to hear Samuel's story. He had only been part of the improv exercise for a few minutes, yet he felt strangely closer to his improv quartet.

Pat blinked hard and squinted. "I'm amazed. In just thirty minutes, Haley delivered a full semester of communication training. I can only imagine how good they will be in six months."

Janine was scribbling furiously and added, "We just witnessed confirmation of several of our own draft core capabilities. 'Creative thinking' for sure, starting with Andrew's five things he heard in Central Park. Foo Fighters, Andrew?"

"I actually saw them play there. Free concert."

"Ah . . . you really love those guys." Janine continued. "The 'effective speech' capability as well. Sandra's choice of details from the Foo Fighters' catalogue really illustrated what that show might've been like."

Pat picked up the thread. "And Samuel—wow, Samuel felt the story. He responded authentically. You could tell he felt empathy for the little girl whose life had started with fun evenings, ice skating with her older brother, but it ended . . . It was powerful. What a great way to teach."

The group had been following Valerie as if on autopilot. She pushed open the door to a large conference room where the WRP C-Suite members stood waiting to greet them.

Conscious, Capable, and Ready to Contribute

After brief introductions, each member of Warrenton Realty Partners' executive team discussed their roles as stewards of WRP's values, especially value number one— "Development: Your development is our only job."

One executive smiled as he explained the play on words. "As real estate developers, people expect us to create amazing spaces . . . from start to finish. But we wanted a value that played on that word and emphasizes that we develop you—whether you're a client, employee, senior executive partner, anyone. Yeah, we're still in development, but we're no longer thinking only in terms of real estate development."

Janine's counterpart explained that she had helped the executive team codify a set of leadership principles, especially about learning and development. "So everyone in the organization can have a common language that can be applied again and again. I'll be happy to email the principles to you if you'd like."

"Yes!" Janine, Pat, and Elena said in unison.

"Eager bunch," Andrew laughed. "So how did you get here?"

"Well, in part, we have Dave to thank. One day he was leading a retreat for us. We were doing well, financially strong, but we knew something was missing. He had us do an exercise. He told us the following. 'Make a list of all the traits and characteristics you would attribute to yourselves individually and collectively up until today. Then look deep inside and answer the same question about traits and characteristics and roles you want to be known for from this day forward.' We came to realize as we shared that each of us wanted to be known differently from that day forward. We were feeding the financial wolf, but the spiritual wolf was starving. And as the parable says, the wolf who will thrive is the one that gets fed. So we pivoted and started feeding a different wolf."

Pat jumped in. "What was on the 'go forward' list?"

The WRP chief HR officer typed on her laptop, which then projected words on a screen at the end of the conference room. "Here's what I recall."

Development
Kindness
Health and well-being
Community leaders

Egalitarian
Growth mindset
Teachers
Conscious Capitalists
High growth/Strong financial returns

"Look about right, team?"

"Yes, and of course Development was first on the list," added Valerie.

Andrew looked at the list. "I'm curious how you reached the idea of people development first. Why not real estate expertise?"

Valerie smiled. "Real estate skills would have been thinking too small. When you really look at it, real estate skills *are* people skills. We had an 'aha moment.' What we really do is build relationships—yet we didn't talk about relationships or work at getting better at them. We realized that the overall quality and reputation of our business depended on how our people interact—with each other and our clients. And that, we realized, happens when we are consciously growing our people skills."

"That makes sense," Andrew said. "We have also been working on a list of core people capabilities that we believe humans need today. 'Adaptability' and 'creative thinking' are two of them."

For the next thirty minutes, the WRP leaders talked about how each of them was embracing this way of thinking and discussed specific development activities and actions that had helped create the development culture at Warrenton Realty Partners. When the conversation wound down, Valerie gestured to the door. "I've got one more thing to show Andrew and his team before we wrap up the day."

After "thank-yous" and a few business cards were exchanged, Valerie led the Shift team to a window, which looked into another cavernous space, painted like it was inspired by Lily Pulitzer. "I promised you Playtime."

The four Shift leaders pressed close to the window and looked into the lounge. One corner was full of Legos and wooden building blocks. About one-third of the room was taken up by an array of video game consoles, screens, and leather chairs from which twenty or so gamers were aggressively working their controllers.

Elena giggled. "Look at the mini dance floor and the private karaoke booth."

Conscious, Capable, and Ready to Contribute

"And Risk, Monopoly, and Backgammon for us old schoolers. Check out the crew in the corner playing Texas Hold 'em," Pat said.

"Let's not just stand here," Valerie said. She opened the door and walked into the colorful space. "I asked any employee who wanted to speak with you to pop in here today. I figured you'd want to hear from the employees themselves. And, anyway, I haven't had my Playtime yet."

With a wink, Valerie headed straight for the bingo table.

Andrew found himself drifting toward an arcade game when a red-bearded man stopped him. "Hey. You must be part of the Shift team. I work in sales here. Valerie mentioned you might have some questions for us all?"

Janine jumped in before Andrew could reply. "Yes, I was really hoping to get employees' perspectives on development culture. What is the experience like for employees?"

A petite woman in a wheelchair rolled up, her smile wide. "Ooh, I wouldn't mind giving you some ideas. I work as an admin."

Andrew listened as the two colleagues spoke. The woman was animated as she spoke about her experience. "I'm going to be honest. It was weird for me at first. This is nothing like any other place I've worked. In the interview, they told me this company was all about learning and growing every day. I remember I nodded and smiled. I mean, who would argue with that? And I wanted the job. I figured they meant something like going to workshops or maybe taking online courses."

The woman laughed. "I was way off. First day I'm here, I think I've gotten my fifteen minutes of fame. People start coming up to me in halls, in my workstation. Telling me about themselves and asking how I am. My manager stopped by, and we created an individual growth plan for me. Not just admin stuff but communication, empathy, creativity. And everyone kept asking what I thought, and when I suggested something—kindness camps—they actually did them."

The sales rep nodded. "My experience was like that, too, though I got tipped off in the interview. They asked a lot of questions in my interview about how I viewed challenge, continuous learning, and feedback. I had to really think to answer because my previous job didn't really do continuous learning, but the interviewer seemed to be genuinely interested in the fact that I like to draw and that I was self-taught. I remember I was asked, 'Development is a big part of our culture here, and part of your job performance you'll be evaluated on is how you grow and help others grow—are you okay with that?'"

The admin leaned forward. "What did you tell them?"

The man shook his head. "I wanted the job, and I said 'yes.' I mean, it sounded good, though I didn't really know what it was all about until my first day when I got my development plan worked out. That was almost—well, I got kind of emotional. The head of sales sat down with me and asked me what I wanted to work on developing. She seemed to really care and wanted me to have what I needed to develop—not just sales expertise. But also stuff just for me as a person. The more I got to know people here, the more I realized that's true of almost anyone you meet here—people care about you and want you to grow and succeed. It's not like that at the other companies where I've worked."

"Bingo!" Valerie yelled. Andrew looked up in time to see her holding her bingo card and doing the shuffle dance on the dance floor.

The sales rep continued once the mayhem quieted down. "It took me a while to get used to how honest and open people are here. In meetings, we are encouraged to disagree and challenge each other for the sake of making the best decisions. I'm not gonna lie: sometimes it feels uncomfortable to be challenged by my peers. But every morning on my way to work, I look forward to spending time here. I've never had that at any other job."

Valerie wandered over, still grinning, her cheeks pink and her hair a little shook-out-of-place by her impromptu dance. "Getting the answers you were looking for?"

Pat addressed her first. "Valerie, this is really cool, but I'm not sure I see the value."

"Value? You mean for WRP?"

Pat looked like she'd been caught trying to sneak a cookie off her brother's plate.

"Hmm, well, yes."

Valerie smiled.

"Sorry if you feel I was unfairly judging your question. Let me tell you where Playtime all started. I read a book about ten years ago by Dan Pink called *A Whole New Mind: Why Right-Brainers Will Rule the Future*.

Conscious, Capable, and Ready to Contribute

Written in 2005, the book was Pink's relatively early voice about the macro implications of the changes brought on by technology and globalization. And this was before the iPhone came out! He made a case for leaning into what he called the 'conceptual age' by embracing 'six senses.' They all grabbed me right here." Valerie patted first her gut and then her heart. "But two have become core to how WRP operates: 'Story' and 'Play.' You saw Story in action with Warren Haley.

"Play is just what it sounds like. Pink, and so many others, make compelling arguments for the value of play. Health and overall well-being top the list."

While Valerie spoke, Andrew tried to recall the last time he really saw Shift employees—or himself—having fun.

"Janine, you will also love this answer," Valerie explained. "We have amazing employee engagement scores. Our turnover is next to nil. Our brand in the marketplace on things like Glassdoor is exceptional. Every time we survey the employees, Playtime gets called out as one of their favorite parts of working at WRP. Of course, everyone loves Warren Haley. These things may not seem like something that has an impact, and maybe to some they seem silly. But we're seeing the tangible results."

Andrew didn't hear the last few words. *Glassdoor, Leo, ugh.*

"But at least some of your partners must have pushed back. How did you convince them to invest in all this?" Elena said as she opened her arms wide with fingers outstretched.

Valerie smiled. "Well, now the results speak for themselves. But before we implemented everything, we started small. We added one program at a time and tracked the employee responses. We saw our engagement scores rising—and our client satisfaction scores, too. Over time, there was a groundswell of voices invested in this way of thinking. And, like with employees, those in leadership who were not getting it, self-selected out. Of course, to be transparent: it wasn't always this good. Thanks to people like Dave Edwards, and the partners who did rally around our mission, we really feel like we are on the right track."

"You should be proud, Valerie." Andrew looked at his watch, blinking twice when he saw that it was nearly 5:30. "Wow, we've taken up so much of your time. Thank you so much. If there's ever anything that we can do, please don't hesitate."

As they all hugged Valerie, she said, "For now, please join the CC chapter. We need great local businesses like Shift, and this city sure needs Conscious Capitalism now more than ever."

The group spoke very little on the drive back to Shift. An observer would have reported that the noise from their mental gears turning was deafening. For Andrew, much of his internal chatter was visualizing how he was going to translate all this for his partners, few of whom he'd describe as Conscious Capitalists. And behind Valerie's words was the reality that not everyone would be supportive. *Plus, we don't have the luxury of going one program or idea at a time. We're not even feeding the financial wolf right now. Can this idea still work if we try to push it all at once? What kind of fight will I have on my hands?*

Pat led the way into Andrew's office, where she and the others plopped into chairs at the conference table. After a few moments, Janine started the conversation.

"I love the idea of the annual three-hundred-and-sixty-degree feedbacks and quarterly pulse surveys. I've just finished reading *Scaling Leadership* by Bob Anderson and Bill Adams. Their Leadership Circle Profile is the tool I'd recommend if we adopt WRP's approach."

Andrew said, "That entire process was one of the most significant proof points of their commitment to live their 'everyone and everything are opportunities for learning' mantra."

Elena was vigorously nodding her head.

"And the way the staff we talked to made it clear that it was 'safe' to get critical feedback. Everyone has an 'individual development plan,' including Valerie and the other owners. Wow."

Janine said, "All stuff we can do here at Shift. Andrew and Pat, what do you think about their coaching program? I'd love to add that. What a great way to embed development."

Pat started to respond directly, but instead turned toward Andrew. "What do you think?"

"First, I think we should bring Dave in to help us set up a coaching program similar to WRP's. Obviously, I believe in having a coach. What I hadn't thought of before today was the power of training *all of us* to be coaches. Valerie's right. Coaching is not the same as being someone's boss.

To really make this a development culture, we need to think bigger. Not just teaching employees or developing them but giving us all the tools to become developers of each other."

Pat was bouncing up and down in her chair. "Imagine if we all had IDPs built around the capabilities of mind skills, people skills, and technical skills? And a coach to help us grow and develop . . ."

"And hold us accountable," Elena added.

"Speaking of accountability, Dave has been pushing me to take the Leadership Circle 360 assessment for a while now. So I'm sure he'd be thrilled if we all used it as the leadership assessment tool."

"And I love the idea of him helping us create our 'Leadership Principles,'" Pat added.

Janine cleared her throat, causing the others to look her way.

"Andrew, this is going to be pretty expensive."

Andrew responded without any hesitation. "You're right, and I do have a plan for getting the capital we need. I'm going to run it by the partners tomorrow. And once every leader is trained to be a coach, the cost for outside coaches will come down."

"By the way, Janine, are we adding 'kindness' as one of our people skills?" Pat asked.

Janine laughed as she passed around the new version of the core capabilities as well as the employee life cycle. "I already added it in, so I sure hope the answer is yes."

They spent the rest of their time together sharing their favorite parts of their exhilarating day and brainstorming about how best to get the partners' buy-in at the next day's breakfast meeting. Optimism flowed along with a heavy pour from a bottle of chardonnay Pat fetched from a small fridge she kept in her office.

As Andrew watched the others relax into the evening, he kept his fears to himself. They were having such fun. But deep down, he knew the partner meeting was going to require one of his best performances as CEO to date. *And I still need to deal with Victor and the board.*

Eighteen

"Good morning, everyone," Andrew said from his usual seat at the head of the oversized mahogany conference table. As the agendas and financial reports were passed around, Andrew made an effort to make eye contact with each of the twenty-seven other partners. Most smiled back at him or nodded their heads. A few partners sat stoically, arms crossed, while two or three perched in their chairs like large cats preparing to pounce at the most opportune moment.

Andrew took a sip of water and leaned in over the table. He wore a light-blue cotton shirt with no tie. As he had dressed earlier that morning, he was feeling 'softer,' as Meg put it. No Canali or French cuffs with shiny links today. Black jeans and Ecco loafers completed the look. He felt younger than he had in a long time. *That's it. Younger, not softer.*

"We've got lots to cover today. Before Pat reports on our financials, I'd like to set the table for today's discussion. Look around the room. What do you see? For sure, we see seven fewer partners—our friends and really strong performers. I miss their smiling faces."

Andrew paused to allow his fellow partners to absorb the absences. Then, in a voice just a notch on the dial louder, he said, "I see each of you. I see what's here, not what's gone. I see an amazing future for Shift built on a foundation of an exceptional past.

"After the financial report, I want to get into a conversation about our future, why we need to change, and some ideas about how to do it. For now . . ." Andrew held up a small blue-and-white book, its cover and

Conscious, Capable, and Ready to Contribute

spine worn from use. "Remember lessons number five and seven from Bill George's *Seven Lessons for Leading in Crisis*."

All eyes were on Andrew as he said, "'Never waste a good crisis'[3] and 'Go on offense. Focus on winning now.'"[4]

Andrew could feel the partners' energy shift and align. A few "amens," "right-ons," and "let's do its" came forth. Even the few stoics responded by unlocking their arms and dropping the frowns from their faces.

"Pat, the floor is yours."

"Thank you, Andrew. Okay, partners, in front of you is a hard copy of the monthly financial report. I want to start by thanking each of you for your near-Herculean efforts over the last month. You've served our clients well—as usual—and you've reached out to virtually every client and member of your team. Those efforts have stabilized us. We aren't out of the woods yet, but we're on a good path."

For the next fifteen minutes, Pat reviewed the income statement, cash position, and forecast for the rest of the year. As soon as Pat said, "Comments? Questions?" Will Parsons's baritone cut the brief silence.

Looking at his notes, he spoke as if he were speaking from a PowerPoint, each point appearing after the next. "Let me see if I understand. One. The Change Management group was on track to do thirty million in revenue this year with eighty-five partners and staff. Two. So far, we've lost between eight and ten million in annual revenue and twenty-six employees and partners. Three. The CM group is very profitable, so the lost profits, before paying partners, could be as high as five million dollars when you factor in the stay bonuses, fixed costs, and excess payroll. That's a lot more than what we were paying those partners, so the difference is coming out of our pockets. And we have had minimal new work and it's clear that the employees are nervous. Headhunters are calling every day. One called my assistant this morning and said he heard 'Shift was about to collapse.'"

A long silence filled the room. Will said. "This is the 'good path' you are speaking of?"

Pat didn't rush her response. "I appreciate your worry, Will. This whole

---

3   Bill George, *7 Lessons for Leading in Crisis* (San Francisco: Jossey-Bass, 2009), 75.

4   George, *7 Lessons for Leading in Crisis*, 105.

situation has not been what any of us would have chosen. But things *have* stabilized and now it's time to focus on how we move forward. And again, thank you Will and all of you for persevering through this ordeal. The teamwork has been impressive."

Pat looked at Will, an open smile on her face until he frowned and glanced down at the notes in front of him.

"Andrew, you said that it's time to go on offense," said one of the partners from the Strategy team. "What actions do you have in mind—and can we afford them?"

"Good questions, Barbara. Naturally, we are going hard at the market. We are beginning to win some new work, and several of you are seeing some growth opportunities with existing clients. But for us to really 'win,' I believe we need to rethink our entire people strategy. Let me run through some ideas Pat and I have been working on with Janine and Elena."

"Elena?" Will sputtered. "One of our newest partners? She's not even on the executive committee."

Several heads swung around to find Elena smiling, fingering the small cross she always wore around her neck. Andrew knew she wouldn't take the bait.

Andrew had also anticipated Will's outburst. "Will, as we move forward, I'd like to see all of us be a little less focused on titles. We're *partners*. As for Elena specifically, she single-handedly saved about ten of her colleagues from going to Axxcel, and she's taken the initiative to give Pat, Janine, and me some really valuable insights about life here at Shift."

"Makes sense to me," Barbara said with a stern glance at Will. "And thank you, Elena. Now, I'd like to hear some of those plans."

As heads nodded around the table, Will's cheeks turned red. He looked over at Barbara, as if ready to snap at her, but then melted back into his chair. Andrew hid his smile as he recalled Julia's description of "Dear Will. All hat, no cattle."

Andrew waited a moment until it was clear that Will would have no rebuttal for Barbara. He looked around the room and said, "I want to start by thanking Pamela Turner." He held up the business section of the *Washington Post*. "I imagine you've seen the local business reporter's article from Sunday about Axxcel. Apparently, we should just fold our tents and go home. Pamela has hired all our best people and is going to crush us and all the other consultants in town."

Andrew put the paper down. "But I want to thank her, because I didn't know how bad our problem was until she appeared on the scene. And you can't get going in the right direction until you know you're lost."

"And you think we're lost?" Will said angrily. "What I think is she stole our clients, our people, our profits. And *you* let it happen."

"Yes, Will. She did all those things. And at first, I was really pissed. Still am at times. But I got to thinking about why it was so easy for her."

Andrew stood up and began recounting all the things he'd learned in recent weeks, starting with Leo's commentary about how Shift put profits ahead of people and clients. Several partners reacted with vehement denials and nasty remarks about Leo.

Andrew put his hands up as if to shield himself. "I get it. That's certainly how I felt at first. Then I looked at Glassdoor, and I studied Janine's HR reports. The truth is: turnover was rising well before Pamela Turner started poaching our people."

As the partners listened, Andrew told of his encounter with Mitch, the former employee, now happily working for a former client. He also admitted to blowing off Leslie Weaver, which undoubtedly helped her decide to join Axxcel. He also shared what some of the six change management consultants had said about Shift's priorities. "Billable work and profits. That's all that matters to the partners, Andrew."

"And our client satisfaction scores have been dropping for months now. My calls to clients, as part of the Axxcel counterstrategy, have revealed erosion in some clients' confidence in Shift. They say we are too busy and don't seem to care about results as much as we used to."

Andrew sighed. "I told Pat it reminded me of our final days at BCC." He looked over at his cofounder, who was nodding in agreement, her lips taut. Sensing that he'd made his points, Andrew walked to his left and grabbed the projector remote off the corner of the table.

A large screen behind Andrew slowly dropped from the ceiling. When Andrew pressed the remote, Shift's core value statements appeared on the screen.

"I want to start here. Leo said that I had lost sight of our core purpose and core values. I think he was wrong about our values. I still believe in all these," he said as he pointed to the screen. "Going forward, I'd not recommend that we change any of them."

"I totally agree," said one of the Strategy partners. "These still represent what I believe in." Others nodded, and there were multiple murmurs of agreement.

"However," Andrew began as a new slide came into view, "we need a new purpose statement."

Higher purpose: Consciously Develop our People's Capabilities so they can Contribute.

"What the—" Will blurted out, catching himself before he completed the expletive. "What about clients? For years we've been telling them we are there to help them '*shift* into high gear.' I told you this was a waste of time when you first raised all this several weeks ago!"

"Hear him out, Will," Pat said, her palms pushing down toward the table in a way that said *calm down*. "I was skeptical, too, at first, but it didn't take long for me to see that the key to exceptional service is fully developed professionals."

"Okay," Will grumbled. "So we up the training budget so clients get better service. Pretty simple stuff."

"Well, that's a good start, of course. One thing I truly regret is our decision to eliminate the leadership development program." Andrew shook his head. "Not sure what I was thinking."

"The whole executive committee agreed. It seemed like a no-brainer," said one senior partner.

"A no-brainer indeed," Andrew agreed. "*Un*—conscious."

The partners sat quietly. Andrew scanned their faces. Later he would say it was the point where he started to feel like they would buy into the plan, when Shift really started down the path toward having a conscious development culture.

"For the last few weeks, Janine, Pat, Elena, and I have been meeting after hours to flesh out our proposal for you." Andrew looked at the door where Janine stood waiting. He waved her in. "Janine knew how to take this overall concept and bring it to life, and I've asked her to walk you through it."

Janine strode to the end of the table next to Andrew. Behind her the screen displayed **Conscious Development Culture**. "Good morning. I'm excited to walk you through two draft documents. Elena, would you please pass them around?" As Elena handed the colorful documents to each partner, Janine said, "We're calling the first one Shift's 'Conscious Development Employee Life Cycle,' and it's built around certain 'Core People Capabilities.'"

"That's the second document," Elena chimed in excitedly. "We see these 'Mind Skills,' 'People Skills,' and 'Technical Skills' as vital to our people's success." Janine's face broke into a broad smile. "You can see this was a collaborative effort!"

"As someone who has spent her career in HR, including the last ten years with Shift, I've always known there are certain competencies employees need to demonstrate to master their positions and advance to the next level in an organization. That's a fairly common way of thinking about development. It's a *good* way to ensure we are designing training that addresses the goals of the company."

Janine brought up a slide of the Capabilities. "I think it will be easier to have a conversation about them if you can see them in large print. You can review the drafts later and give us comments."

MIND SKILLS	PEOPLE SKILLS	TECHNICAL SKILLS
• Executive Function Skills (Core Capability)	• Emotional Intelligence (EQ) (Core Capability)	• Domain Skills
• Growth Mindset	• Authenticity	• Digital Readiness
• Adaptability	• Kindness	• Multidisciplinary Skills
• Critical Thinking	• Balance	
• Curiosity	• Communication Skills	
• Creative Thinking	• Giving and Receiving Feedback	
• Decision-Making	• Teamwork	
	• Influencing	
	• Resolving Conflict	
	• Leveraging Differences	
	• Integrity	

"For years, we have thought of skills needed in the workplace as falling into two categories: hard skills and soft skills. Hard skills are the technical requirements to do the job."

"Really important skills," said one of the partners.

"No doubt. It is where much of our training has been, and will be, focused." As Janine said this, Andrew watched several of the partners nod their heads in agreement.

"When Andrew asked us, 'What capabilities do our people need in order to thrive at work, at home, as citizens?' we had a 'eureka' moment. It became clear we need a new set of soft skills. We call them 'mind skills' and 'people skills.'"

Barbara, the Strategy partner who'd spoken earlier, glanced up. "Is there really a difference between the two?"

"Yes, we feel that both are important and distinct. *People skills* are the vital interpersonal skills that we all need if we are going to be effective leaders. Starting with EQ, we've built our list around communication and teamwork as well as how we expect people to treat each other: integrity, authenticity, and kindness."

"'Kindness.' Seriously? Is this still a business?" Will muttered. A few partners laughed supportively.

Andrew responded, "I get it, Will. Makes me a little uncomfortable too. But let me ask you a question. Over the last thirty years, which airline has seen the most profitable growth?"

Will's face said, "I'm not playing this game, Andrew. I always lose." Out loud, he said, "You tell me, Andrew."

Andrew almost laughed out loud.

"Southwest?" Barbara said, giving Will a maternal raise of her eyebrows.

"That's right. And everyone knows their logo. A big colorful heart. And what's it like to work there?"

Janine jumped in. "Highest employee engagement scores I've ever seen. Turnover virtually nil. That sure helps keep the profits up! Plus, their client service ratings are amazing."

"Like so many, I've always been a huge fan of Herb Kelleher, the founder of Southwest. I first learned about him doing case studies back in business school. Southwest is known for their efficient business model and their culture," Andrew said. He could see that the partners were paying attention, so he continued. "There are so many great Herb quotes, but one that fits this discussion is 'A company is stronger if it's bound by love rather than by fear.' Pretty 'squishy' and 'touchy-feely,' but the results don't lie."

Janine added, "Some of you know that Andrew and I recently met with several of the Change Management employees who were on the fence about leaving for Axxcel. I am happy to report that most are staying. During that meeting, we shared some of the ideas we are discussing today. Markiesha, who is staying, said something I think you should hear. I believe her direct quote was 'Any company that invested in me to this extent . . . Well, I doubt I'd ever leave.'"

After a few moments, Barbara said, "Beautiful. Makes perfect sense to me. And 'mind skills'?"

This time Pat jumped up. "As you can see, each of these *mind skills* is anchored in learning and problem-solving. These capabilities are parts of the brain's cognitive functions. In the twenty-first century, having skills like adaptability, critical thinking, and decision-making are vital. It's an incredibly 'VUCA' world: volatile, uncertain, complex, ambiguous. Our people need to know how to focus, organize, plan, and prioritize."

"I think I heard the word 'investment,'" said one of the partners. "This sounds expensive."

Andrew cleared his throat, "We're going to get to the cost of moving in this direction shortly. But let's have Janine walk us through the Employee Life Cycle first."

As Janine's beautiful chart appeared on the screen, Andrew looked up to see Meg standing at the door, her right hand's five fingers outstretched.

"Let's take a five-minute break. Get refills. I'll be right back."

Andrew walked into the hall, where Meg whispered, "General Pagano called. He said it was very important that he give you a heads-up about tomorrow's board meeting. I told him you'd call him after the partner meeting, but I wanted to give you the option to get him now. It sounded important."

"A board meeting tomorrow?"

Meg's face looked like a beet as she stammered, "That's the other thing I needed to tell you. Victor sent an email calling an emergency board meeting for tomorrow morning at nine. The General forwarded the email so I could confirm it: you and Pat weren't on the thread."

Nineteen

"Okay. Thanks for keeping the break brief. Let's get back to the discussion at hand." Andrew could feel Pat's eyes boring into the side of his face. He knew his business partner; she was silently imploring him to tell her what had caused Meg to interrupt the meeting. He turned his head and whispered, "Let's chat for a few after the meeting. This is way more important."

As Pat settled down in her seat, a few worry lines evaporated from her face, and she said, "Janine, please walk us through the life cycle."

Janine stood up and used the remote to refresh the large screen. "The first thing you should note is the human being in the center and the three sets of core capabilities we discussed earlier."

Elena leaned forward. "That's because Janine realized we need to embed development of these capabilities in every step of an employee's career and tenure at our firm. That's how we will build the culture."

Janine worked her way around the wheel, starting with the Strategy icon, and giving the partners examples of potential activities and actions she envisioned for each stage.

"Letting the world of potential Shift employees know they'll get more professional development here than at any other consulting firm will attract more of the right talent," she said.

Andrew added, "Imagine the power of that employer brand. And once they are attracted, we can assess a candidate's alignment with our culture."

"How do you do that?" one partner asked.

"Well, you might ask about their prior experiences with three-hundred-and-sixty-degree feedback assessments and how they used the results. Or something as simple as 'What do you read?' We're looking for people who embrace personal growth."

"Onboarding?"

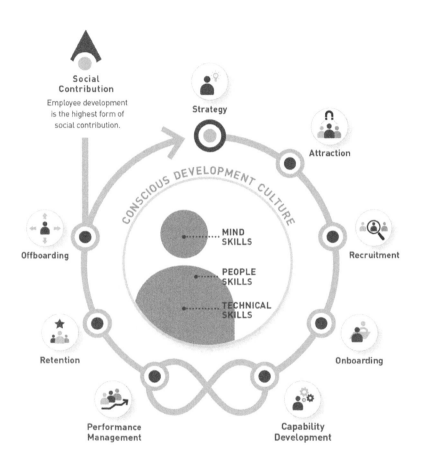

Conscious Development Employee Life Cycle Model

"The best example, from what we've brainstormed so far, is the idea that every Shift employee and partner would create an IDP—individual development plan—starting day one. Obviously, the plans would be created with help from managers and HR. They'd become more complex with time, but if we introduce the idea during the acclimation period, it'll be clear that we are serious about development."

Andrew was watching each partner's reactions. Some were nodding their heads and toggling between Janine and the glossy life cycle documents in front of them. A few sat still. *At least no one is frowning.* Even Will was looking interested. "So what's the deal with the figure eight at the bottom of the chart?"

"Great question, Will," Janine responded. "One thing we learned, as we researched all this, is that performance management—annual reviews, interim feedback, promotions, etc.—is too often thought of as completely separate from learning and development."

"Which makes no sense," Andrew blurted out. "It ought to be a continuous learning experience, a feedback loop. My boss lets me know I need to perform better at a certain capability and helps me get the help I need."

"Is that why some companies are chucking out the annual review process altogether?" Barbara asked.

"Yes, that's one major reason," Janine replied. "Costly and also not very effective."

"That sounds logical, and I'd love to see us do all this. But do you really think we as a company know how to deliver a—how'd you put it—a 'continuous learning experience'? Speaking for myself, I'm not sure I know how to do that."

Andrew scanned the partners' faces. Worried looks and the failure to make eye contact let Andrew know that more than a few were wondering the same thing. He sensed fear. *Are they scared to be stretched out of their data-driven, management consultant comfort zones?*

"Barbara, thank you for being willing to share what we all are feeling, to one degree or another," Andrew began. "So if we all agree that we want a 'continuous learning culture' or, as I learned at Warrenton Realty Partners yesterday, 'a culture where everyone and everything are our teachers,' let's go learn how to be really good at it. The training and development will start with us." Looking each partner in the eye, he again held up the *Washington Post* article about Axxcel and said, "That's how we're going to win."

"But how are we going to learn?" Barbara continued. "I think many of us know about how successful WRP has been. What did they do?"

Elena, Janine, Pat, and Andrew then shared the details of their visit. There were a few eye rolls and raised eyebrows from the more conservative partners as the four leaders described Playtime and the improv workshop. But Andrew watched every partner sit up straighter as he ended the story by explaining Warrenton's financial success and the suggestion of bringing in Dave Edwards to create a coaching program.

"We'd start with all of us getting the Leadership Circle Profile 360 assessment and working with a coach. Then we would add the directors. And we'd get training on how to *be* a coach—from someone who has worked with some of the most impressive businesses in the region."

Looking around at the others, Barbara said, "That's something, I think, that we can all embrace, but can we afford it? That sounds really expensive."

Andrew, realizing she had a few more points to cover, said, "Janine, I think, we ought to tackle the investment question now. Is that okay?"

"Of course, I think now is perfect," she said, handing Andrew the clicker.

A new slide appeared entitled "Financial Implications."

"As you can see, this is a high-level analysis of costs and savings. 'Costs' are grouped in two categories: one-time or ongoing. The 'savings,' better described as return on investment, are ongoing. That being said, the returns will not be immediate."

For the next few minutes, Andrew methodically explained his assumptions, pausing to acknowledge that the initial investment in coaching for fifty or so senior people would exceed $500,000 over the course of a year.

Barbara squinted at the slide. "Wow, that's a big nut, especially given Pat's financial report."

"Indeed it is. I'd like to talk through how I propose to fund it. But first I'd like to offer a few overall thoughts."

"Most of these costs are up-front investments. Once we get the coaching going, we become the coaches and will model coaching conversations to others. Similarly, software and technology investments we will need will be one-time investments."

Scanning the faces, Andrew sensed that he hadn't lost any of them yet. "And while much of the true cost is the value of our time, a valuable asset to be sure, this will require cash outlays, so there must be a compelling financial return from all of this. And all the research supports that there will be."

The Fable

140

"For example?" Will asked.

"Take a look at *Conscious Capitalism* by John Mackey and Raj Sisodia. Another good source is Raj's earlier book *Firms of Endearment*, cowritten with David Wolfe and Jag Sheth. One chart in *Conscious Capitalism* really grabbed my attention. It showed that *Fortune* magazine's 100 Best Companies to Work For had cumulative returns two hundred and seventy-five percent higher than the S&P 500 companies over a fourteen-year period."[5]

"And the 'Firms of Endearment' companies returned eight times the S&P 500 over a ten-year period," Elena added.[6] "These firms invest in their people."

"And who are these companies?" one partner asked.

"Public companies like FedEx, IBM, Marriott, and Nordstrom, as well as privately held brands like Patagonia, SC Johnson, and The Motley Fool. There were well over sixty companies in the study."[7]

Building on the positive energy he was feeling, Andrew continued his presentation. "Let me give you a very direct example. We found many studies about the true costs of turnover: lost productivity, wasted interview time, headhunting fees, and many other factors. Some estimates suggest losing an employee can cost up to two hundred percent of that lost employee's annual compensation."

A few "wows" and one piercing whistle could be heard as every partner seemed to lean closer to Andrew. "So let's be conservative and assume each lost employee costs us one hundred percent of their compensation. We'll keep the math simple and peg that number at one hundred grand, even though we know it's higher. We have three hundred and fifty employees and partners, so each improved percentage point in our turnover rate saves between three and four employees every year."

"Three hundred thousand dollars saved each year—at a minimum," Janine said.

"Right. And what's our turnover rate now?"

---

5   John Mackey and Raj Sisodia, *Conscious Capitalism: Liberating the Heroic Spirit of Business* (Boston: Harvard Business Review Press, 2014), 279.

6   Raj Sisodia, Jag Sheth, and David Wolfe, *Firms of Endearment: How World-Class Companies Profit from Passion and Purpose* (Upper Saddle River, NJ: Pearson Education), 14.

7   Sisodia, Sheth, and Wolfe, *Firms of Endearment*, 19.

Conscious, Capable, and Ready to Contribute

"Factoring out the Axxcel departures, it has been running at eighteen percent. That's up from two years ago when it was twelve percent."

"So assuming all this would get our turnover rate back to twelve percent, you're saying we'd save twenty or so people each year. That's two million dollars." Barbara leaned back in her chair.

"Not to mention increased productivity and better client service," Pat added.

"So, Andrew, the obvious question is, how do we fund the up-front costs?"

"Good question, Barbara. Here's what Pat and I are thinking. This is a special situation similar to when we sought outside investors to fund our expansion to other cities." Andrew felt his solar plexus tighten as he remembered Victor's secret board meeting. Shaking it off with a deep gulp of air, he continued. "We think that each of you should have the opportunity to put in more capital at the same terms Victor Jones has. Completely optional. And I've spoken to Julia, and if there's a shortfall, we can backstop the difference."

"When do we have to let you know?"

"A few weeks sound fair? In the meantime, we will crunch the numbers a bit more and then share what we have."

"Hey, Andrew, before I could decide, I'd need to understand that arrow pointing straight up to 'social contribution.' What's that all about?" asked one of the senior partners who worked with Pat and Will's Strategy group.

Andrew paused.

"A few weeks ago, Dave asked me what my higher purpose was and said whatever it is, it has to be aligned with Shift's. I didn't actually know how to answer the question when he asked me, but I know now. Contribution. That's the key. Our people need to be developing their core capabilities, but that's just the beginning.

"I believe we can take all we learn and do at Shift into our communities. Can you imagine Shift becoming the example of what happens when a business develops its people and they contribute to society, changing the world around them? I can. What if our fully developed people, who provide amazing services to our clients, also contributed all those talents to society, creating high-paying jobs, becoming better parents and spouses, and, as *Conscious Capitalism* says, 'elevating humanity'?

"I was out on a run when it hit me. This Conscious Development Culture, which Janine so elegantly described, could deliver as much or more value to our communities as the best corporate social responsibility program. Just imagine if our team lived every aspect of their lives as better communicators, quicker learners, critical thinkers, and empathetic problem-solvers—always with kindness? The benefits would be immeasurable. Employee development really can be the highest form of social contribution.

"And I want to help make that happen. I'm going to make that happen. Contribution. That's my higher purpose."

Andrew certainly hadn't intended to bare his soul. But as Andrew's final words hung in the air, Will Parsons stood up. "I'm in. I want to be a part of that vision, and I'll put in my share of the capital. I'll admit it: I'm still not sure about the kindness and creativity parts. But if it's good enough for FedEx and Southwest, I'm not about to argue with the financial results. And I want to learn those capabilities." With a grin, he said, "Maybe I could use some coaching on a few of them."

The rest of the room laughed so loud that several of Shift's employees peered around the corner to see what was causing the partners to act like they had just won the Powerball. Barbara and a few of the others began to clap.

After a minute or so, Andrew got the crowd under control by yelling, "One more thing. Do your best to keep this excitement level up. Just know, it's going to be a difficult journey. This journey will be totally worth it, but it won't be easy. Together we can accomplish just about anything. That's who Shift is. Thank you for everything you do. Meeting adjourned."

The partners noisily poured out into the hall outside the conference room, leaving Pat, Janine, and Elena standing with Andrew.

"Great job, Janine. And your sidekick really delivered some well-timed zingers."

"Passion is contagious, Andrew. Way to go, Elena. Your enthusiasm won a few hearts and minds today. Let's go. I'll buy you lunch."

As Janine and Elena walked out, Pat said, "Welcome back, partner. I know the Andrew I saw today. The message is bigger, but the heart is the same one I've known for all these years."

"Thanks, Pat," he said as he embraced her. "You and I can pull this off if we can figure out what to do about Victor."

Conscious, Capable, and Ready to Contribute

"Victor? What's he got to do with this?"

"Apparently, Victor scheduled a board meeting for tomorrow but failed to invite you and me. The General wanted to give us a heads-up."

A trace of fear passed over Pat's face. "Well, what are we going to do?"

"Right now we're going to eat." Then he broke into a sly grin. "Tomorrow we put on our 'visiting the banker' suits and crash Victor's little party."

Twenty

Pat and Andrew met in the lobby of the Jefferson Hotel on 16th Street at 7:45 a.m. The concierge directed them to a private room just off the lobby where several members of the staff were setting up breakfast. A small sign next to the door read, "VJ Capital Strategy Meeting: 9:00 to 11:30."

After choosing two seats at the far end of an oddly thin rectangular table nearly twenty feet long, Andrew said, "Any second thoughts about our plan?"

Pat started to respond just as General Pagano burst into the room. "Victor and the others are walking up the driveway. I was hoping to tell you about a conversation I had with one of your clients, but it'll have to wait until after the meeting." He dropped his papers on the ornate table. "This highfalutin place have coffee?"

A waiter appeared from behind a hidden door and poured him a large mug of steaming black coffee. Pagano took a long gulp and looked at Andrew and Pat. "You two ready for whatever Victor has up his sleeve?"

Andrew thought back to the prior afternoon when he and Pat had learned about Victor's special board meeting. *That had been an interesting conversation.*

• • •

"Thanks, Gus. See you tomorrow. We appreciate the heads-up." After hitting the "end" button to be sure the speakerphone was truly off, Andrew looked at Pat. "Interesting. The General doesn't know much more than we do."

"Just that Victor has a big idea he wants to present to the outside board members," Pat said. "And that he doesn't trust Victor either."

"Certainly no love lost there." Andrew leaned back in his chair. "I wonder . . ."

"What?"

"Let's face it. Even with the partners' willingness to invest in the new strategy and the stabilization of our financials, we still have Victor to deal with. We picked the wrong financial partner. He's only focused on one thing: profit. And while that's not in and of itself a bad thing, we need someone who can think past the next quarter. That doesn't make him a bad guy; we just don't fit together."

"Yes. I also think we are going to need even more capital than Victor committed to support the growth that's coming our way," Pat replied. "So what are you 'wondering'?"

"Well, I was thinking about Victor's partner, Jesse Martin. Remember how he took the time to tell us about his experience at DARPA and how they were always thinking long term?" Andrew thought of Jesse. He rarely spoke, but when he did, he always looked you right in the eye. And he had a handshake Andrew's dad would approve of.

"Yes. So?"

"Imagine if we had him instead of Victor as an investor. Better fit."

Pat shot Andrew an exasperated look. "But he's Victor's partner."

"True. But they don't seem like they're on the same page." Andrew paused. "Based on Victor's 'sixty-day' warning and the way he's sneaking around setting up meetings, I think he's going to pull his investment anyway. I don't think we have much to lose by talking to Jesse and seeing whether working for someone with such different values has left an impact."

Andrew scrolled his contacts, hit "call," and was surprised when Jesse picked up on the first ring. Andrew explained that he was hoping to discuss Shift's financial position, run an idea by him, and see what Jesse knew about the board meeting. Andrew felt a flicker of hope as Jesse spoke. "Uh-huh. Sure. See you at six thirty."

Andrew hung up and said, "We're meeting for drinks at the bar at Zaytinya. He said he didn't know much about the meeting, but he'd love to talk to us." *Maybe this could actually work.*

"Sounds good. I'll swing by here at six fifteen so we can walk together. I think I'll spend the next few hours with Will. Keep the positive momentum going." After a smile that said "wish me luck," she left Andrew's office.

Just then, his phone chirped.

> **J:** How did the partner meeting go?
> **A:** Lots of questions. But in the end, they bought in.
> **J:** Even Will?
> **A:** Yep, the financial case sold him.
> **J:** The others?
> **A:** They liked the Conscious Development Culture ideas. I told them that my mission is now Contribution.
> **J:** CDCC. Just like the crystals I left you.

Wracking his memory, Andrew tried to recall what Julia was referring to. He could see that Julia was typing; then it hit him. Before she could hit send, he rapidly typed a response.

> **A:** Yes! The grid. The first letters of each stone: CDCC. You told me I'd know what they were trying to tell me.
> **J:** The world shows up in strange ways, doesn't it? ♡ ♡ ♡
> **A:** BTW Pat and I are having drinks with Jesse from the board. Home by 8:30. Madly.
> **J:** K. See you then. More.

A few hours later, as he held the door open for Pat, Andrew was still smiling to himself about Julia and her crystal grid. The two partners walked into Jose Andres's popular Mediterranean mezze restaurant and immediately saw Jesse Martin waving from a small table near the long bar that divided the restaurant in half. Jesse stood, shook their hands, and said, "Have a seat. I was hungry so I ordered hummus and baba ghanoush. Help yourselves."

"Looks delicious," Pat said, as a waiter appeared to take drink orders. After agreeing on a bottle of Greek wine to share, Jesse spoke first. "How's the business doing?"

Andrew and Pat gave Jesse a recap of the actions and improved financial results since the last board meeting, including the development culture plans, the visit to WRP, and the partner meeting earlier in the day.

"Excellent," Jesse said. "That should calm Victor down some."

"Speaking of Victor," Andrew began, "do you know why he called the board meeting for tomorrow and failed to invite the two of us?"

Jesse placed his wineglass down just hard enough to cause some to splash out on the table. "I don't know why he needs to act like this. He's always playing mind games." With an eyeroll, he said, "His favorite book is Robert Greene's *The 48 Laws of Power*. Anyway, until you called, I hadn't noticed that you weren't invited." Dabbing the spilled wine on the table with his napkin, he continued. "All I know is he has some possible merger he wants to discuss."

"Merger?" Andrew said. "How does he expect to do that without the two of us weighing in?"

Jesse shook his head. "Maybe he wants to test the waters before he tells you more? You now know everything Victor has told me. I went by his office earlier today to get more info. He said, and I quote, 'Jesse, go back to finding *my* next big game-changing technology.'"

Andrew grimaced. "Ouch. If it makes you feel any better, I sure wish I'd been more careful choosing our financial partner. Even though we got the investment we needed to expand, he'll never go along with our new plans for people development, even though the financial analysis I told you about is rock solid."

"Yeah, and it sounds like we'll all make more money your way. Until you mentioned them, I had not heard of *Conscious Capitalism* or *Firms of Endearment*, but I will be downloading those books as soon as I get home tonight. The idea of harnessing the power of business to do good while becoming stronger financially? I want to read about that."

Jesse swallowed a bite of bread loaded with dip, followed by a gulp of water. He exhaled loudly. "The one thing is: What those books talk about, I think—what you spoke about—well, it requires long-term vision. And Victor . . . He's overly focused on short-term financial results."

Andrew put his wine glass down, shot Pat a glance, and said, "Jesse, I know it might seem out of line, but after our partner meeting today, Pat and I were brainstorming ideas about potential new financial partners."

He paused. "We believe that you are the perfect partner for us."

Jesse stopped moving, his wineglass frozen between the table and his mouth. It was if a Ferris wheel had come to an abrupt stop, the riders not sure when or whether it would start up again. After a few seconds, he slowly returned the glass to the table and said, "Whoa. I did *not* see that coming."

Andrew folded his hands and placed them on the table. He smiled at Jesse but remained silent. He badly wanted to keep explaining, but he knew Jesse was not a man to be rushed. Pat fidgeted a bit but also let Jesse think. Andrew could practically feel Jesse process a wide array of emotions.

After about thirty seconds, Jesse took a sip of wine and smiled. "It doesn't hurt to listen. Walk me through the details."

For the next few minutes, Pat and Andrew took turns explaining to Jesse how they proposed to deploy any investment he would make, emphasizing how his investment would be used for long-term people development.

"We'd offer the same terms that Victor agreed to. As I mentioned, several of us would also put more capital in at the same terms. Realistically, the vast majority of the costs should be one-time investments—like setting up the coaching program, the cost of coaches for the senior leaders, apps to support things like performance management and behavior-based interviewing, and hiring a few outside consultants to help with organizational design and development of specific training in some of the core capabilities. As we explained to the partners, once the benefits of reduced turnover and higher productivity kick in, the net cost will be minimal."

Jesse nodded. "Sorry to be cynical, but how is this different from all the ESG pitches I've heard before? You know—environmental, social, and governance programs—all of which will 'save the planet' but are really just about increasing stock prices."

"Higher purpose," Andrew said, sitting up a bit straighter. "That's the difference. Pat and I are taking Shift in this direction because we truly believe that when we consciously develop our people's capabilities, they will contribute more to society. And because Shift will also be more successful financially, it will contribute by creating more jobs, paying taxes, and increasing the well-being of all of our employees. Make no mistake; this is not a corporate social responsibility program. This is about business itself making a difference."

Jesse sat back in his chair, deep in thought. After a moment or two, he said, "So we buy Victor out. I can already visualize his beet-red face when we drop that bomb. And I agree to a further commitment of up to three million to assist with all the culture changes and growth that we expect to come from this."

Jesse paused. "Anything else to cover?"

Andrew replied, "Of course, we'd need to get this all properly papered." He took a deep breath and said, "It occurs to me that we need to ask you one more question."

"Fire away."

"What's *your* higher purpose?"

Jesse broke into a wide grin. "That is the best question of the night!" He reached into his sport coat, fumbled through his wallet, and held up a yellowed, tattered card. "Remember when we discussed my DARPA boss who really pushed us to think long term?"

Pat and Andrew nodded, as Jesse continued. "Well. One year, we did a strategy exercise where we had to come up with our personal vision. You could call it 'higher purpose.' I've kept mine all these years." With that, he put it on the table in front of Pat and Andrew.

They leaned over the table as Pat read it out loud. "Use my brains, energy, and wealth to improve the lives of as many humans as I can."

"What do you think?"

Andrew broke into a wide grin, feeling warm and hopeful. He picked up his wine glass and held it out toward the center of the table. "I think we need to drink to a new partnership!"

• • •

Now, back in the five-star hotel's conference room, Andrew thought of that discolored, wrinkled card. *How different this would be if we had started with Jesse as a financial partner.*

Andrew heard Victor's angry voice booming in the hall. "What do you mean 'the others are already waiting in the room'?"

"Well, sir, they said they were here for the meeting with Mr. Jones starting at nine. It didn't occur to me to . . ."

"Just get out of the way."

The Fable

150

The door flew open and Victor entered the room accompanied by Jesse, the other outside board member, Roger Coyle, and three men dressed in conservative business suits. Victor stopped dead in his tracks when he saw Pat, Andrew, and Pagano sitting at the table, smiling and sipping coffee. His glare came to rest on General Pagano.

"Yes, Victor, I told them. After all, it is *their* company."

"You had no right to do that, Pagano." Thumb outstretched, Victor flicked his wrist over his shoulder, like a baseball umpire calling a third strike. "Get out, Andrew. You too, Pat," he growled. "This is a private meeting."

"Victor, you sent an email calling a board meeting. As you are well aware, Pat and I are board members."

"This is a private meeting. Call it a VJ Capital meeting, if it makes you feel better. Just leave."

"Just let them stay, Victor. You're going to need to talk to them eventually."

"Be quiet, Jesse," Victor sputtered, his eyes blazing. Then seeing that Roger Coyle and Pagano were nodding their heads in agreement, he turned to one of the men in the dark suits. After brief whispering, Victor sat down and said, "Fine."

"Victor, since all the members are here, let's just make this an official meeting. That will help speed this along, assuming things go as you want. Make sense?"

Jesse's conciliatory tone seemed to calm Victor, who then leaned over to one of the men who had joined him. After a minute of back-and-forth with his colleague, Victor said, "Yes. Let's treat this as a special board meeting of Shift Advisors."

Pat said, "Who are these men?"

"My lawyers." Victor stood up, barely sparing Pat a glance. "The purpose of today's meeting is to discuss a merger that I recommend Shift enter into." Victor looked right at Andrew. "This company is in serious danger of collapse unless Shift gets serious help: new leadership, new thinking, and new sources of revenue. I found a company that will bring all of those and more."

Pat started to respond, "What . . . ?" but Andrew stopped her by gently placing a hand on her shoulder. He looked directly at Victor and said, "We're all ears."

For the next few moments, Andrew's eyes never left Victor's face. Like two prizefighters at a weigh-in, they stared at each other, neither wanting to be the one who showed weakness by looking away. Andrew could see that Victor was confused by Andrew's calm demeanor. Victor was used to people cowering in fear or pushing and shouting back, and Andrew was doing neither of those things. He had been through a lot in the recent weeks, and he was ready for whatever Victor brought his way. Finally, Victor blinked and marched to the door. He swung it open and said, "Come on in. We're ready."

A swath of sunlight covered Pamela Turner as she walked into the room, Leo Vincent and Gary Norris close on her heels. Her blond hair was pulled back, and she wore stylish glasses. She had chosen a conservative navy blazer, blouse, and skirt ensemble, which exuded confidence. Holding her hand up to block the sunshine, she cheerfully said, "Good morning, everyone. We're so glad to be here."

When she saw Andrew and Pat sitting at the table, Pamela's face fell, and her head swiveled to look at Victor. "I had understood this was a meeting of the outside board members."

Victor glared at General Pagano and said, "Don't sweat it, Pamela. Just run through the plan."

Andrew watched Pamela's body soften. It was as if Victor had pressed the "charismatic CEO" button on some invisible remote-control panel. She glided around the table greeting everyone. "Hello, Andrew. Pat, so good to see you. Good morning, Jesse. You must be General Pagano. I've heard so much about you. And you're Roger Coyle. So nice to meet you, too. I've so many Deloitte and Wharton friends. We'll have to compare notes."

As she returned to the head of the table, she continued. "Many of you know Gary Norris. He's our investment banker. We have him to thank for introducing Axxcel to Victor." Andrew watched Gary try to smile. "So nice to see everyone." Gary's slight eye twitch called into question the truth of his words.

Pamela continued to gain momentum, her voice rising and becoming more confident with each word. "And this is Axxcel's COO and managing partner of Change Management, Leo Vincent. He joined us after a nice run at Shift."

Leo looked like he'd eaten a few bad oysters. Andrew detected some gray hairs at his temples, and it seemed as if Leo's black sport jacket hung a bit looser than normal. His obvious discomfort saddened Andrew. *I hope he's okay.*

Andrew felt peaceful, despite sensing Pat's blood boiling to his left. He could sympathize. He was watching someone try to take apart what he and Pat had built, and he knew Pat well enough to know that, for her, watching this was like watching the attempted abduction of her own child. Yet he knew that Dave would coach him to just let it play out. He recalled the skills he picked up at the improv workshop at WRP. "Stay in the moment. Listen with all your senses. Just let it come to you, Andrew."

Pamela opened her laptop and plugged it into the projector, which sat in front of Victor. "All set, Victor. Do you want to kick this off?"

"Yes. As I made abundantly clear, this discussion was supposed to be private. But here you are, Andrew. So you'll just need to hear the truth. Pamela, Gary, Leo, and I have prepared a presentation outlining a merger of Axxcel and Shift. The merger documents are drafted, and we're all confident that due diligence can be finished within a few weeks." He looked at the three suits, who were nodding vigorously. Andrew tried to catch Gary's eye, but his friend had buried his head in a pile of documents.

Victor continued. "The most important part of this deal—and the only way I'll keep my investment in Shift—is for Andrew to step down as CEO. Pamela will be leading Shift into its new, profitable future."

As Pat gasped, Andrew said, "Hmm, and what plans do you have for me?"

"Anything. You can choose any role you wish to craft for yourself. Except CEO. Oh, and you're also off the board. Maybe we should call you a special advisor and have you do business development and client relations."

Andrew stood up. "What makes you think that our partners and our team members will want to work for Axxcel?" He held up a flash drive. "We've got a presentation, too. We've overhauled our strategy. Our partners are 'all in' on building a new Shift: a Shift that puts our people at the forefront of the stakeholder ecosystem; a Shift where profits are plentiful because we have consciously developed our people and they deliver exceptional client service; a Shift that makes a difference in the world."

Conscious, Capable, and Ready to Contribute

Victor turned to look at Pamela and laughed. "What do you think, Pamela?"

"I'd laugh too, but I can't find the humor in it." She looked around at Leo, Gary, and the other board members. "This is a business. All this do-gooder stuff is important as part of any PR strategy. Of course, customers expect to see a brand that cares; showing a softer side is a good strategic move. And businesses make contributions all right—to their shareholders. That's where it counts. Businesses exist to make a difference for the investors who have risked their funds for them."

Pamela continued her diatribe. "I'd say Andrew's making this easy. What is he offering investors? He's going to run this business into the ground chasing some pie-in-the-sky idea. Leadership change is coming not a minute too soon. If this development and contribution nonsense is what he's all about, it's even more obvious that I should be in charge."

"I wouldn't put you in charge of keeping track of the Jeeps, much less a company," General Pagano barked.

"How dare you," Pamela snapped.

"How dare *I*? Let me ask you a question. Do you know much about the culture of the Marines? How we think, how we support each other?"

Andrew sat back down and leaned over the table in Pagano's direction. Pamela Turner tried to look defiant, but Andrew detected a sense of foreboding overtake her body. In a voice a full decibel quieter, she said, "Not really."

"Honor, courage, commitment, integrity. Semper Fi—always faithful. Once a Marine, always a Marine."

"So what?" snapped Victor, as he looked at his watch.

"Well, Victor, Marines stick together." He paused, looked at Andrew, and winked. "I had a nice dinner last night with William Baxter. You know him, right, Pamela? CEO of Logistics International."

Pamela's eyes narrowed. "Yes, of course."

"Baxter and I served together. You did know he's a Marine, right?" Not waiting for an answer, he continued. "Well, you probably don't listen much to the 'nonsense' stuff about clients. He called because he knew I was on Shift's board of directors."

"And?"

"He wanted to know if I could get Andrew to agree to take over the contract you stole from Shift."

"Stole? That's slander."

Shuffling the papers he had thrown on the table earlier, Pagano held up several documents. "I've got bills you sent to Logistics International's accounting department, which don't come close to matching the time records that your own internal auditors provided to us. Looks like you tried to get two hundred fifty thousand dollars for work you and your team never did."

Pagano pulled more papers from the pile. "And here I have proof that you lied on the proposal that won you the work in the first place. Your bid said it would cost eight hundred thousand to do phase one. But in this internal memo Baxter got hold of, you wrote that it would only take half of that. You even adjusted your projected annual profits to reflect the 'windfall from the LI contract.' All your actions are summarized in this affidavit that William Baxter's lawyers have already sent to the Department of Justice. So yeah, I'd say 'stole' is the right word. I think the DOJ will agree. But if you want to call it fraud, that works for me. Either way, you might want to spend less time trying to arrange sneaky mergers and more time working with a team of defense lawyers."

Pamela didn't move. She seemed to be unsure about where to look. Andrew recalled Julia's comments after reading the *Business Weekly* profile. "I feel sorry for her. Her life must have been awfully lonely."

"Let me see those papers." Victor made a move for the paperwork.

"Actually, I have copies for everyone," the General said, as he passed the pages around. Victor scanned the papers quickly, his face turning fire-engine red.

"Well?" he said, looking at Pamela.

"Just a simple accounting error, Victor. I'll clear it up with Baxter."

"Not going to happen. Baxter knows you phonied up the bills and that you lied to him about the cost of the contract in the first place. DC is a small town, Pamela. We military types are especially tight. How long do you think it will be before your clients start checking Axxcel's bills? I'm curious what they'll find."

Before she could respond, Pagano looked at Leo and then Andrew.

Conscious, Capable, and Ready to Contribute

"Baxter also said he's sorry he won't be working with Leo. 'That kid is strong. Too bad he didn't stay with Shift.'"

All color had left Leo's face. He had taken a seat and was rubbing his forehead with both hands. Pamela was pacing. Andrew could sense the nervous energy that had likely fueled her rise to the elite echelon of college soccer and the business world at large.

"Victor, this deal still makes sense. You know you need to make a change. I can get you the returns you need on your investment. Don't let some stupid typos on a few documents rob you of your ROI."

Victor looked at the documents again, his whole face taut. His empty gaze fell on the far wall of the room. After a few seconds, he said, "No, Pamela, that won't work. You'd better leave. I didn't get this far by investing with dishonest people. I had too many friends lose money with Madoff. I may be a hard-ass, but I don't tolerate this kind of behavior. You need to go, too, Gary. I recommend you improve your due diligence process going forward."

Pamela's full swagger returned, as though another switch had been flipped. "You'll regret this Victor. Axxcel was your last chance to save your investment in Shift. And *you*, Andrew . . ." Pamela sneered. "You and your Marine sidekick will be hearing from my lawyers. They'll love going after you for spreading these lies. Your reputation won't be worth two nickels when we get done with you. "

Pamela stormed from the room with Gary Norris at her heel. Leo followed a few paces behind, slowly.

After Leo pulled the door closed, the group sat silently. Victor stared at his papers and then whispered something to the lawyers, nodding his head in response to a comment from his senior counsel. He said, "Well, since we're all here, let's talk about the Shift numbers."

When no one responded, Victor looked around the table and said, "Look. Pamela was clearly a mistake." Turning his eyes on Andrew, he continued. "You do need the help. It's why I wanted to bring her in. I was doing you a favor. I still feel like this could be a great investment. But, hey, you are going to have to drop this contribution crap. Now let's talk about the financials."

Andrew and Pat both looked across the table at Jesse Martin. He discreetly offered a thumbs-up and mouthed, "You go first."

"Victor," Andrew began. "That won't be necessary."

"Well, I'd say that it's up to me. I'm the guy most at risk here."

"Yes, about that . . ." Andrew reached into his backpack and pulled out a thick document. He flipped to a page marked by a pink Post-it note. "Our contract is quite clear. Either party can unilaterally end this arrangement by September thirtieth. Today is the tenth."

Victor's brow furrowed as Andrew slid a one-page document to him. "This is our formal notice that Shift Advisors is exercising its option to return your investment, with the required ten percent return, effective today. All we need are wiring instructions."

"Good thing you brought your legion of lawyers," Pagano said with a snicker.

Victor had already handed the document to the lawyers who were feverishly flipping through the contracts. After a few minutes, the senior lawyer handed it back to Victor. "Yes, this is legitimate. Legitimate, that is, assuming they have the financial wherewithal," he added.

Victor's face shifted from anger to smugness. "Which I know you don't have, so it seems the leverage has shifted back to my end of the table."

Jesse cleared his throat loudly, which caused Victor and the others to turn his way. "Actually, Victor, they've got plenty of capital to buy you out and invest in their new strategy. I'm their 'financial wherewithal.'"

Victor stared at Jesse, his face frozen in stunned disbelief. "You can't do that. It's a conflict of interest and a violation of our partnership agreement. Don't forget: You work for me."

"Not really your day, Victor. I can afford lawyers, too. Although, it only took *one* attorney to review my agreement with you and also set up my own investment fund. It's all—how did your lawyer put it? Oh, yes. It's all 'legitimate.'"

Pagano slapped the table. "Dang, this is fun. See what happens, Victor, when you treat people like dogs? After a while, they bite back."

Victor was sweating profusely. His eyes darted back and forth from Jesse to Andrew to Pagano. He suddenly stood up and yelled, "Jesse, I will put up with lots of things from people, as long as they deliver results. But I will never accept disloyalty. You're fired."

Conscious, Capable, and Ready to Contribute

"Too late. If you check your email inbox, you'll find my resignation letter."

After a quick check on his phone, Victor started for the door. After a few steps, he stopped and spun around. "Jesse, you're a fool. These two will bankrupt you." And then he was gone.

After the reverberation from the slammed door subsided, Pat said, "I just have one question, Jesse. I never saw you touch your phone during the meeting. Not once. How did you send the resignation letter?"

Jesse's face beamed like he'd won first prize at the science fair. "I got home last night, and I couldn't sleep. Everything you and Andrew talked about—consciousness, development of capabilities, contribution—I knew I needed to be a part of it, more than just as an investor. To do that, I needed to get away from Victor. So I talked to my wife, who is a lawyer, and then I drafted the resignation letter. I hit 'send' just outside this room. One good thing about Victor: he always makes everyone turn off their phones during meetings."

Andrew laughed and said, "Well, thank you. We're thrilled to have you as our partner. And, General Pagano, where do I start to thank you?"

"Just call Baxter, make it right, and keep me on your damn board."

"That's it?"

"And hire Leo and his team back. Poor kid. I've seen men more chipper after thirteen weeks of boot camp."

"Yes, I feel like Shift's been given a second chance. Leo deserves one too."

"Now that we've gotten all that handled," Jesse said, "let's see the presentation you have on that flash drive. I want to see how my investment is going to contribute all these fully capable people to this great city."

"The city? Oh, that's just the beginning."

Twenty-One

Shift Advisors Turns Fifteen
DC consulting firm leads by consciously developing its employees' capabilities

BY ROBERT JACOBY

I'll admit it. I was wrong. A few years back, while working for a leading business newspaper in Washington, DC, I wrote an article describing an up-and-coming consulting firm, Axxcel, and its charismatic CEO, Pamela Turner. Ms. Turner seemed to be taking the DC business community by storm. It seemed at the time there was no stopping her company. Without coming right out and saying it, I essentially predicted the demise of Axxcel's competitors. They just didn't seem to have a chance.

I was wrong. (My wife will love seeing that written twice.) While perhaps not rising to the level of such famous frauds as Enron or Bernie Madoff, Axxcel's collapse, brought on by Pamela Turner's avarice, narcissism, and hubris, dominated the headlines and airwaves at the end of 2019. Who could forget seeing Pamela, in her charcoal power suit and oversized sunglasses, not a hair out of place, being perp-walked down K Street? Or the tell-all interviews given by many Axxcel staffers? My only comfort as a reporter is the realization that I was just one of many duped by this charming and glamorous operator.

Sometimes a mistake leads you to an important realization. In fact, that does seem to be the human condition. We grow by failing and trying again. After all, the truism isn't "trial and success."

What I now know is that five years ago, I was looking at the wrong consulting firm. I should have been examining another local success story: Shift Advisors, founded by Andrew Hyde and Patricia Carter. At the time, Shift was not yet the shining star it is today, but the foundation was there.

Two weeks ago, when I called his office, Andrew Hyde answered his phone on the first ring. Not only was he quite pleasant, but he offered me unfettered access to Shift. "Robert, our mission here includes inspiring others to contribute, so we'd love for you to write about what we do. We're holding a Fifteenth Anniversary celebration next Thursday. We'd love to have you join us."

A week later, I walked into the lobby of the iconic Shakespeare Theatre Company's Sidney Harman Hall on F Street in Northwest DC. Meg Green, Andrew's long-time executive assistant, escorted me into the auditorium, just as a somewhat ruffled, diminutive fellow, who appeared to be in his mid-sixties, walked across the stage.

"Good afternoon, everyone. For those of you who don't know me, I am Dave Edwards. I've had the privilege of helping build a coaching culture here at Shift. And today, I will, once again, be serving as master of ceremonies for a very special Shift annual meeting."

As the words left his mouth, large "Happy Birthday Shift!" banners unfurled around the room. The audience erupted with cheers, whistles, and thunderous clapping. Edwards let the noise die down on its own. Smiling broadly, he continued. "We have a fun program planned. To start the occasion, we put together a short video entitled 'The Shift Team: Conscious, Capable, and Contributing.' Enjoy."

Two large screens on each side of the stage burst to life as the sound system blasted the Foo Fighters' "My Hero." Videos and still photos of Shift team members at work and play filled the screens. A Shift partner teaching a class on financial planning for twenty adults in a Southeast Washington classroom. Shift employees in the spotlight in an improv workshop about honoring differences. Shift employees sitting in lotus position as Andrew led them through a guided meditation. An employee recording a podcast about how to show empathy in the workplace.

The final scene showed Julia Hyde, Andrew's wife, getting off the elevator pushing a cart full of freshly baked chocolate chip cookies—apparently a long-time tradition. (No wonder Andrew has kept his job all these years!)

When the music stopped, the screens went black before slowly coming to life again. Giggling voices of children could be heard as the screen lit up to display a man and woman standing behind three squirming kids, two boys, and a girl. The woman spoke first.

"Andrew and Pat, Steve and I are so grateful to work at Shift. Thank you for investing in our development. Training in the technical skills is crucial, and I am so grateful that Shift helped me obtain my Certified Change Management Professional designation. But it's the learning we've received on communication, especially listening," she said with a wink and a head-bob toward her spouse, "that has made our lives better. We're better consultants, for sure, and better parents. We have a better marriage. We're kinder. And the two of us work better as a team. And we sure need teamwork to handle eight-year-old triplets."

The crowd convulsed with laughter as one of the boys stuck out his tongue at the camera and the little girl blew a pink bubble the size of her head. The husband sighed and said, "Thank you, both. Congrats on fifteen years of success. We'll be there when Shift hits thirty!"

The film continued for another few minutes, with clients, peers, and philanthropic leaders from across the country speaking directly to the camera. To a person, they called out the high quality of Shift's people. I heard many great client service stories and tales of big projects completed successfully, but what each client called out most were the special capabilities of Andrew and Pat's team members.

The CEO of a major software company was my favorite. "We were at a turning point as a company. I'm so grateful to my colleague, Valerie Maguire, CEO at Warrenton Realty Partners, for recommending that I call Shift. I could go on and on about how Will Parsons, Markiesha Charles, and Elena Núñez and their team truly delivered solutions that helped us shift course. But that's not why I recommend them to potential clients and potential employees. No, what makes them different is their across-the-board commitment to those special capabilities they talk about all the time. They demonstrate emotional intelligence, kindness, and integrity in everything they do. Their in-house training professionals and coaches must be exceptional because Shift employees are the best communicators ever. They're curious, creative, critical thinkers. They miss nothing."

"Let me tell you a little story. Will was looking at ways we could leverage our new product line, and during our meeting he noticed one of our partners was upset. After the meeting, he reached out to her to lend an ear and learned that the woman's estranged son had just become homeless. A colleague later told me that Will had personally met with her son to coach him and get him into a program to get him back on track. He met that young man every week to mentor him, and he did it all while absolutely crushing our launch and our brand shift. I've never seen anything like it in my twenty-five years in this industry. So thank you, Will and Shift. Congratulations on fifteen years. We look forward to many more together."

As the screen faded to black once again, David Edwards took center stage once more. "Ladies and gentlemen, Andrew Hyde and Pat Carter."

The dynamic duo rocked the house for the next thirty minutes. It was electric; like being at some sort of revival. And like any good show, it had an unexpected finale.

But you'll have to wait for the exciting reveal. I think it's best to give you more context by sharing the highlights of my interview with Andrew, which took place in his office the day after Shift's birthday.

My interview with Andrew started out where you'd expect: facts. I learned that Shift had tripled in size in just five years. Company revenue will exceed $325 million this year. As a result of several large acquisitions, they now have eight offices in most of the largest cities in the US. There are currently nearly one thousand team members. Employee engagement scores are in the nineties, and turnover has dropped to just under 10 percent. Andrew shared his perspective on how they built the culture I'd seen on display the day before, as well as business challenges they'd faced in the last few years.

I then waded into a few tough topics.

"So, Andrew, how did Shift handle that wonderful year of 2020: COVID-19, social unrest, political turmoil?"

"It was quite a year. And 2021 wasn't so fun either, was it?"

Hyde paused. "Just as we'd started down the path toward reinventing Shift, Jesse Martin on board, Leo Vincent and his team back in the fold, Wendy back on our team, COVID-19 hit. On the bright side, we were better equipped than many to survive and thrive. We had a financial partner who wanted to play the long game. We'd embraced the mantra that 'everything is our teacher.' So we had the company-wide attitude of 'Oh, well.' We'd survived the Axxcel/Pamela Turner fiasco. We figured we'd be able to tackle just about anything.

"Years ago, Pat and I were driving to a client. She blurted out, 'There's only life.' I can't even recall what we were talking about to elicit that response. The point she was making is that work and 'outside of work' should be integrated. 'Is work-life balance even the right concept?' she mused. 'The term implies that there are two separate things—work and life—vying for our time and energy. I see work as an integral part of life.' You know what, Robert? Pat was right. And we sure relearned that in 2020.

"So when the pandemic hit, our goal was to help Shift team members be equipped to be better parents, spouses, partners. Everything was happening at home. At first, it was kind of fun. I remember a *New Yorker* cartoon, 'Do I work from home or do I live at work?'"[8]

"It wasn't long before we realized that one of the hardest issues we were going to face was how to support our folks at home. We had technology kits delivered to our team members. Everybody who needed an upgrade got a new laptop. We arranged food delivery. Remember all the trouble school systems were having with virtual learning? Well, our IT folks helped parents get the virtual classrooms set up."

In case you're wondering, I thought about interjecting a few questions, but I was swept up in Andrew Hyde's passion for Shift and his people.

"Speaking of education, we continued all of our coaching and development programs virtually. We even continued our yoga and meditation practices. We all needed those!

"And many of the mind skills and people skills we were embracing—they were so needed. We all needed to be curious about what was going

8   David Sipress, "I Can't Remember—Do I Work at Home or Do I Live at Work?" *New Yorker*, May 8, 2017.

on and come up with creative ways to adapt. With video conferencing and virtual work, we had to become better communicators and do that while communicating in a whole new way—virtually. Clearly, we needed to be kind to ourselves and kind to each other. It was a tough period of time. And that meant lots and lots of teamwork."

"What about clients?" (I figured I better ask at least one question.)

"The core capabilities we had developed really helped us better relate to our clients' needs and fears. We were generous with our time. As our coaches would say: we met them where they were. We invested time and dollars: discounts, write-offs, payment extensions. And you know what? Our clients thrived. We began to offer our internal content for free, especially our mind skills and people skills training. Sure, we could have charged, but we wanted to share what we had. We only had one request: That they not horde it. That they also pass it on to their clients, their partners, and their employees."

As Hyde took a sip of water, I saw my chance to ask more. "What about all the social unrest?"

"Robert, do you mind if we walk and talk? There are a few things you will enjoy seeing, and I don't want to just drone on."

I grabbed my notebook and phone, and we headed off. As we passed one team member's workstation, I noticed an entire wall covered in bright blue and green cards. I paused for a closer look. "Kindness Kard" was printed on each. I turned to Andrew, who had been joined by Meg.

"This is Meg's work station—the command center where she performs her special magic act. Efficiency and technical expertise combined with some of the highest EQ I have ever seen. And these cards—she's too modest to tell you."

I looked at Meg, who was indeed blushing and looking as if she wished she had returned a few minutes later. Hyde continued. "One of our practices is to celebrate acts of kindness by sending these Kindness Kards. You can see that Meg has quite an impact on people. Oh, and you can be sure that she sends them out as well. I have one that I keep in the desk drawer where I put my car keys each morning. I never tire of seeing her words of encouragement."

Meg had obviously had enough. "Andrew, don't you want to continue Robert's tour? I really have a lot of work to do."

Andrew and I tried not to laugh and continued on our way. As we rounded a corner, Hyde stopped abruptly. "Hey, one of the Kindness Workshops is starting in five. Let's pop in."

Andrew led the way up a set of internal stairs, which opened in front of a glass room in which about twenty employees were standing in a semicircle on a large mat in the center of the room.

In the front of the room stood an extremely fit-looking woman with brown hair pulled back in a French braid. She gave me the impression of a college professor who spent her vacations training as a triathlete. Andrew whispered, "All of our workshops are led by Shift team members. Heidi's one of the best technology strategists you'll ever meet. She's also a nationally ranked masters level swimmer."

"Good afternoon, everyone," Heidi began. "Welcome. For the next few hours, we're going to have some fun as we learn some things about being kind and why we think it's important to how we operate at Shift." Once she caught sight of Hyde and me, she said, "Hi Andrew. You know the rules. No observers; only participants!"

And that's how I ended up in Kindness Camp.

Suddenly flushed and feeling feverish, I noted that most of my fellow participants were also doing their best not to make eye contact with Heidi. A few stared down at their own feet; others gazed at a spot some five feet over the speaker's head. Clearly a nervous bunch. Andrew just grinned at me when I glanced over at him.

"I promise you, no one is going to be asked to do anything embarrassing. We're simply going to share our kindness with each other. And when we're done, I predict you'll begin to have more productive, fulfilling relationships here at Shift and in your personal lives."

Some of the fidgeting stopped as the peer leader continued. "Okay. Our first exercise is one I brought with me to Shift. I first experienced this at a seminar led by the British author and psychologist Robert Holden. It's drawn from an invocation used by the Zulus of South Africa. It's pretty simple. Turn to the person closest to you. Look them right in the eyes and slowly say, 'I'm here to be seen.' And the response is 'I see you.' Be sure to pay attention to how the experience affects you. Head, heart, and gut," she said, changing the position of her right hand with each word.

"Give it a go. After each person meets, move along to someone new. You'll get around to everybody in a few minutes, and then we'll talk."

For the next few minutes, we cycled around the room. As instructed, the only words spoken were the Zulu greeting known as Sikhona and Sawubona. Yet everyone reacted differently when speaking. Some bowed slightly. Others clasped their hands in namaste pose as they finished each greeting. One tall man placed his hands gently on each of his colleague's shoulders as he stared deep into their eyes. I found myself smiling and nodding my head slightly after each encounter. Let's be clear: it still felt pretty awkward at first, and my face must have been bright red for the first few minutes. But since everyone was saying it, it quickly became less strange.

After we had greeted everyone, we all stood very still. I felt my body slow down, as if some unseeable force had infiltrated my being, like a CT scan moving slowly from head to toe. It was the way I felt after a particularly good deep tissue massage. My internal assessment was interrupted by Heidi's words: "Who wants to share? What did you experience? Just shout them out."

"At first it was weird . . . looking into their eyes. But when I relaxed, I began to feel their personality."

"The eyes. I could see what a nice person was in there."

"We were one."

The instructor said, "Excellent. Can you elaborate?"

"Sure. No titles; no hierarchy. Just humans experiencing each other. We were equals."

"Wonderful! Anyone else?"

"Yes. I can't wait to get to know these people. Just slowing down to see them and to feel that they saw me . . . well, they seem like a nice bunch of folks, and I want more."

A few "folks" clapped while others laughed and offered "woo-hoos."

"Great start on our afternoon," Heidi said with a broad grin and a few claps of her own. "The punch line is pretty simple. One important way to be kind is to take the time to consciously see the other person."

For the next half hour, we interviewed each other and then shared about what we learned. The message was clear: kind people listen with intention to learn about the other person.

The Fable

After the listening exercise, everyone sat cross-legged on the floor as the instructor guided us through a meditation. As I slowly opened my eyes, Heidi said, "One person you should all be kinder to is yourself. Meditation is one of many practices that are pure gifts to yourself." She paused to give our cohort time to reflect.

"And you can't give away what you don't have."

Andrew whispered, "The next exercise is individual gratitude letter writing. It's a wonderful exercise, but I've got other things to show you, so let's go."

We stood and Andrew turned to Heidi and said, "Thank you so much for allowing us to join in."

"My pleasure." Then she took my hands and said, "Robert, thank you for joining us. I can see the kindness in your eyes." I wanted to ask her if she'd call my mother-in-law to tell her, but instead I replied, "And I see you."

Once in the hallway, I scanned my notes. I was trying to figure out how to ask about this all feeling a little cultlike, but I had to admit: I noticed a continuing calmness that I hadn't felt in a long time, maybe ever.

Luckily, Andrew didn't need prompting and started to speak. "Some of the curriculum comes from personal experiences. Others come from our research. For example, there is a Random Acts of Kindness Foundation. They have many resources to help businesses. And of course, we're not the only business doing this kind of thing. There are many good models out there."

"For example?" I asked.

"Well, I suggest reading *The Healing Organization: Awakening the Conscious of Business to Help Save the World* by Raj Sisodia and Michael J. Gelb. They profile over a dozen companies who lead with love."

"What happens to people who aren't kind? Who don't play nice?" I thought of the schmuck who stole my parking spot this morning.

"We talk to them. With kindness, of course," he said, once again with *that* grin. "Then we look to see if they can own the behavior, make amends, and act differently in the future."

"And if they can't change?" I asked.

"Well, they usually self-select out. That's one great thing about a strong, well-understood culture. People who don't fit actually prefer to not stay—to them, it's weird to be thinking about kindness. Of course, sometimes we have to counsel them out. But that's pretty rare."

"How do you know who's kind, anyway? Does Heidi sit in on your interview process?"

Andrew turned from where he had walked a little ahead. "Close. When we first started on this Conscious Development Culture journey, we figured our training would cover it. But too many employees made it through the doors without being at least open to learning kindness. Now we embed 'tests' of each of our core values into all recruiting activities. For example, we keep track of how potential hires interact with everyone, from assistants to the cleaning staff. Anyone who has an interaction with the candidate gets to chime in about how they were treated by the prospect."

It seemed too simplistic, but I couldn't deny there was a certain positive energy in the halls that made it all seem true.

As we reached the hallway, I reminded him of my unanswered question about all the tumult of 2020 as companies and citizens confronted the reality of racism in America.

"Well, again, we had a bit of a head start since we were already working on how to contribute. And we knew that companies who embrace diversity of thought and who build diverse cultures outperform those who don't. We went back to the capabilities we were working on. We were leveraging differences, helping people learn how to resolve conflict. We were teaching critical thinking.

"We'd always been fairly diverse, but I came to realize that despite our best efforts, we were missing a major point. We had many unconscious biases that were holding Shift back. I had the opportunity to hear a president of a historically Black university speak to a group of CEOs about systemic racism. It made me realize that CEOs drive the strategy. We set the vision. We rally our people around a higher purpose. Therefore, we need to lead the diversity, equity, and inclusion efforts."

"What did you do?" I asked.

"I started by calling my friends and colleagues of color and asking for help. And I admitted I'd been blind to a few things. They were very kind and reminded me that life is a journey. We're all at different stages. The key is just to keep moving on the journey. I read everything I could. I made

The Fable

myself feel really uncomfortable, and I asked the other partners to do the same. I hired a Black coach to work with us. She brought in a bunch of coaches of color, and we added diversity, equity, and inclusion into the topics covered in our improv workshops and communication training.

"We consciously recruited diverse talent. The historically Black colleges and universities have become one of our primary sources for talent. We built all this into our onboarding. We basically worked it into our employee life cycle that we've already talked about. And after we bought Victor Jones out, we wanted two new board members. We made sure to consider only Black, Native American, and other minority candidates. We ended up selecting two Black professionals: one man and one woman."

Andrew stopped at the window of a large training space filled with Shift team members. "This is good timing," he said as he glanced inside the room. "That speaker is from the DC Council. You may remember the story I told you about a former employee who had the courage to confront me one day on the street. Well, we connected with his company, and we joined forces to expand a financial mentoring and job coaching program for Ward 8, the city's poorest community. In return, community leaders agreed to lead a program here at Shift called 'What It Means to Be Black in America.' That's when the real change started to happen."

"And you are still offering it? Five years later?"

"It's a journey. We need to keep learning and growing."

The talking and walking continued for another thirty minutes. When we got back to his office, I asked Andrew about the political environment of 2020.

"Robert, I'm a Conscious Capitalist. Capitalism is apolitical. I care about people, and I want Shift to help make this world a better place. That's apolitical, too. So we just let the whirling dervishes of political DC whirl. We stayed focused on what counts: making a difference for our people."

I concluded the interview by holding up my phone. "Would you like to see last night's birthday party for Shift? I caught the very end on my iPhone."

He seemed taken aback by this. Then he flashed his signature grin and said, "Well, I guess we did say 'unfettered access.'"

We leaned over the small screen together and I hit "play."

Conscious, Capable, and Ready to Contribute

Andrew stood up at the front of the room. "Pat and I want to thank everyone who made today such a success. And thank you all for fifteen amazing years. The scavenger hunt will begin in fifteen minutes. Janine's team has concealed fifteen contribution-themed prizes throughout this beautiful city. Pay close attention to the clues in your goody bags, and we'll see you at the Old Ebbitt Grill at seven."

"But before I let you go, I've got three important topics to cover. First, I'm excited to let you know the research has started on our contribution index, which will measure all the ways companies contribute to society. Thank you to Elena Nunez, who dreamed up the idea. Our contribution index will let leaders see how companies are changing the world for the better."

"Second, speaking of Elena, on behalf of all the partners, I am pleased to announce that Elena has been elected CEO of Shift Advisors, effective January first, 2025. Pat will become the board chair, Leo Vincent will become chief operating officer as well as the head of Change Management, and Will Parsons will become the managing partner of Strategy."

The crowd went very still. Andrew looked around and chuckled.

"I guess that does raise a question, doesn't it? What am I going to do if someone else is CEO? It's time for me to step aside. You all are in capable hands! I've formed a new venture, and my goal is very simple. I want to carry the 'contribution' message to the business world at large. But first, my lovely bride Julia and I are going to make a long-planned and often-postponed trip to Machu Picchu. I've been working hard on my fitness—after that mild heart attack last year—so I think I'm ready for the climb! Julia's been patient as we got Shift and my health squared away. She really deserves this trip, and we're looking forward to getting away—just the two of us. So thank you for this wonderful experience, and I wish everyone the best."

Just then, Julia appeared to Andrew's left, prompting cheers from the audience. She smiled and waved, radiant. "I just want to strike while the iron is hot and get this handsome man away from you," she laughed. The two hugged for a minute and then walked off the stage, arm in arm.

After a long standing ovation, the rest of the Shift team headed out into the DC evening air in search of hidden treasures. I sat still in the emptying room, allowing all that I had seen and heard to settle in.

The Fable

It has taken me five years, but this time I think I got it right. I've learned what really makes a great company is not a single-minded, hard driving, flashy leader. No, what you need is an egalitarian culture built on development, kindness, and generosity of spirit. Maybe it doesn't make as many headlines, but it gets much better results. And I can find no better example of a culture to emulate than Shift's. These people are truly conscious, capable, and ready to contribute.

How to Shift

Build it so they will want to come, flourish, and stay, knowing that someday they may leave.

Thus, it is imperative to define what you want them to say about their growth experience with your organization and what you want the outside world to say about how you invest in and contribute capable people to society.

You've likely arrived at this final section of the book because you are a leader who understands the importance of developing people capabilities for the sake of your business's success and your people's well-being and future. We imagine you are intrigued by the idea that your company's efforts to develop your employees' full capabilities not only has benefits for your business and culture but could actually be recognized as a more conscious form of societal contribution.

You may know firsthand what it looks and feels like to work in an organizational environment where challenging yourself and your colleagues to learn and grow and realize full potential, with love and compassion, is not only expected but encouraged and incentivized. Or you may want to know that experience for yourself and your employees but are wondering how to make this a reality. And this may seem like a daunting shift, especially for a well-established company that does not currently embrace a conscious development culture.

Wherever your business finds itself, we welcome you and hope you will find inspiration and support to begin or continue the journey toward a more conscious practice of people development in your company's workplace.

We wanted to convey through Andrew's story that leaders are becoming more conscious of the business imperatives and the higher purpose opportunity to contribute more capable people to society. But as you saw play out at Shift Advisors, awakening to this vision is only the first step. How a company creates and sustains a conscious and fully integrated development culture is a much bigger challenge. And as Andrew's story makes abundantly clear, it really is a journey.

Andrew and his team had to think through how their company's existing culture (including values, attitudes, behaviors) needed to shift to make learning and development a more consciously integrated and natural part of the everyday business strategy and work experience. They faced a lot of skepticism and resistance from the executive leadership and some board members, which in turn meant Andrew, Elena, Pat, and Janine needed to have difficult conversations to explore Shift's needs and opportunities. And they had to seriously weigh the risks and rewards, especially since the firm was going through a major financial crisis. It's significant that Andrew and his team went ahead with the development culture work anyway, despite the crisis. It can be tempting to wait until a company grows or is financially thriving to start creating a development culture. A number of leaders at Shift wanted to wait, but Andrew had the vision and foresight to realize there is no perfect time. By fighting to create a development culture as the company was changing and facing challenges, Andrew was able to position Shift to grow profitably by taking advantage of the human, financial, and business benefits of a development culture. We saw some of the results of that experience in the final chapter of Andrew's story.

It's equally important that Andrew, despite his enthusiasm, waited until he understood more and until he had buy-in before launching a people development culture. Like many conscious leaders, Andrew understood this type of culture has to start at the top. This was not something he could outsource to his HR professional. It was not enough to launch an improv class or a meditation session; for people development culture to work, Andrew had to work on himself as a leader and had to change the relationship Shift had with its employees. This culture is not about implementing a "program" or a few fun ideas and calling it a day. A people development culture is about doing the work to thoughtfully alter the way the company shows up for its people and the way the team interacts with leadership and the company.

A core message of the fable is that realizing the full potential of people development in the workplace requires committed leadership, starting at the very top. Andrew's story underscores a common characteristic of companies with committed conscious development cultures: the senior-most leaders, often the founders, are the chief champions of a development culture.

But what if you are not the company founder, but a CEO, a president, or an executive-level leader who wants the organization you lead to experience the benefits of a conscious development culture? And what is the driving motivation of leaders who successfully build conscious development cultures, anyway?

Our experience and research show that leaders who build successful development cultures understand how their own development journey has benefited every aspect of their lives. They are very clear that people development goes hand in hand with operating and navigating their business successfully. And they understand that they need to have a culture that creates personal and collective accountability, community, and strong relationships to make continuous learning and growth feel psychologically safe, fulfilling, and worthwhile for everyone.

When it comes to creating a more conscious development culture, there really is no one-size-fits-all approach. Every organization needs to figure out what makes sense for the nature, size, and maturity of their business. But our experience and research suggest that the five approaches we outline in this chapter can serve as a practical roadmap to help leaders get started.

The five approaches can be summarized as follows:

1. Understand the Role of Leadership
2. Align Business and People Strategies
3. Define Conscious Development Culture Principles
4. Identify Core People Capabilities
5. Embed Conscious Development throughout the Employee Life Cycle

Understand the Role of Leadership

In the story you've read, Andrew, Pat, Elena, and Janine lead the shift toward a more conscious and holistic approach to developing their people. This is a *shift* because in many companies, business leaders defer to human resources (HR) or learning and development (L&D) to lead people development (training, education, and leadership) in support of the business priorities. After all, HR and L&D are considered the learning experts. Frequently, the CEO's role is to communicate the importance of learning and development. This is a vital role for a CEO or executive leader to play, but for a shift to occur, it takes more than lending verbal support. Leaders also need to model and actively cultivate the organizational conditions to sustain a true development culture. In some cases, they need to become different leaders to enable such a culture to thrive—just as Andrew had to change his leadership approach.

At Shift Advisors, Janine, the chief human resources officer (CHRO), worked closely with all the company's leaders to develop a conscious people development culture. This meant having quite a few conversations among the senior leadership about what it would mean to make developing people capabilities a more central part of Shift's values, beliefs, business strategy, and learning and performance practices throughout the whole company.

This "leader-led" approach to development is embraced by many progressive companies today. In our experience, it's only when all the senior leaders, starting with the CEO, collaborate with HR to *own*, *model*, and *drive* the learning and development culture that conscious development can really take off.

Why?

In an organization, learning and growth can often feel scary for everyone, but especially for employees, because it means confronting what we don't know, taking risks, allowing our ideas or perspectives to be challenged, and making mistakes that we learn and grow from. This can be uncomfortable for some, but it also all happens in a sandbox of relationships with other people. We are constantly battling our ego's fear that others will see and judge us if we fail, admit we don't know, are wrong, or make a mistake.

This is why leaders need to model what owning learning and growth looks like. We all need to feel it's safe to test out ideas, speak up, and be open and vulnerable in learning. In virtually all organizations today, some level of hierarchical structure exists, creating a power dynamic between leaders, managers, and employees, so when leaders make mistakes—and admit they don't know or were wrong—they give permission for others to do the same. People need their leaders to model what it looks like to be vulnerable in their own learning and to be compassionate in supporting others on their journey of learning and growth. They need to model how a leader can recognize their own triggers and reactive tendencies and do the inner work necessary in order to continuously learn and grow from the inside out.

So how can senior leaders *own* and *model* their learning? Bob Anderson and Bill Adams,[9] in their book *Scaling Leadership*, describe "learning out loud" as a practice that involves people sharing with others their mistakes and realizations as well as areas of their leadership they are working to improve. It is also very powerful for employees to know their leaders are working on their own practice of leadership with the support of a leadership coach and peers. When teams can see a leader learning in real time and showing commitment to their own development journey, it inspires and invites everyone in the company to also be open to learning and development opportunities.

Finally, senior leaders need to actually *drive* the development culture for the company. What we mean by drive is that leaders have to take responsibility for ensuring that the values, beliefs, incentives, structures, strategies, processes, and practices that support a conscious development culture are understood and embraced by employees at every level of the organization.

The CEO of one company we work with not only embraces his own leadership development journey by working with a coach but is consciously driving a development agenda of more conscious leadership within his leadership team and then integrating leadership principles more holistically within the company's talent maturity model. The CEO started by

---

9   Robert Anderson and Bill Adams, *Scaling Leadership: Building Organizational Capability and Capacity to Create Outcomes That Matter Most* (Hoboken, NJ: Wiley & Sons, 2019).

engaging with his own leadership coach. After six months, he offered his executive team the opportunity to hire their own coaches and to work as a team on their collective development. This resulted in each executive devoting more of their focus on mentoring and developing the next level of leaders in their business units. From there, the executive team looked for ways to strengthen the leadership culture. They gathered a lot of feedback from different levels of leadership and then worked collaboratively with the HR and L&D teams to create new processes to help them select and develop leaders who embrace their leadership principles. This hands-on commitment has taken the companies' focus on fostering a development culture to a whole new level.

When every level of leadership gets involved in developing people and instills that goal into the mission, values, culture, and daily operational practices of the company, learning and development really comes alive.

We believe the *own, model,* and *drive* concept will help remind senior leaders that their roles as champions and full participants are crucial to building and sustaining a vibrant and effective development culture. Our executive clients who embrace the *own, model,* and *drive* concept tend to have two initial reactions. The first reaction is that it takes time and energy to focus more consciously on development, whether at the individual, team, or organizational level. They realize how little they actually slow down to have mentoring or development-oriented conversations with direct reports. But the second reaction we hear from executives is their discovery of how incredibly effective, meaningful, and rewarding it is to have more focused mentoring and development-oriented conversations with their direct reports and teams. What seemed like a sacrifice of precious time turns out to be an incredibly valuable practice—one that transforms and scales the business.

It's not important or desirable for leaders to figure out or dictate all the practices that support people to intentionally learn and grow every day. What is important is for leaders to clearly communicate the big picture of what the company is trying to achieve through a conscious development culture and what core skills and capabilities the company values and encourages employees to develop. This clarity is what will unleash the creativity and cooperation, allowing everyone to contribute to creating practices and tools that best support people in learning and developing their capabilities.

When team members get involved in creating a development culture—rather than just being told about it—they become excited. They get to help shape a culture they then become invested in. Involving more people in the discussion also brings out powerful ideas—ideas leadership alone may not have considered.

Visionary companies like Shift embrace the idea that developing a conscious development culture is a vital part of their purpose and overall strategy. **For some businesses, it will be the most important strategy they employ.**

So it's time to ask yourself some questions. How does your leadership team talk about people development at your company? How do your company leaders define what it means to *own, model,* and *drive* a development agenda at your organization? How might your company be affected if you did take this type of ownership or embraced it in new and different ways?

Answering these questions is especially helpful and useful when part of regular executive meetings or retreats. When executive leaders incorporate these questions as part of an ongoing conversation, it deepens their relationships as a team. It also lets them practice and support each other to model learning and development and helps drive the development culture and practices. Here are some questions to get a strategic conversation going about development:

1. What does "owning" my personal development as a leader mean to me, and in what ways have I committed to my development journey?
2. How do I model to my team and employees how I learn and develop as a leader?
3. How often do I openly discuss mistakes I have made?
4. How often do I experience joy and satisfaction when I see a leader or employee blossoming in their roles?
5. In what ways do we, as senior leaders, talk about our own development?
6. To what degree do we talk about the importance of learning and development in our day-to-day operations and as part of our business strategy?
7. How might our business performance be hampered by employees with underdeveloped people skills capabilities?

8. What would be the benefits to our business if people development was a core value in our company?
9. How important is it that our employees learn skills at work that also help them be better with their families and communities?
10. What is our vision for developing our people?

Align Business and People Strategies

Once you've completed the deeper work of thinking about how a more conscious commitment to people development could better serve your business, your people, and society, you will then want to examine how people development is reflected in your business and people strategies. In our experience, one of the most common weaknesses we see in business strategy development is that the people strategy, which is meant to guide all the talent management and development elements supporting the business, is not well articulated or integrated into the business strategy. Our experience is validated in research findings presented in 2018 that only 40 percent of companies say their learning strategies are aligned with business goals. This means that for 60 percent of companies, learning and development has no explicit connection to strategic business objectives.[10]

So how can we better align and integrate business and people strategies? By focusing on conscious people development. Delivering on the people capabilities and competencies a business needs to thrive is the most important driver and indicator of a successfully integrated business and people strategy. You can think of learning and development as the function in the company that serves as a fulcrum because it plays a central role in both the way you grow the business and the people.

This is why more and more companies are pursuing business excellence and the growth of people as one integrated strategy. In other words, how people practice learning and development in a company is explicitly tied to business improvement, growth metrics, engagement, and organizational health. A positive learning environment fuels the creativity, energy, and agility associated with organizational change and business growth. So the logic goes that the more you grow and develop with your people, the stronger your company will become overall.

This is the view and a key message of the three companies profiled by Robert Kegan and Lisa Laskow Lahey[11] in the groundbreaking research

---

10 Human Capital Management Excellence Conference (West Palm Beach, FA: Brandon Hall Group, 2018).

11 Kegan and Lahey, *An Everyone Culture*.

presented in their book *An Everyone Culture: Becoming a Deliberately Developmental Company* (2016). They argue that "Business growth requires people who are developing; developing people requires the rich context for growth that business provides . . . 'this approach to business is not first about attracting and retaining talent, or merely doing the right thing by people in an abstract sense, making principled sacrifices in the name of corporate social responsibility. Rather, it's a choice, fundamental to the company's identity, to see the pursuit of profitability as requiring the continuous growth of the people joined in the pursuit.'"[12]

We encourage executive leaders and their teams to make learning and development the fulcrum that closely ties people and business strategies together. Here are some ideas for ways to incorporate consideration of people development in elements of your business strategy:

1. Consider how people development might factor more prominently in your overall goals and aspirations, including a clear Higher Purpose, Vision, Core Values, and High-Level Financial Objectives. You might start by asking the following:

   - Might your higher purpose evolve to include helping people develop and thrive?

     Take for example, Decurion Corporation, a California-based company and one of the three "deliberatively developmental" companies profiled in *An Everyone Culture*. Decurion CEO Christopher Forman describes how he formulated an evolved purpose to help people flourish, and this became the animating purpose of Decurion. Here is what Forman and COO Bryan Ungard say about what it means to have a purpose around people flourishing: "When people hear 'flourishing,' they think of appreciation and good feelings. But growth and development does not always equal 'feeling good.' Our culture is not about maximizing the minutes you feel good at work. We don't define flourishing by sitting-around-the-campfire moments. We ask

12 Kegan and Lahey, 198.

people to do seemingly impossible things. . . . We've learned, also, when we are onboarding people to our culture, we have to manage their expectations. We say, 'It will be hard, but it will be rewarding.'"[13]

- Do your core values support a conscious people development culture? If they do not, how could they be updated to do so?
- Which of your financial objectives are tied to people development? What financial incentives exist in your organization to encourage people development? Are there any disincentives that could inhibit a more conscious approach to development? How could your bottom line grow if people development is an articulated expectation, daily practice, and goal?

2. Develop a concise statement that connects creating a conscious development culture to your business strategy. Think of it as an elevator pitch. If you had to explain your conscious people development culture to someone quickly and succinctly—including what it is, how it shows up, and what it does for your company—what would you say?

3. Incorporate L&D goals and objectives as part of your company's Balanced Score Card[14] and Key Performance Indicators (KPIs).[15] This approach will help drive focus on measuring the influence of L&D programs and practices on things like whether employees are demonstrating the right skills and behaviors in performing their job functions and how they impact organizational performance and culture. These and other measurement strategies will be critical enablers of a learning and development culture.

13 Kegan and Lahey, 35.
14 Robert S. Kaplan and David P. Norton, *The Balanced Scorecard: Translating Strategy into Action* (Boston: Harvard Business School Press, 1996).
15 "What Are Key Performance Indicators and How Do They Relate to the Human Resource Function?" Society for Human Resource Managers, August 16, 2019, https://www.shrm.org/resourcesandtools/tools-and-samples/hr-qa/pages/whatarekeyperfindicatorsandhowtheyrelatetothehrfunction.aspx.

Conscious, Capable, and Ready to Contribute

Examining these areas individually and as a leadership team can help you appreciate how a conscious development culture is already showing up in your organization right now. It can help you target any roadblocks that prevent your company from enabling more conscious people development opportunities at every level.

Define Conscious Development Culture Principles

Everyone in your organization has their own idea of what "learning," "growth," and "development" look like and the degree to which it is expected in their job. But the ideas and assumptions people have tend to be unstated and largely undefined in a company. This creates challenges around expectations. If the CEO or HR leader assumes development is about work-related skill training, but employees see development as a chance to pursue passion projects, you're not speaking the same language. Even as more companies embrace the concept and practices of a learning culture, it can be hard to leverage the full benefits of a continuous learning environment until everyone is on the same page with the vision, goals, and expectations for what it means to operate in this kind of culture.

Defining a set of principles gives you a common language and expectations that can be applied by all employees. Defining your company's own principles is also a good way to clearly articulate the values, beliefs, expectations, and behaviors that create the everyday conditions that support your employees' ability to learn and develop their capabilities. In our client work, we have observed that companies and teams who take the time to create these guiding principles are the highest-performing organizations.

Let's look at some examples of development-centered guiding principles, which you could adapt to your own organization:

1. **Learning and development as a core value.** Learning and developing capabilities should be a key focus at the individual, team, and organizational level. Unless learning and development is articulated and understood as a value that is core to the business, they will not be taken as seriously as other core values.

2. **Learning and development are integrated with business strategy and results.** As part of the business strategy development process, leaders identify the specific people capabilities employees need to achieve specific business results. By calling out these specific capabilities in the business strategy, businesses elevate their relevance and create expectations for developing and using capabilities in performance. This principle makes it clear that learning and

development is key to achieving the company's purpose and goals. While learning is important in and of itself, research shows that L&D investments lead to better ROI when they are integrated with strategy, operations, and performance measures and incentives.[16] In other words, by linking learning and development to strategy and business goals, people development becomes a powerful way to improve business performance and contribute more capable people.

3. **It is safe to learn and develop.** Make sure the work environment is "psychologically safe" to learn for the sake of improving oneself and helping others improve on a daily basis. A psychologically safe work environment, according to Harvard's Amy Edmondson,[17] is one where all employees feel confident that they will not be embarrassed, rejected, or punished for speaking up. This means your employees feel safe to admit when they make a mistake or get something wrong and feel able to challenge the status quo for the sake of improving individual or collective knowledge, skills, and performance. A climate where people feel comfortable being themselves and trust and respect the intentions of each other is absolutely essential to achieve the full potential of what a true conscious development culture can deliver. Quite simply, learning and development means taking risks, and employees need to feel safe to take risks. Executive leaders have to be truly conscious that they have the biggest influence on whether their company values and creates a safe learning environment.

4. **Expectations for learning and development.** In a conscious development culture, everyone is expected to embrace the many opportunities to learn and develop their capabilities. Additionally, when everyone receives support and encouragement for ongoing learning and development, a safer and more relaxed learning culture naturally animates a spirit of generosity instead of competition. Mentoring, teaching, and coaching among peers is acknowledged

---

16 Edward D. Hess and Katherine Ludwig, *Humility Is the New Smart: Rethinking Human Excellence in the Smart Machine Age* (Oakland, CA: Barrett-Koehler Publishers, 2017).

17 Amy C. Edmondson, *The Fearless Organization* (Hoboken, NJ: Wiley & Sons, 2019).

and valued. Regularly soliciting feedback informally accelerates and fine-tunes growth for oneself and others. Learning to give and receive feedback nonjudgmentally and compassionately is itself a capability that catalyzes growth. Aside from benefitting individuals and groups within the organization, L&D serves business outcomes and the customers it serves.

5. **Learning and development is incentivized, rewarded, and celebrated.** Individuals and teams are incentivized, rewarded, and recognized for how well they learn and contribute to learning at the individual, team, and organization levels. Rewards can range from bonuses to praise and recognition and increased advancement opportunities. And importantly, this helps tie an employee's learning and development efforts to their performance in a specific function or activities. From a higher purpose perspective, when companies celebrate learning and developing their employees' human capabilities as a form of individual and collective joy, everyone can take pride in their contribution to human capability and society.

6. **Embrace a growth mindset.** A "growth mindset" is a term developed by psychologist Carol Dweck.[18] A growth mindset refers to the idea that our abilities can be cultivated. This means we can continuously improve our skills and capabilities through practice, perseverance, learning from feedback, mistakes, and inspiration from others. More and more companies embrace the concept of growth mindset as foundational to their learning culture and as a quality they look for in employees. Team "hot wash" meetings that emphasize learning from failures and successes are one example of a growth mindset practice.

7. **Leaders *own*, *model*, and *drive* the development agenda of the company.** Leaders _own_ that they must be willing to learn and share what they are learning and how they are growing as leaders. They _model_ through the way they talk about their learning and demonstrate

---

18 Carol Dweck, *Mindset* (New York: Ballantine Books, 2006), 50.

their own development, so employees feel inspired and empowered to take ownership over their own learning and development. Leaders _drive_ development in a company by ensuring that the vision, culture, and everyday practices of learning and development are part of the company's values, business goals, and results.

A helpful place to start the process of identifying guiding principles is to assess how your company culture currently values and approaches development. You might already have recent climate data around creating a psychologically safe learning environment, for example. How do your employees perceive or experience the work environment when it comes to having a growth mindset toward work and challenges, giving managers feedback, making mistakes, speaking out, managing conflict, being vulnerable, and support for continuous learning and development? Starting where you are currently and looking at the information you do have can help you see where you might want to make course corrections.

If you don't have data on hand to shape your guiding principles, you could conduct a 360-degree culture assessment to get a sense of how every level of the organization views the presence of a development culture. This will be very helpful information to determine what principles or practices already exist and which ones will be new and require more adaptation.

Identify Core People Capabilities

We want to begin this section by briefly explaining why we use the term "Core People Capabilities." We are all fairly accustomed to the shorthand terms, coined by the US Military, to describe the two big buckets of skills we use in the workplace: "hard skills," the job-specific technical skills that require dedicated training or education; and "soft skills," the interpersonal and behavioral skills we need to relate and work well with others.

While these two general skills categories are useful, they have limits. "Soft skills," for example, are sometimes pushed aside as less important or somewhat vague. And most leaders have had to answer a question like this: what do we do with the brilliant employee who no one wants to work with because he lacks empathy, has no self-awareness, and is a poor listener?

Companies are increasingly finding that such employees who "don't play well with others," no matter how genius their technical skills, are liabilities unless leaders have the will and the knowledge to develop them. We know from our own experiences that hiring talent with the right combination of technical skills and soft skills poses two ongoing dilemmas. The first is how to accurately screen for the right soft skills for what the role and the company culture requires. The second is making the difficult call as to whether a candidate with strong technical skills can develop one or several soft skills that may be lacking. The underlying challenge is that soft skills tend to be subjective to assess, challenging to screen for, and frequently hard to teach.

We believe it is time to embrace a more holistic and overarching set of terms for the soft skills and abilities we need at work: "People Capabilities." For us, the term *People Capabilities* affirms the real goal of intentional learning in the workplace: using the knowledge, skills, *and* abilities developed at work to grow more fully as humans. We encourage the empowered growth within people to use their abilities capably with wisdom, confidence, and humility. And we're not just trying to teach specific skills like, for example, active listening, with some skills seen as more important than others. We're trying to elevate the range of a person's potential by growing their human capabilities across the board.

Identifying a set of core people capabilities is hardly a new idea for most businesses. Virtually all companies offer some level of learning and development for their employees, and that means starting with the basic ideas of "what do they need to know and do to be successful in our business?" and "how do we help them learn and develop?" These questions are especially important as companies consider how to develop the next generation of leaders, where strong people capabilities are strongly correlated with effective leadership. And more and more companies appreciate that developing people capabilities is increasingly a strategic business imperative that needs to be happening much earlier in every employee's career.

The challenge we often see at many organizations, however, is that outside of the HR or L&D functions, few other leaders stop to really think about what core people capabilities really matter in the business and which are valued in the culture. Take the skill of *critical thinking*, for example. How do we build an employee's ability with this skill? When only the people working in HR or L&D functions are thinking about capabilities from a "how to develop them" standpoint, you get limited insights from the front line on what skills people need to know to do a job or work together well with others. But when you create an organization-wide development culture, the conversation shifts. You get marketing asking, "What do we want our people to know about the hard and soft skills of the job?" Employees ask, "What skills do I need to know?" This creates more common understanding and a richer and more varied learning experience—one that helps workers develop the full range of human skills they actually need to succeed.

As we know, the key to developing any new capability is to focus on context, practice, and measurement. At AO People Partners, we have developed a Core People Capabilities Model to help employers and employees focus on developing the most critical human skills and abilities people need to work and collaborate successfully in the twenty-first century workplace. The Core People Capabilities Model organizes skills into three overarching buckets: Mind Skills, People Skills, and Technical Skills.

We developed this model to help streamline the seemingly endless possibilities of capabilities your employees may need. Our experience and research also shows that these three categories of skills are nearly universal; these are the categories of skills all workers and people need to be successful in their lives at work and outside work. In practice, companies can emphasize the capabilities that are most important for meeting their business needs. We envision that this capability model could be used as an overarching foundation or integrated if your company already has an existing comprehensive employee capability competency framework.

Mind Skills

Mind Skills are embedded in the brain's cognitive function and are closely associated with learning and problem-solving. Virtually all jobs performed today and, in the future, will require higher use of our mind skills. Formal education begins the process of developing and cultivating mind skills, but to be competitive in today's complex and fast-changing world, employers and employees need to understand and foster these skills further.

Based on our research, these are the Mind Skills considered foundational:

CAPABILITY	DEFINITION
EXECUTIVE FUNCTION SKILLS (CORE CAPABILITY)	The brain-based skills enabling focus, organizing and planning, understanding of different points of view
	Focus: Centering one's attention on a task or project and bringing it to completion
	Organizing, Planning, and Prioritizing work or project
	Different points of view: Surfacing and challenging underlying assumptions
GROWTH MINDSET	Belief that most basic abilities can be learned through dedication and hard work[19]
ADAPTABILITY	Capacity to reflect dynamically amid constantly shifting work landscape
	Ability to be resilient and recover from setbacks
	Ability to think, move, and change quickly (i.e., agility)
CRITICAL THINKING	The objective analysis and evaluation of an issue in order to form a judgment
	Testing claims for truth
	Surfacing and challenging underlying assumptions
	Widening the scope of inquiry
	Awareness of unconscious bias

19 Dweck, *Mindset*, 50.

CURIOSITY	Desire to learn, know, and understand. Fueled by inquisitiveness.
CREATIVE THINKING	The process of generating new and imaginative ideas and solutions. Happens best in psychologically safe[20] environments, which enable inspiration or innovation.
DECISION-MAKING	Ability to make quality decisions in a timely manner, taking into consideration uncertainty and the possibility of not having complete information

Here are some examples of how you might see Mind Skills showing up with an employee. Imagine Vicki is a software coder and project manager who loves to learn new things about coding (growth mindset) but wonders why a problem keeps cropping up (curiosity). She raises a question that challenges an assumption her colleagues are making (critical thinking) and asks her colleague to say more about his idea because she doesn't see his point (appreciating a different viewpoint). In planning her day, she prioritizes her tasks and realizes she will need to turn off all distractions and finds a private place to work so she can concentrate. Then she sets her timer for forty-five minutes so she can completely focus on getting an assignment finished in the time she set (executive function: prioritizing/planning, focus, boundary setting). Upon hearing the news that her best programmer is needed to work on a fast-developing new client project, she pulls her team together to figure out how to quickly backfill the role to manage workload and continuity (adaptability).

It isn't likely that Vicki, or any of her colleagues for that matter, are aware that she is deploying these Mind Skills. But if the company made these skills more visible and valued, it would be easier for Vicki to hone her use of them and help model and support growing them in others.

People Skills

People Skills are the interpersonal and behavioral skills and abilities, such as the ability to know oneself and to communicate and relate to others effectively on a personal and professional level.

Employers are becoming acutely aware that people skills are key to

20 Edmondson, *The Fearless Organization.*

effective leadership and to the collaboration, innovation, problem-solving, and adaptability skills employees need to compete successfully. For example, in our client work, we hear many employers worry about undeveloped communication skills among the younger generation workforce, who are more accustomed to texting than talking.

Based on our research, these are the People Skills we consider foundational:

CAPABILITY	DEFINITION
EMOTIONAL INTELLIGENCE (EQ)	Ability to manage one's emotions in the workplace, home, and community through self-awareness, self-control, self-motivation, empathy, and compassion
(CORE CAPABILITY)	**Self-Awareness:** Awareness of what one is feeling and thinking and how it informs thoughts and behaviors, understanding the impact on others. Understanding one's strengths and weaknesses. Clearly seeing how others perceive us.
	Self-Control: Expressing one's emotions at the appropriate time and degree; anticipating consequences
	Self-Motivation: Ability to take initiative, achieve, and persevere
	Empathy: Ability, through listening and seeing, to perceive from another's point of view and to feel moved to act on someone's behalf
	Compassion: Ability to recognize the suffering of another and willingness to take an action to help alleviate the suffering
AUTHENTICITY	Ability to be true to oneself. The ability to relate to others in a genuine, courageous, and high-integrity manner.
KINDNESS	Ability to be gentle or considerate of another. The act of goodwill.
BALANCE	Ability to manage commitments and make trade-offs to keep a healthy balance between business and family, activity and reflection, work and leisure. Tendency to be self-renewing and handle the stress of life without losing the self.[21]

---

21 The Leadership Circle Profile 360™. This definition comes from the Balance competency.

Conscious, Capable, and Ready to Contribute

COMMUNICATION SKILLS	**Active Listening:** Fully concentrating on what is being said rather than just passively hearing the message of the speaker. Listening with all senses.
	Effective Speech: The ability to verbally advocate, inquire, illustrate, and frame one's thoughts and ideas
	Effective Writing: The ability to use written words to convey information clearly and persuasively
GIVING AND RECEIVING FEEDBACK	The ability to receive and hear a person's feedback with the intent to improve and achieve
	The ability to give feedback with the intent to help another person to improve and/or achieve a goal
TEAMWORK	The ability to work cooperatively or collaboratively as part of a group of persons acting together as a team or in the interests of a common cause or goal
INFLUENCING	Ability to persuade others and cause desirable and measurable actions and outcomes. Opening others to possibilities.
RESOLVING CONFLICT	The ability to reconcile opposing views in a manner that promotes and protects the interests of all parties concerned
LEVERAGING DIFFERENCES	Ability to appreciate and incorporate diversity of thought, experience, and culture in a way that engages and encourages better collaboration with one another
INTEGRITY	Ability to adhere to a set of values and principles that one espouses; follows through on commitments and leads by example

Here are some examples of how you might see People Skills showing up with an employee. Marty, an outgoing, talkative director for a twenty-five-person manufacturing division, notices that he is talking a lot in a team meeting and that two of his colleagues are sitting quietly observing the discussion. So he stops and asks them if they have any thoughts about the subject to share (self-awareness). Discussing the best response to a customer service problem, Marty respectfully offers his perspective on why his team members should consider his alternative idea (influencing). While Marty is walking by the training room on his way back to his office, he sees his team member, Tanya, frantically trying to put the fifty chairs and eight tables back into the correct formation. He looks at his watch and thinks, *I can spare five minutes to duck in and help her finish this task more quickly* (empathy, kindness, teamwork). In another meeting later that same day, Marty sees that his two colleagues are stuck in their points of view about an issue, so he suggests an alternative to help them resolve their differences (resolving conflict). Again, these examples illustrate that People Skills can be observed and experienced by others. And importantly, when a company makes them known and valued across the organization, it becomes easier to practice, recognize, and model them in action to other employees.

Technical Skills

Technical skills are the abilities and knowledge needed to perform tasks within a specific field or discipline. Because most companies have a pretty good handle on training and development in relevant domain skills, we simply reference what our research suggests are the three high-level categories of technical skill capability categories employees need to develop to succeed in the twenty-first century:

CAPABILITY	DEFINITION
DOMAIN SKILLS	Specialized knowledge or ability needed to perform a specific task or function
DIGITAL READINESS	The knowledge, skills, and ability to use technology to effectively perform one's job
MULTIDISCIPLINARY SKILLS	The appreciation for and ability to engage different disciplines and perspectives to solve problems and create new solutions

Embed Conscious Development throughout the Employee Life Cycle

You are probably familiar with the "employee life cycle," the HR model used by most companies to support employees through the stages of their employment in an organization. This life cycle provides a reliable structure and roadmap for HR and talent development functions to manage, support, and measure each employee's career journey, from recruitment to offboarding. Our use of the life cycle is slightly different. We believe the employee life cycle is a practical and effective means to embed, leverage, and reinforce more development opportunities.

In our fable, Janine is the one who suggests to Andrew that Shift could leverage more conscious development through the employee life cycle. It makes perfect sense. If you want to really foster the conditions for a people development culture at your company for all your workers, don't you need to make sure development is supported and reinforced from candidate selection through every stage an employee is with you?

We believe that embedding the principles, practices, and incentives of your conscious development culture throughout the employee life cycle is one of the most reliable, sustainable, and effective ways to cultivate continuous learning and development for every employee from day one. It is quite simply a game changer. And with more of the routine administrative HR functions now automated or outsourced, HR and L&D professionals are able to focus more on improving the employee experience and culture, especially around continuous learning and development.

We created the Conscious Development Employee Life Cycle Model, illustrated below, to provide a holistic, employee development-centric roadmap. Our hope is that this roadmap will validate how you are already using the employee life cycle for development and will encourage creativity by helping you come up with new ways your company can leverage the employee life cycle to support better people development in your organization.

You might want to start, like Janine and Andrew did, by looking at the life cycle on a whiteboard and imagining how you can create or build upon more opportunities for developmental conversations with employees at every stage of their stay. But first, let's take a closer look at what leveraging development through the employee life cycle can look like.

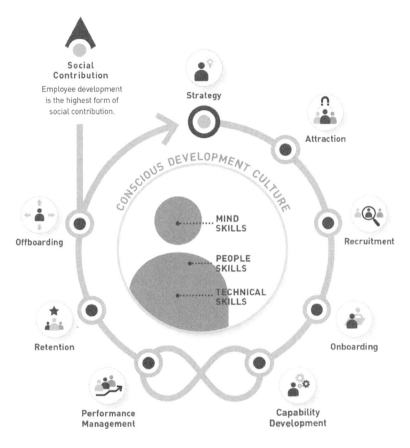

Conscious Development Employee Life Cycle Model

Strategy

As we mentioned earlier, we believe that creating a conscious development culture is ultimately a strategic decision. Building a development culture has to start with the recognition that people development is core to the business strategy. Therefore, we include strategy as the first step in the Conscious Development Employee Life Cycle to signal the importance of leaders fully integrating business and people strategy from the start.

Attraction

Organizations use many methods to attract the right kind of talent, and it's important to include information about a company's commitment to a development culture in all these methods. It is an opportunity to build a strong employer brand in the marketplace and to attract the right employees. Today more than ever, top talent and early career prospective employees associate a company's commitment to learning and development with its employer brand proposition.

Candidates know what to expect when they are clearly told employees are expected to embrace the company's conscious development culture. More focus on the front end of the employee life cycle pays dividends at all other stages of an employee's experience in the company. When candidates understand what a development culture is and what their place within that culture will be, a company is more likely to attract potential workers who are excited about the prospect of growing this way. As more development-ready employees are hired, the development culture gains momentum.

Consider incorporating the messages and stories about your company's commitment to conscious learning and development into these common employee attraction methods:

1. Overall Branding: messaging via website, advertisements, social media, blogs
2. Current Employees: video interviews sharing their stories on how they are learning and growing their *People Capabilities*; formal employee referral programs and informal networks where employees can incorporate messages about the conscious development culture
3. Recruiters and Search Firms: briefing materials and hiring conversations

Recruitment

Integrating conscious development principles into this stage will make it easier to find the best quality candidates to fit with the company culture. There are a few ways conscious development principles can be integrated into your recruiting and hiring processes:

1. For each role, identify and map out the key people capabilities. Knowing which capabilities are important for each role will help ensure a good fit between a candidate and your culture, values, and business goals. It also helps guide interview questions and assessments so you can assess the level of skills and capabilities for the role.

2. Include questions that assess a candidate's orientation toward development in the candidate interview. For example,

   • Questions that give insight into a candidate's mindset about personal learning, growing through challenges, as well as their ability to give effective feedback to help others learn and grow. To do this, use behavioral-based questions that ask an interviewee to reflect on when they demonstrated specific skills. For example, "When is a time you had to give a colleague hard feedback? How did you deliver it? How did it go? What learning opportunity for the colleague did you intend to support?"

   • Questions that assess a candidate's fit with your company's learning culture. We recommend asking a candidate about their past learning and development experiences at their current or previous employers. If the candidate is being considered for a leadership role, consider interview questions based on your company's core values to gauge how they embody the values presently and in previous experiences. You might ask what experience they have had with 360-degree leadership feedback assessments and how they used the results. It will be useful to learn how a candidate relates to the concept of a growth mindset. Also, consider asking the candidate about any specific skill and ability they are interested in developing.

   • Questions that assess a candidate's ability to adapt and grow into requirements of the role. This can mean asking a candidate about how they grew into a role and their plans for growing into the role if selected. For example, you could ask, "Can you share what was the biggest adjustment you had to make when you were first promoted to a supervisory role?" or "What questions would you want to ask the person whose position you are taking?"

3. Communicate with prospective candidates (verbally and in writing) about the company's

   - Culture
   - Commitment to each employee's personal and professional development
   - Expectations around learning and development at the individual, team, and leadership levels
   - Benefits that they receive from their commitment to employee learning and development

4. Don't overlook the development opportunities for the team members involved in screening and assessment. Consider what the selection panel is learning from the selection experience, individually and collectively, on issues such as

   - Diversity, equity, and inclusion
   - Areas to tweak and improve the candidate assessment and selection process
   - What they are learning from candidates about the company's brand
   - What they are learning about their own capabilities in assessment and screening
   - The team involved in assessing candidates, for example, may find your organization needs to include personality style tests as part of the screening process. Or one employee may realize they need training in interviewing techniques to better evaluate candidates. All these can be powerful insights.

Onboarding

Having selected someone who is a fit for the role and culture, include components in the onboarding process that help set up the new hire for success in a continuous learning environment. One option is to hold one or a series of orientation sessions with HR and the new hire, where you

1. Explore the principles behind the company's conscious development culture, explaining what it means and what it looks like in terms of mindsets, behaviors, and daily practices.
2. Communicate expectations of all employees around engagement in the company's conscious development culture. This means engaging in the employee's individual learning and development and also their role in helping others learn and grow, whether they're functioning as a peer, a team member, a manager, or leader.
3. Introduce the company's Core Capabilities Model (i.e., Mind Skills, People Skills, and Technical Skills) and how successfully executing the company's strategy and daily operations relies on employees developing the core capabilities.
4. Share that all employees are expected to develop an individual development plan (IDP) tailored to the specific core capability needs of their role. It would include their career aspirations and goals, developed with the support of their manager.
5. Discuss how the company integrates learning and development with performance management objectives. Explain how the approach to performance management emphasizes continuous learning and its impact on achieving results.
6. Introduce your company's internal learning and development technology platforms. These may be designed to track and support employees' individual learning and development resource needs as well as their learning milestones and achievements.

Another important orientation activity is to enable existing employees to share with new employees their experience getting used to working in a development culture. This effectively shows new employees some strategies for learning to learn and can also reassure them that other team members have gone through the same journey. If your company has mentoring and/or buddy programs, this is another good way to help new employees learn about the development culture.

Integrated Capability Development and Performance Management

The strategies we have outlined thus far are intended to help you create the cultural conditions that enable and sustain dynamic development of your people and your business. It is such an exciting time to be a company committed to conscious people development because there is so much excellent research, technology, and expertise to help companies evolve everyday practices that support optimal learning, development, and performance. What we want to highlight now are aspects of development culture that help integrate development and performance management activities.

But first, you may have noticed that we slightly changed the traditional employee life cycle model. There's an infinity loop on our version. We included this to suggest a more seamless relationship between talent development and performance management. Talent development and performance management are naturally linked but are frequently pursued as largely separate activities.

We often see this disconnection in the manager-employee performance review conversation. Managers and employees may sit down, for example, to talk about skills training, a leadership development program, or stretch assignment opportunities for career advancement. This is all good, but with the exception of stretch assignments, developmental opportunities are generally discussed as separate activities that take the employee away from their day-to-day work routine. It is not uncommon, in fact, for a manager to have little knowledge of their company's learning and development resources. They often simply encourage the employee to talk with HR because they see employee development as HR's job. The trouble is this prevents a holistic approach to employee development, especially since research shows that many L&D functions have at best only loose connections to annual performance reviews and often lack a structured approach to better support more development-centric performance management practices.[22]

Equally problematic is when a manager doesn't employ coaching conversation techniques. Without doing so, they may not understand how an employee approaches continuous learning around an issue or challenge or how they use and develop a particular skill or capability in performing their job. Research shows that developmental-oriented conversations about performance are far more helpful and enriching for both the employee and the manager than simply reviewing performance accomplishments or misses. Furthermore, employees today, especially millennials and Generation Z, want and need clarity on how they are progressing in learning or improving their skills. They want to know how the skills they are learning and working on, particularly if they are identified in their development plan, tie to how they perform in their job and work with peers, and how the skills will help them progress in the company and their career.

If the performance review process is oriented more toward the employee's learning and growth, rather than solely on how well they performed their responsibilities, the manager and employee will have a more engaging, productive, and helpful performance conversation. This shift in focus is happening as more and more companies embrace the manager's role as coach and invest in developing their manager's coaching skills.

We are observing managers using capability development mindset in performance reviews to highlight an employee's efforts and learning opportunities, such as in the following examples. Note the parenthetical references to Core Capability being displayed.

- "I was impressed to see how you skillfully challenged us to examine the other solution approach on the Jones project." (Critical Thinking)
- "Over the past six months, your direct reports shared with me that they feel encouraged that you are consistently being more present

22 Jacqueline Brassey, Lisa Christensen, and Nick van Dam, "The Essential Components of a Successful L&D Strategy," McKinsey & Company, February 13, 2019, https://www.mckinsey.com/business-functions/organization/our-insights /the-essential-components-of-a-successful-l-and-d-strategy.

in staff meetings and listening more attentively when they talk." (Active Listening)

- "You mentioned in your self-evaluation that you did not achieve your goal to recruit new team members on to your team. When we meet to go over your performance appraisal, I would like to hear more about what got in your way to keep you from achieving this goal, what you are going to do to get back on track, and ways I can help you be successful." (Organizing, Planning, and Prioritizing—Executive Function Skills)

From these brief examples, you can begin to appreciate how a manager using basic coaching skills can help an employee improve particular capabilities identified in the employee's individual development plan. It's one way that companies can create a more integrated, effective, and mutually satisfying approach to capability development and performance management.

Furthermore, emerging development-oriented performance management software tools and resources on the market provide ways to enable managers to easily tailor development-oriented performance conversations for whatever forms and frequency in which they occur.

Of course, we know that managing individual and team performance is also an everyday responsibility for managers. This is actually where more conscious integration of development-oriented practices (such as healthy and consistent feedback loops between managers, individuals, and teams) has the best impact on performance.

But let's break down the relationship between development and performance even further. In a conscious development culture, performance is not limited to how well you perform a function or a role or even the outcomes you deliver. Rather, performance is also measured by how well you embrace the journey of continuously learning and developing your capabilities every day in that function AND how well you contribute to helping the people you work with develop their capabilities.

As Kegan and Lahey note,[23] development activities shift from a primary focus on providing learning and development resources for only

---

23 Kegan and Lahey, *An Everyone Culture.*

high-potential workers and leaders outside the normal flow of work to designing a work environment where everyone is consciously working on developing capabilities in the course of their daily work. As Andrew learned, _everyone_ and _everything_ become sources of learning and developmental growth for the individual, the team, and the business.

Now, are we suggesting that embracing informal development practices in the way we work every day will replace the need for formal, separate learning and development activities like online learning platforms, individual coaching, workshops, leadership development programs, or other special experiences? No. But what we are suggesting is that it's time to stop relying so heavily on formal learning events and activities to do the work of "teaching" work capabilities and embrace the many ways social learning and development (e.g., peer learning, coaching, mentoring, and shadowing) happens for employees that are in many respects more effective and produce better results in both sustained learning outcomes and repeated application in job performance.

Learning about and growing our People and Mind Skill capabilities are really developmental processes that happen over time, as we mature and practice capabilities in daily real-life settings.

It's not enough to try out new techniques in role-play exercises. In fact, more than a few participants in leadership programs have shared that, while they loved getting away from the daily grind and having powerful learning experiences with colleagues, they became demoralized upon returning to their work environment because they felt awkward trying out their newly learned skills, or they don't see the skills and behaviors reinforced in the work culture and, most importantly, modeled by their leaders. What made role-playing work in chapter seventeen of our fable is that Valerie, the CEO, made sure her employees were empowered to use what they learned in their everyday work.

Formal training experiences are well-suited environments for introducing skill concepts, but the work of practicing and mastering the skills needs a work environment where everyone is experiencing the stretch and mutual support for developing and performing higher capabilities in their work. It requires leaders who are very conscious of their responsibility to consistently drive the cultural norms and practices that everyone must embrace to develop and perform at the levels the business needs and the people want.

To be clear, for both employers and employees, this way of looking at daily work as the curriculum for continuous learning and growing of human capabilities can take some getting used to and may not always be easy or even welcomed at first. This is why implementing daily practices to help people get really, really good at speaking up, challenging perspectives, admitting when they're wrong, seeking out feedback, and giving and receiving constructive feedback becomes so important. It forces everyone to tap into their higher humanistic skills—wisdom, compassion, and courage—to create learning moments with colleagues—direct reports, peers, and bosses. The result is much stronger working relationships and engagement. Employers and employees soon discover that the benefits extend beyond improved performance and engagement; helping each other learn and grow creates a deeper sense of meaning and joy for employees, managers, and leaders alike.

Retention

This stage on our roadmap includes various activities aimed at retaining employees, including employee engagement and feedback surveys, recognition and rewards, promotion and succession planning, and other specific retention strategies. Integrating more conscious development conversations into these functions helps prepare employees for new roles and for changes in the organization and industry, making them—and your company—more agile.

The following ideas may help you find new ways to incorporate more learning and development in each of these functions:

1. **Engagement and Feedback Surveys.** Go beyond common development-oriented survey statements such as "I have access to the learning and development I need to do my job" or "I believe there are good career development opportunities for me at this company." Consider asking more specific questions about each employee's learning experience and the learning culture, such as the following:

- "We regularly take time to talk about what we are learning as a team."
- "I hear my leaders talk about or reference our core people capabilities."
- "My supervisor is helping me improve my practice of particular core people capabilities."
- "My manager regularly asks me what I am learning about myself."
- "I feel comfortable giving my manager specific feedback as a learning opportunity for them."
- "I see an improvement in the way my peers give me feedback."

2. **Recognition and Rewards Programs.** If you don't already, recognize and reward employees who model a conscious development culture. The goal is to positively reinforce individual and team efforts and the learning opportunities that come with them. Another goal is to show that learning and growth are expected and are safe to pursue. Rewards often uncover great stories of how employees and the company are benefitting from the conscious development culture, and these stories can further inspire employees or can even be used in branding or in training.

3. **Promotion and Succession Planning.** The place where conscious development practices and tools can have the most significant impact is in promotion and succession planning. Whether it's for filling key positions or managing a talent advancement pipeline, conscious development conversations are vital to ensuring continuity in capabilities and closing identified skill gaps in a position. If, for example, you use a 9-Box talent review grid model,[24] a well-known talent management tool often used to help evaluate employee performance and potential in succession planning and development, the team doing the evaluating should be more conscious in examining the core people capabilities needed for a role. Greater focus on capabilities will

24 "Succession Planning: What Is a 9-Box Grid?" SHRM, March 9, 2018.

also increase the quality and objectivity (i.e., with less bias) of the conversations around the development opportunity for the candidate.

4. **Retention Strategies.** Consider conducting periodic "stay interviews" where HR and business-line leaders interview employees to understand what is working, what is keeping an employee at the company, and what learning and developmental support the team member desires. Increasingly, employees are citing lack of learning and career development opportunities as a key reason for their decision to leave a company. Stay interviews can gather feedback to pinpoint ways to retain high-value talent, which can result in improving learning and development practices.

Offboarding

The offboarding process provides an opportunity to grow your employer brand and reputation as a company that truly invests in helping employees grow their capabilities. Too often employees are "shown the door" when their tenure at a firm comes to an end. Imagine how strong your employer brand would be if former employees raved about your development culture and how it helped them grow.

For starters, the exit interview or survey can be a very helpful source of feedback about an employee's specific development experience during their tenure at the company. It's also a great opportunity to demonstrate to a departing employee the company's commitment to improving the learning and development experience itself. It allows the employee the opportunity to reflect in a constructive way on what capabilities they improved upon during their stay. Even if the separation is involuntary, a development-oriented conversation can create greater value for both the employee and employer.

Consider how the company could provide the separating employee with a summary of the development journey the employee took while working with the company. We recommend a portable individual development plan file or development summary. It would be a reminder of the company's efforts to support the employee's capabilities development—a true gift to any departing employee.

Progressive companies have long recognized the value of building a strong alumni following. Proud former employees often become customers and can be a rich source of employee referrals. Imagine how strong these relationships would be if you continued to offer learning and development to these raving fans. Sure, there is a cost to this, but we posit that the benefits to your company far outweigh these investments. And the continued contribution you'd be making to the growth of the community outside your four doors would be immense.

Why Go Down the Path of Creating and Sustaining a Conscious Development Culture?

As we see in the story, Andrew and Pat spent time exploring for themselves why becoming a more consciously developmental company was worth the commitment and investment. Then they made the business case to the partners and the board. And as they described and we captured in a table below, the benefits for an employer and for employees are pretty tangible and impressive.

FOR THE EMPLOYER	FOR THE EMPLOYEE
• More conscious, effective leaders	• Tangible lifelong marketable and portable skills
• Healthy growth culture	• Stronger Mind Skills, People Skills, and Technical Skills
• Increased ability to adapt and change	• Stronger collaboration abilities
• More creativity and innovation capability	• Stronger adaptability and agility
• Effective collaboration	• More intentional and meaningful professional growth leading to advancement opportunities
• Continuous business improvement	• Leadership mentality and ability
• Better internal and external customer relationships	• More engagement in work
• Stronger employee engagement	• More fulfillment from supporting others to grow and develop
• Enhanced employer brand and value proposition	• Ability to be more effective using people capabilities more consciously outside of work
• Reduced voluntary attrition	
• Improved financial results	

The great news is that more and more companies can validate the connection between their commitment to developing their people and their overall organizational health. But we all know it is easy to start a practice of something. It's harder to make it a habit. And as many of you probably know from experience, it is very exciting to start down this path of creating a more intentional and conscious development culture, but it takes consistent work and commitment to stay on the path. This is why we believe it is very helpful to keep your "whys" in mind on those days when consciously practicing people development feels too darn hard to sustain. Because there will be lots of days that you and everyone in your organization will inevitably say, "It seems so tedious to have to be so conscious about seeing everything and everyone as opportunities to learn and grow. Can't we just focus on doing the jobs we're getting paid to do?" Knowing *why* you want to keep investing in people development can help you stay the course and move past those days.

First, we have to start appreciating that developing human capabilities requires a long-game mindset, a process of application, practice, realization, and mastery that spans our adult lives. It is fundamentally a developmental journey. Think about how your own people skills have developed since you started your career and what and who helped you develop them along the way. How well working adults develop their full capabilities throughout their careers is highly influenced by the quality of the human relationships and organizational culture in which they work. People are always learning and growing in the workplace. The question organizations need to be asking is what mindsets and behaviors are we reinforcing? Do they support positive performance and engagement? Or discourage it? What capabilities do we want to be consciously shaping in the people we employ?

So if we all agree that developing people capabilities will be a lifelong requirement of working adults and the organizations that employ them, then perhaps it's time to expand the purpose of modern organizations (whether a business or not-for-profit) from a singular focus on delivering value to people through products and services to also include contributing to the development and potential of people as well. When we elevate developing people to the level of organizational core purpose—why the organization exists in the first place—then it becomes easier for employers and employees to embrace all the implications that come with creating and sustaining a conscious and vibrant development culture. It rationalizes and invites a broader role for the function of learning and development in your organization. And it bridges the relationship between the work adults perform every day and the developmental journey each adult is on to learn and grow the full capabilities they need to be successful at work, at home, and in society. We envision a world in which the conscious practice of people development becomes a recognized and incentivized social contribution of twenty-first-century organizations. We firmly believe that *employee development is the highest form of social contribution.*

Managing the Shift

As you start your own journey toward creating a conscious development culture, we know you'll find the process rewarding and inspiring. You can expect the process to evolve with many iterations as you find the right practices for your organization. We offer the following tips to keep you and your employees moving forward:

- Stay anchored in your purpose and vision for developing your people. It will be the source of your passion, inspiration, courage, and the patience you will need to continuously drive the vision and agenda for people development in your company. Your sense of purpose and vision will help you *own*, *model*, and *drive* the development agenda in your company.

- Communicate often and honestly about why the company is shifting toward a conscious development culture, how things are going, and what the organization is learning. Employees will need to see and hear their leaders talking about conscious people development in order to embrace the mindsets, behaviors, and practices that enable it.

- Tap into and welcome the wisdom and creativity of your leaders, managers, and employees to come up with ideas for simple practices that support everyday learning. Although there is more and more external expertise available to assist with ways to design a conscious development culture, your own leaders and teams will often have the best insights on ways to leverage learning and development conversations and practices in the flow of daily work.

- Be patient with the pace of culture shifts. A conscious development culture is not meant to be a destination but an ongoing journey of personal and organizational learning, growth, and evolution.

- Embrace the fact that developing ourselves and each other is often hard AND it is a source of great joy and satisfaction for the individual, teams, and organization.

- Don't be afraid to ask for help when you need it. Fortunately, there are many resources and lots of advisory expertise to help your company make the shift toward a more conscious way to grow your people and your business.

Thank you for taking the time to go on this journey with us. We hope you have enjoyed experiencing Andrew and Shift's evolution. Thankfully, not every leader must go through all of the ups and downs that Andrew faced to build a conscious development culture! It will take hard work, of course, but it will be worth it when you are the leader of a company whose people thrive because of the capabilities you have helped them develop. You will join the rising chorus of leaders who realize that businesses with conscious development cultures are the ones who truly contribute to society.

Behind the Fable

From Ed

During a rewarding career in consulting and public accounting, I served in many leadership roles, including CEO. I was blessed to have many great mentors throughout my career—bosses, peers, clients, business leaders, and one amazing executive coach, named Dave. (And, yes, he is the inspiration for the character David Edwards.) These relationships have infused me with a desire to help others develop their full professional and personal capabilities.

Much of the inspiration for Shift Advisors came from my experiences in public accounting and consulting firms. We believed we had a responsibility to be stewards in cultivating leaders. My partners and I were committed to the idea that we could develop "leaders at every level." We understood how essential this commitment and investment was to the success of our business and our employees' ability to advance in their careers. Our commitment was rewarded with consistently high engagement survey scores, multiple-year recognition as a best place to work, and financial success.

So when Catherine came over to see me one day with the question "What if the ultimate benefit of all professional development is social contribution?" I was intrigued. I already knew that development of people is the best way to ensure business success. Add to that the premise that fully developed employees create value at home and in society at large? That seemed fresh and exciting. A real win-win. As we talked more, the ideas about what capabilities humans need in the twenty-first century evolved. You now know them as Mind Skills, People Skills, and Technical Skills. And as you read in the fable, and you experienced in the "How to Shift" section, many other ideas rolled out as we kept our conversations going.

One last thing from me. I have my maternal grandmother and my mom to thank for my love of the word, especially fiction. I'd always planned to write, once my public accounting days were done. So when Catherine suggested I write a fable about all this, I was in! I am grateful to Catherine for many things but none more than offering me the opportunity to write Andrew's story. I hope you enjoyed it.

From Catherine

I have devoted my career to helping individuals and teams build the foundation of awareness and skills they need to communicate and collaborate more productively.

For over twenty-five years, in my capacities as a workplace mediator, organizational and leadership development consultant, and leadership coach across multiple sectors, I have personally experienced and witnessed the positive and negative impacts of people skill capabilities on employees' well-being and organizational performance.

Like many of you, I have seen how workplace cultures can bring out our best human qualities and reinforce our worst tendencies. To me, few things are as satisfying as being a part of or watching a high-performing team of people in action. Do you know that feeling of looking forward to being with your colleagues? When you enter the room or virtual space, the energy feels light and relaxed as everyone is getting situated with playful banter and genuine laughter. How about when conversation or debate is intense and everyone is listening with rapt attention, but you sense everyone is respecting the points or ideas being put forth? And then there is that most alive feeling of all, when you relate to someone who is being vulnerable with their feelings and you feel really connected, like we're there for each other—we're in this together.

And few things are as heartbreaking as witnessing a team environment where the energy feels heavy or flat because people are afraid to express themselves, afraid of not being accepted, or focused on protecting themselves by saying arrogant or hurtful things to make themselves feel smart and better. Or not speaking up with a different point of view or not wanting to press a difficult issue for fear of confrontation and conflict, for fear of being penalized or shamed because you don't see what everyone else does. And maybe the most frustrating is seeing colleagues checked out, not in the conversation, not really giving their best attention and effort.

The point is that we spend a lot of time and valuable resources trying to develop the people capabilities that create more of the former and less of the latter experience.

As a people skills development practitioner, I provided many of the traditional resources—such as workshops and leadership programs—to develop people capabilities. Employees who took part enjoyed these opportunities to get away from their work environment to learn how to lead people and collaborate effectively. And employees did apply and improve their skills and work performance after coaching and training.

But then what? Many employees pointed out that after a training or workshop, they were excited and motivated to try out what they had learned but sometimes got lost when they considered how to practice or apply the concepts and skills to daily work. How do we get people skill concepts to stick so we act on them every day?

In some cases, employees became disillusioned; what they learned wasn't always observable in their leaders nor fostered in the work culture. There was training for the employees and then there was what the leaders did. Separate from that was what really happened in the company. What's more, an organization's leaders were rarely the ones at the front of the room leading conversations about leadership. In my experience, this disconnect between the learning environment and the work environment is common, and companies don't see much lift from traditional training.

These insights inspire my focus today—helping leaders and their organizations create organizational cultures that support holistic and integrated learning and development approaches so all employees can better integrate and practice what they learn not only in their daily work but also in their daily life after they come home from work and when they are taking part in their communities.

My focus on creating more awareness about the importance of "practicing" mind and people skills development in the course of daily work is informed by my daily Buddhist practice over the last thirty-three years. I have come to appreciate that becoming a truly happy, capable person in every sense is not only a developmental process that occurs over the course of our lives but also requires conscious effort and commitment to daily practice. Each day I get the chance to try again!

From Us

We joined forces because we share a passion and sense of joy in helping leaders and teams connect to the power of their own development and that of their people and their business. We believe conscious leaders are the key to elevating humanity in the workplace. We are happy to see and be a part of the explosion in research and application into the art and science of human development and performance in the workplace. And yet, there is still much work to be done. Human capability and performance development are still largely untapped assets in the workplace and in communities.

And there are other dynamics driving our point of view. Two imperatives are converging in our twenty-first-century world of work. The first imperative is the growing realization among leaders that organizations need employees at all levels to operate consistently at higher levels of cognitive, emotional, and social intelligence in order to adapt continuously in a fast-changing, complex, and technically driven world. To be competitive and successful in business, people need to work together, in person and virtually, in ways that maximize creativity, innovation, and execution. People need to embrace continuous learning and personal growth to adapt to new kinds of jobs. We believe this need will only intensify in the years ahead and will be a key determinant of business success. In other words, it's not business as usual, and we all need to become more flexible and more skilled across many areas of our human potential if we are all to succeed in this new world.

The second imperative is a growing consciousness among all generations, but especially the emerging generations, that the workplace can and must become an environment where people of *all* backgrounds grow all their capabilities and realize their full potential to experience acceptance, well-being, meaningful purpose, contribution, and fulfillment. Attracting the best employees is increasingly tied to the overall quality of the "employee experience." And the experience we seek is to work in company cultures that support our desire to be part of a supportive community where relationships help us grow and succeed.

In twenty-first-century organizations, we can't just read about these ideas. We have to practice them.

There is also an emerging idea—and it's crucial: it's the key role business can play in meeting the developmental needs of working adults. We believe it is time to recognize that the workplace can and often does contribute significantly to human growth and flourishing. The workplace is where adults not only spend the bulk of their waking lives but also where they have the opportunity to develop and grow their full potential. Developing people, equipping them with the intellectual, emotional, and social capabilities they need to thrive in the twenty-first century, is not only key to business success but is what will make the most positive difference in our world. It is the ultimate contribution an organization can make to society. We envision a world in which developing people in the workplace is truly recognized and incentivized. We know that employee development, done well, is the highest form of social contribution.

Through the fable, we introduced the idea that companies make an important contribution to society when developing their people's full capabilities—which in turn helps their people become better at being human and better at human relationships at work, at home, and in society. As the world looks to business to be a force for good, we believe leaders will increasingly see the opportunity and responsibility to consciously develop their people for success AND for contribution.

For organizations to realize any or all of these imperatives, and the full potential of optimal work environments on human performance and growth, a shift is needed toward a more conscious, holistic, and integrated approach to developing people in the workplace. The good news is that a growing number of companies are making shifts in their culture and daily practices to pursue business excellence and the growth of people as part of an integrated business and people strategy. What business now knows, and research shows, without a doubt, is that the environment that is best for human learning and development is also best for optimal productivity and engagement. It's time to elevate the role of the modern workplace as a place for conscious human connection and development.

Conscious, Capable, and Ready to Contribute

But you might be thinking to yourself about now (or even way earlier than now!), how will all this great everyday development at work happen in a new workplace paradigm accelerated by the emergence of the COVID-19 pandemic? How relevant will a more conscious people development culture in the workplace be now that remote and virtual work and learning is here to stay for many more companies? We say it will be more relevant than ever!

Like many of you, by spring 2020, our world shifted to working completely from home. Initially, we had to adapt just about every aspect of our coaching and consulting business to serving clients 100 percent virtually. Yet, like many professional service businesses, we discovered that this pandemic-induced shift happened almost seamlessly. But we also discovered what virtual meeting fatigue feels like and what it means to be "Zoomed" out.

Now, more than a year later, as vaccines roll out, we see many companies reimagining their office spaces for when they fully reopen. When teams do come together, it will be imperative that they maximize their productivity together—to use that precious time to nurture the needs humans have for positive connection and growth. To also adapt and thrive in every aspect of our world, we will need more mind and people skills, not less; more conscious human development, not less. And the workplace, consciously designed for people development, will be the key. And just as we all successfully figured out how to Zoom and use other technology to connect, we are optimistic that conscious leaders will take this opportunity to rethink the ways in which their employees collaborate in person and virtually.

We wrote this book to share our message and vision for the conscious practice of people development in the workplace. We used the medium of storytelling to engage and inspire the hearts and minds of conscious business leaders. We hope the story of Andrew and Shift Advisors validates your own journeys and beliefs about developing your employees.

We look forward to hearing from you.

Ed Offterdinger
Catherine Allen
www.aopeoplepartners.com

About AO People Partners

AO People Partners is a premier leadership development and people strategies firm.

Our mission is to inspire and support the conscious practice of people development in the workplace. With a team of experienced coaches and consultants who bring business, leadership, and adult development expertise to the table, we help leaders and their organizations create the cultural conditions and sustainable practices that enable their people and their businesses to grow and flourish.

AO PEOPLE PARTNERS

SHIFTING MINDSETS, PERSPECTIVES & PRACTICES

To learn more, please visit www.aopeoplepartners.com.

Acknowledgments

Conscious, Capable, and Ready to Contribute: A Fable reflects our common vision of an evolving world of work. While each of us took a primary part in creating this book—Ed writing Andrew's story; Catherine doing the vital work of offering practical ways to create a conscious development culture—every page reflects our shared point of view. And we have many to thank for helping us make this book a reality.

We are grateful to our clients who teach us every day. Thank you for showing us what conscious leadership looks like.

Projects like this require a great team. Thank you to the AO People Partners team, led by Amanda Karst. She kept all the plates spinning throughout this process, always with a smile. Thanks also to Nicole Adams, Dan Brown, and Deb Smith for their help during the early research phase of this project, as well as Bill Bressette and Diane Kelly for fact-checking important details about life at Shift Advisors.

Thank you to the Conscious Capitalism community, especially the movement's founders, John Mackey and Raj Sisodia, and the current Conscious Capitalism, Inc., team, led by Alexander McCobin. We are also grateful to our Conscious Capitalism DC partners. You inspire us.

We started this with a big idea and a desire to use a book to get it out into the world. Thankfully, we met the team at Round Table Companies, who showed us how to do it. You are all amazing at what you do and the most joyous group we have ever encountered. Thank you, Corey Blake, for assembling such a world-class team and for your extremely direct feedback!

There are many on the RTC team to thank, but none more than our gifted editor and coach, Agata Antonow. Agata, your wisdom, patience, sense of humor, and overall calm demeanor were beyond invaluable. In addition, we thank Sunny DiMartino, Keli McNeill, Yolanda Knight, Christy Watson, Adam Lawrence, Christy Bui, Carly Cohen, Liz Bauman, and Kristin Westberg.

We offer a special thanks to Ken Gillett and his team at Target Marketing Digital, as well as Jake Group and Laura Evans Media, for helping us get the word out about our book. We are especially grateful to Rafe Sagalyn for his friendship and behind-the-scenes advice about the mysterious world of publishing.

We fervently believe that developing people and equipping them with the capabilities they need to flourish is not only key to business success but is what will make the most difference in our world—the highest form of Social Contribution. We honor the great thinkers who are a part of a rising chorus of voices who are helping to illuminate the infinite possibilities of people to grow and flourish everywhere. Thank you to the following authors and thought leaders who have especially inspired us: The Leadership Circle's Bob Anderson and Bill Adams, Daniel Pink, Robert Kegan and Lisa Laskow Lahey, Amy Edmondson, Bill George, Carol Dweck, and Thomas Friedman.

Ed

My personal gratitude list always starts with my wife and fifty-fifty partner, Donna. No one contributes more to this world than you do. I am the lucky recipient of many of your gifts, and you always know when it's the right time to push me into the abyss or catch me as I fall. Thanks for the prayers, sprays, candles, and, of course, the crystals.

Our kids, Bobby and Cara, now busily sharing their capabilities around the globe, teach me new ways to think, create, and contribute. Thank you to both of you and the loves of your lives, Kerry and Kiel, for the many conversations, texts, and emails filled with creative ideas. For the record, the score is now Ed – 1; CK – 1.

Throughout a very full life, I have been blessed to have many mentors, spiritual advisors, business colleagues, and friends who have positively impacted me in ways small and large. I am grateful to each of you for your support and for showing me how to be a better person. To keep egos right-sized and because the list is really long, I have decided not to name each of you. Please know I am so thankful for our relationships.

Finally, I thank my long-time coach and friend, David Maguire. I miss your wise observations about life and your seven-minute voice mails, which always started with "Well, I slept on our conversation and . . ." Thank you for being my thinking partner. You always knew when I needed a kick in the ass or an arm around the shoulder. Throughout the writing of this book, I could feel your love and guidance. Thank you for continuing to help me grow.

Catherine

As every author knows, writing a book takes a lot of dedicated time, energy, and focus. I want to begin by thanking my family who supported me with their gracious understanding, patience, and love during the long stretches of quiet time I needed to focus on the book, especially when crunch times collided with our vacation time. To my darling husband, Tom Walsh: your loving encouragement and well-timed good humor helped me keep perspective and on track. Spencer and Sydney, you are my pride and joy and, without a doubt, the contribution to society I am most proud of. You both inspire my vision and motivate my dedication to creating workplaces committed to conscious people development.

I am grateful to other members of my family who have also inspired and supported me during the writing of this book. Thank you, Christine, for all the ways you have taught me to stay determined and persistent. To my cousins, Sam and Angie Allen: there are no better role models and mentors than you for how to continuously learn, grow, love, and contribute generously and open-heartedly. Angie: "Putting it Together" has been my anthem song. And I'd like to say a special thank you to Dewayne Welch and Kevin Allen, my brothers from another mother. My brother David is a testament to how much a person can grow and flourish when surrounded by love, faith, and endless positivity. And thank you to all the Walshes for your interest and warm support while I was working on the book.

I, too, have been blessed throughout my life to have had mentors, colleagues, and friends who have helped me to appreciate how everyone and everything can be a teacher and source of learning and growth. This mindset is a central theme in our work and in this book. To my friend, Chrystal Murphy, thank you for teaching me how to win in the morning.

Thank you, Dr. Jennifer Wild, for all the ways you have inspired and mentored me throughout my career. Thank you to my mentor coach, Rick Tamlyn. Even more than modeling for me the art of coaching, you gave me a road map from which to imagine and play a bigger game. I am forever grateful to you and Chuck. And to my friend, business partner, and now coauthor, Ed Offterdinger: the universe could not have brought me a better partner to bring the vision and mission of AO People Partners into the world. Those early days cocreating around Donna's kitchen table will forever be golden memories.

And finally, I want to acknowledge with deepest appreciation my spiritual mentor, Daisaku Ikeda, the world's leading voice of Nichiren Buddhist philosophy who teaches the practice of inner transformation as a means to achieve individual and collective happiness. From his writings, his vision, and his example, I can see how the daily practice of consciously developing ourselves and helping others to become truly capable, happy people is what will make the most positive difference in our world.

ELEVATE HUMANITY THROUGH BUSINESS.

Conscious Capitalism, Inc., supports a global community of business leaders dedicated to elevating humanity through business via their demonstration of purpose beyond profit, the cultivation of conscious leadership and culture throughout their entire ecosystem, and their focus on long-termism by prioritizing stakeholder orientation instead of shareholder primacy. We provide mid-market executives with innovative learning exchanges, transformational storytelling training, and inspiring conference experiences all designed to level-up their business operations and collectively demonstrate capitalism as a powerful force for good when practiced consciously.

We invite you, either as an individual or as a business, to join us and contribute your voice. Learn more about the global movement at www.consciouscapitalism.org.

Printed in Great Britain
by Amazon

83951716R00140